The Ultimate

BEER LOVER'S
HAPPY HOUR

Over 325 Recipes for Your
Favorite Bar Snacks and Beer Cocktails

JOHN SCHLIMM

Award-winning Author of *The Ultimate Beer Lover's Cookbook*

CUMBERLAND HOUSE™

Published by Cumberland House, an imprint of Sourcebooks, Inc.

P.O. Box 4410, Naperville, Illinois 60567-4410

(630) 961-3900

Fax: (630) 961-2168

www.sourcebooks.com

Library of Congress Cataloging-in-Publication Data

Schlimm, John, 1971- author.

   The ultimate beer lover's happy hour : over 325 recipes for your favorite bar snacks and beer cocktails / John Schlimm, award-winning author of The ultimate beer lover's cookbook.

      pages cm

   (trade paper : alk. paper) 1. Snack foods. 2. Beer. 3. Cocktails. 4. Happy hours. I. Title.

   TX740.S3253 2014

   641.5'3—dc23

                                        2014019698

Printed and bound in the United States of America.

SB 10 9 8 7 6 5 4 3 2 1

Praise for *The Ultimate Beer Lover's Cookbook*

"More than a decade in the making, Schlimm's mammoth culinary valentine to beer is worth the wait...Schlimm has compiled a definitive beer recipe sourcebook that will be appreciated by beer-lovers for years to come."

—*Publishers Weekly*

"There's much to be admired (and by admired, we mean ingested) within the pages of a new modern-day classic called *The Ultimate Beer Lover's Cookbook*."

—*Urban Daddy* (Los Angeles edition)

"Want to experience the joy of cooking with beer? Then check out John Schlimm's *The Ultimate Beer Lover's Cookbook*."

—Playboy.com

"The cookbook that will take beer to another level!"

—*OK!* magazine (Father's Day Gift Guide)

"[A] masterful cooking tome...conversational, breezy, engaging tone...beautifully designed...recipes impressive from a beer perspective or otherwise."

—*Beer Advocate* magazine

"John Schlimm...invokes his beery bloodlines...bubbles with love for brew...offers a wide range of dishes you probably wouldn't think of using beer in."

—*Pittsburgh Post-Gazette*

"Do you love beer? I mean, do you really love beer? If that is the case, then you have to read this book...It's the most comprehensive and impressive cooking resource using beer as an ingredient...If you can eat it, *The Ultimate Beer Lover's Cookbook* lets you do it with beer."

—*Tailgating Ideas* Blog

"It's a book that'll keep your favorite beer geek puttering happily in the kitchen for hours."

—*The Oregonian*

Also by John Schlimm

To all the animals—
So you know that you have not passed this way unloved.

"There is nothing in the world like the first taste of beer."

—*John Steinbeck*

CONTENTS

Contents

Contents

NOTE FROM THE AUTHOR

The food and beer pairings and the drink recipes in this book are meant to be enjoyed and savored responsibly and safely. Please do not drink and drive.

INTRODUCTION

T he love of beer literally flows through my veins.

Not only do I drink it and cook with it, but I also stand on the shoulders of a legacy that reaches back almost a century and a half to a great-great-grandfather who brewed this liquid gold with little more than wholesome, earthy ingredients and fresh mountain spring water. And one of my favorite places to be in the world will always be at a bar on a Friday night, with a beer bottle in one hand and something to eat in the other, music cranked, and a circle of friends laughing all around me—that's life at its best!

The Ultimate Beer Lover's Happy Hour raises the ultimate toast to beer at its best by pairing the mouthwatering joy of bar food with an eternal tap of brews for you to enjoy and indulge in anytime you want right in your own home. With more than 325 easy food and drink recipes, and over 1,000 related suggestions for using traditional, seasonal, and craft beers, this book demonstrates how pairing and cooking with a brewski have become versatile and buzz-worthy art forms anyone can master.

For starters, "The Midas Touch: Beer's World Tour through History" explains the backstory on the world's most famous and beloved drink—one that we humans have been consuming for centuries. This section will give you the lowdown on what all the fuss is really about when it comes to beer and will change the way you look at this culinary icon, especially at mealtimes.

"The Ultimate Beer Lover's Pantry" and the "Beer Style Guide" sections, which are also in the beginning of this book, show seasoned home chefs, pint guzzlers, foodies, beer snobs, and first timers alike how to stock up on all the essentials to get cooking, drinking, and chowing down with beer. It's easy, and once you've stocked up, you'll be set to get your party on at any time!

Then, no matter the occasion, I've got you covered with all the ultimate comfort snacks and beer you and your friends could ever want.

In other words…welcome to Beer Town! You most definitely will enjoy your stay—in fact, with this book in hand, you now never have to leave. Handfuls of Cinnamon & Brown Sugar Bar Nuts and Alehouse Agave & Chipotle Mixed Nuts, Dilly Lime Thyme Pretzels, Marinated Olives at the Tap, and snacks from The Tavern Chips Bar and The Pub Crawl Popcorn Bar will make sure all your days and nights get lit with fun and flavor. As will Friday night–inspired party starters like Bar Top Poppers, Deep-Fried Dills, What a Jerky!, Cheesy Speakeasy Sticks, and crispy, golden nuggets from The Deep-Fried Veggie Basket and The Roadhouse Fries Bar.

Party time will be brew-charged with spicy-to-sweet selections from The Game Day Sauce Bar, The Party Salsa Bar, and The Hoppy Hummus Bar, along with Guac 'n' Roll and other spirited dips like Plastered Pimiento Spread and Spiked & Spicy Cheddar Spread.

For heartier tapas, serve up Potato Skins Stuffed with Chiles, Tomatoes & Green Onions; Avocado & Onion Quesadillas; Greasy Spoon Grilled Cheese Sandwiches; Taproom Tacos with Green Sauce; and Bruschetta Brewski; or selections from The Slaw Platter; The Mash Up! Platter; and The DIY Kebab Bar, with offerings like Worcestershire & Peace Marinade, Brown Sugar & Spice Marinade, and Brew & BBQ Marinade. Or head straight to The Beer & Pizza Bar and The Beer & Burgers Bar, where everything you know about pizza and burgers gets taken to a whole new level of tipsy gratification.

Plus, to ensure every bite is indeed happy, all the dishes are paired with your choice of brew styles—Altbier, American Pale Ale, Barley Wine, Belgian Abbey Dubbel & Tripel, Brown Ale, India Pale Ale, Kölsch, Rye Beer, Saison, Amber Lager, Doppelbock, Dunkel, India Pale Lager, Maibock, Oktoberfest, Pale Lager, Oatmeal and Russian Imperial Stouts, American Wheat Ale, Dunkelweizen, German Hefeweizen, Chili Beer, Fruit Beer, Herb/Spiced Beer, smoked Rauchbier, and many, many more. So whatever your pint of preference, you'll be able to find it here.

Also, for a round of thirst-quenchers no one will forget, chapters 6 to 10 offer endless inspiration via beer-infused mixed drinks, chuggers, shots, shooters, chasers, punches, and even floats and shakes. The names speak for themselves—Buzzy Navel, Hootinanny Sunrise, Red-Headed Mary, Daredevil's Brew, Skip & Go Naked, Dive

Bar Mimosa, Eeking Monkey, Beertini, Under the Table Daiquiri, Sweet Home Amaretto, Depth Charge, Jäger Beer Bomb, The Rebel's Yell, Barroom Blitz, Sake Boom Boom, Atomic Diva, Hoot & Holler, Drunken Leprechaun, Citrus Sunsation, Gin Mill & Ginger Punch, Beach Party Punch, Strawberry & Ale Float, Chocolate Beershake, and Vanilla Cream Ale Float. And there are so many more where those came from.

It all really comes down to what one of my best friends always says: "BEER = FUN!" Perhaps no truer words have ever been spoken. And that's exactly what this bar-in-a-book is all about—beer, great food, friends, laughter, and fun.

Like the immortal *Cheers* bar anthem says, "Sometimes you want to go where everybody knows your name, and they're always glad you came." Well, my friend, you've come to the right place!

THE MIDAS TOUCH:
BEER'S WORLD TOUR THROUGH HISTORY

Beer is the indisputable and ultimate rock star of the culinary world. Boasting world-wide sales today in the hundreds of billions annually, this hearty concoction of barley, hops, yeast, and other earthy ingredients has dominated the ultracompetitive food and beverage circuit for millennia.

Needless to say, beer has a *past*. Dating back several thousands of years, what is known is that this illustrious icon started its journey in primitive villages and ancient civilizations in the far reaches of the world, where it was created in various versions almost simultaneously.

The first recorded recipe for beer is 3,900 years old and is of mythical proportions. "The Hymn of Ninkasi," originally found etched into a stone tablet, is devoted to the Sumerian goddess of brewing: "Ninkasi, you are the one who soaks the malt in a jar." She shares this billing with Siris, also a Mesopotamian goddess of brewers. Likewise, the traditional Greek and Roman wine god, Dionysus, is said to have started out as the god of beer, but the debate rages on about that one.

Of all the many gods and goddesses of beer throughout different cultures, Ninkasi's main competition may be Mbaba Mwana Waresa, the beloved South African Zulu goddess of beer. Many believe she was the first to invent beer for us mere mortals to savor.

Beer even rolls with its own posse of patron saints! One of them, St. Arnold, once declared, "From man's sweat and God's love, beer came into the world."

Regardless of who has the rightful claim to its origins, beer has been beloved for centuries. Sumerian women were the first people to brew beer. Mesopotamians sipped beer together through reed straws from a single bowl. Babylonians wrote beer recipes on clay tablets. Chinese villagers discovered the joys of individually brewing their favorite new beverage with millet and using it in religious rituals. In ancient Egypt, the pharaohs had "royal chief beer inspectors" to ensure the beverage's quality, the pyramid builders were paid with beer, and the dead were buried with one for the road—to the afterlife, that is. And Noah was even said to have served beer on the ark. What a way to ride out the great flood!

Cherished Old World texts tell of beer's near mythical status as an elixir for prince and pauper alike. One of mankind's earliest known literary works, the *Epic of Gilgamesh* from Babylonia, extols the virtues of beer. As King Gilgamesh's friend, Enkidu, puts away several pitchers of the local brew, much like many a reveler might today, the author notes, "His heart grew light, his face glowed and he sang out with joy."

The fourth-century BC Greek historian Xenophon recorded, "For drink, there was beer which was very strong when not mingled with water, but was agreeable to those who were used to it. They drank this with a reed, out of the vessel that held the beer, upon which they saw the barley swim."

The Egyptian *Book of the Dead* speaks of beer, relating it to such qualities as truth and eternity. Another popular ancient Egyptian saying held that "the mouth of a perfectly happy man is filled with beer."

Even the Bible recognizes the godly attributes of a good brew in Proverbs 31:6–7: "Give beer to those who are perishing…let them drink and forget their poverty and remember their misery no more." In Isaiah 56:12, it is also written, "'Come,' each one cries, '…Let us drink our fill of beer! And tomorrow will be like today, or even far better.'" Also, many beer scholars believe that at the famed wedding feast at Canaan, Jesus actually turned the water into beer, not wine.

The art of spinning this liquid gold in ancient times traveled through Greece, where Plato heralded, "He was a wise man who invented beer." From there, the secret to brewing was given to the Romans, who honored its chief ingredient, barley, on their coinage. Even Julius Caesar declared beer a "high and mighty liquor." Historians have long credited beer, along with bread, as the driving impetus behind the development of early technologies and civilization itself. One might then say that beer took us out of the caves and into the pubs of progress.

During the Middle Ages, creating and feasting on beer were favorite activities in the cottages, monasteries, and castles of Europe. Whether king or priest, laborer or barbarian, while weathering Crusades or societal evolution, life was made easier by drinking beer. Often synonymous with beer, Bavaria, Germany, boasts the world's oldest commercial brewery still in operation, the Bayerische Staatsbrauerei Weihenstephan (translated as Bavarian State Brewery Weihenstephan), which dates back to 1040, when it was originally part of a Benedictine abbey.

Also in Bavaria, beer made its early mark on the law when the Duke of Bavaria passed the cleanliness or purity law regarding the creation of beer, known as *Reinheitsgebot*, on April 23, 1516, which makes it one of the world's oldest food regulations. Earlier still in the annals of law, an eleventh-century edict in the northern Polish city of Danzig stated, "Whoever makes a poor beer is transferred to the dung hill." That should give you a sense of how seriously people took the art of crafting good beer.

Of course, beer and its boozy buddies had their most headline-worthy brush with the law centuries later during Prohibition in the United States. Brewing was halted by the Eighteenth Amendment to the U.S. Constitution, which prohibited the "manufacture, sale, or transportation of intoxicating liquors" and their importation and exportation. The amendment was ratified by the necessary number of states on January 16, 1919, and then formally certified by the secretary of state on January 29, 1919.

At that time, many thought beer's low alcohol content would exempt it from this amendment, believing that "intoxicating liquors" referred only to beverages with high alcohol contents, such as whiskey, rum, and other distilled spirits. However, an ultrareligious congressman from Minnesota named Andrew J. Volstead defined "intoxicating liquors" as any beverage containing more than one-half of 1 percent alcohol. Volstead's position prevailed in Congress, and, despite President Wilson's veto, the period known as Prohibition went into effect on January 17, 1920. Because of Congressman Volstead's advocacy concerning this issue, the Eighteenth Amendment is also called the Volstead Act.

During this time, many breweries relied on making near beer, a nonalcoholic take on the original, while other breweries were forced out of business. Of course, what would a golden rock star be without a few skeletons in the closet? And our sudsy celebrity had its share, especially during this time. More than a few rebellious brewmasters out there continued to mine the alcohol-infused brew in all its glory and covertly distributed it to devotees on the sly.

It was only a matter of time, though, before beer would once more have its day in the sun. Fourteen years later, on December 5, 1933, the highly failed tenets of the Eighteenth Amendment were officially repealed when Utah, Ohio, and Pennsylvania ratified the Twenty-first Amendment, the only amendment to ever be adopted to repeal a prior amendment. Beer enjoyed a resounding comeback in the states as brewing once again officially commenced. Beer lovers everywhere lobbed a collective sigh of relief. Among them was President Franklin D. Roosevelt, who announced, "I believe this would be a good time for a beer!"

Speaking of relief, throughout the ages, beer has also been praised for its supposed medicinal value, challenging that of its main rival, wine. Sumerians washed wounds with hot water and beer. Ancient Egyptian physicians had about a hundred medical prescriptions calling for beer, and used beer to treat gum disease. Anthropologists from Emory University discovered that the bones of ancient Nubians from along the Nile River contained tetracycline, an antibiotic that was produced as a result of the beer they consumed. And the famous sixteenth-century Swiss physician Paracelsus declared, "A little bit of beer is divine medicine."

Modern-day research has lent credibility to this theory. Numerous studies have shown that the vitamins in most beer—such as antioxidants and the B vitamins niacin, riboflavin, B6, and folate—the soluble fiber, the protein, and the other natural ingredients could be good for the heart. One such study yielding these results was conducted by the Beth Israel Deaconess Medical Center and the Harvard School of Public Health and reported in the *Archives of Internal Medicine*. Furthermore, beer's high potassium and low sodium content may help maintain a healthy blood pressure, while a brewski or two could possibly help protect moderate drinkers from ulcers, stroke, hypertension, diabetes, some cancers, and other conditions.

To the delight of avid beer drinkers, researchers from the University College London and the Institute of Clinical and Experimental Medicine in Prague discovered that the term "beer belly" is incorrect. In the *European Journal of Clinical Nutrition*, they revealed how one's expansive belly is not caused by beer. In addition, for the ladies who love their brews, the study also showed that women who drink beer actually weigh less than women who refrain. A study conducted by the University of Naples showed similar results, pointing the finger of blame for so-called beer bellies at—*gee, surprise!*—poor diet and lack of exercise.

Results from other studies on beer's link to good health have also been widely reported in such prestigious medical journals as the *Journal of the American Medical Association*, the *New England Journal of Medicine*, and the *British Medical Journal*. A study published in the *American Journal of Psychiatry* even heralded the benefits of "beer sociotherapy," or enjoying beer in a group, in geriatric mental patients. Likewise, the potential health benefits of beer have also been noted by other organizations, such as the American Dietetic Association.

Finally, consider this: the late Hermann Doernemann of Germany, who died in 2005 at age 111 years, 279 days, credited his trek to becoming the second oldest man on the planet at the time to enjoying a beer each day. Not to mention my great-great-aunt Reggie, who frequently enjoyed a whiskey shot and beer chaser (see page 274), and she lived to be 104! Just maybe then, like apples, a beer a day also keeps the doctor away. So drink to your good health…in moderation, of course.

Beer has earned the presidential stamp of approval again and again. Our first president, George Washington, understood its power. He not only had his own brewing operation at Mount Vernon and served beer at dinners, but he was even known to sway voters with a brew or two at campaign events.

Close to a century later, President Lincoln said, "I am a firm believer in the people. If given the truth, they can be depended upon to meet any national crisis. The great point is to bring them the real facts, and beer." During his tenure, President Eisenhower once observed, "Some people wanted champagne and caviar when they should have had beer and hotdogs." In 1978, President Jimmy Carter signed the bill *H.R. 1337* into law, legalizing homebrewing, which ignited the art form and the ensuing legions of beer hobbyists.

More recently, Barack Obama campaigned in barrooms, sipping a brewski, during his historic 2008 campaign. As president, he invoked beer-diplomacy at his famous 2009 White House "Beer Summit," and, in 2011, President Obama bought a home-brewing kit for the White House kitchen, marking the first time alcohol of any kind had been brewed or distilled on White House grounds. The resulting brews heard around the world were the White House Honey Brown Ale and the White House Honey Porter. Other 1600 Pennsylvania Ave. brewskis have since followed. Ale to the chief, indeed!

Although the ales of England and the Netherlands became some of the most popular transplants to our shores during the earliest days of the American colonies, eventually the influx of German immigrants also brought their newly invented lagers.

It's at this benchmark in the genealogy of beer that my own family's story begins. It is a nineteenth-century German immigrant and his fellowship of brewmasters who are also owed due credit for sparking this cookbook nearly a century and a half later.

In 1869 at age nineteen, with only a few gold pieces sewn into his jacket, my great-great-grandfather Peter Straub left his family in Felldorf, Wuerttemberg, Germany, in search of the American dream. With a last name whose origins date back to 530 BC in what would become Straubing, Germany, young Peter left everything that was familiar to him—the security of his parents, brothers, sisters, relatives, friends, and home. He had an immigrant's drive within him to pursue a better and more fulfilled life. This is undaunted humanity at its best, and a story that has been repeated in many American families in one form or another.

Peter also carried one other thing with him on that long journey across the raging seas, something he would rework, refine, and develop into 100 percent liquid gold: a recipe for beer. Although he didn't know it at the time, Peter possessed the Midas touch, just like beer's other burgeoning kingmakers and his contemporaries of the same era—Milwaukee's Jacob Best, who in 1844 founded what would later become Pabst Brewing Company; Frederick Miller, who founded Miller Brewing Company in 1855; August Schell, who established the August Schell Brewing Company in 1860; Joseph Schlitz, who created Joseph Schlitz Brewing Company in 1856; Detroit's Bernhard Stroh, who opened Stroh Brewery in 1850; Golden, Colorado's Adolph Herman Joseph Coors, Sr., who founded Coors in 1873; St. Louis's Eberhard Anheuser and Adolphus Busch, who launched Anheuser-Busch Company in 1852; Louis Koch, whose 1860 beer recipe launched the Samuel Adams brand in 1985; and Pottsville, Pennsylvania's David G. Yuengling, who started D. G. Yuengling & Son in 1829.

Local Pennsylvania writer Roswitha Cheatle wrote of this pivotal time: "Up to 1840, [the] 'British' type of beer dominated the American scene, but enough is enough, the Germans said, and took it upon themselves to educate the Americans on real beer, the lager variety, which is today America's basic taste bud whetter. And this in turn brings us to the story of Straub Brewery."

Upon arriving in his new homeland, Peter settled in Allegheny City, Pennsylvania, working at the Eberhardt and Ober Brewing Company. There he enlisted his skills as a cooper, which is a craftsman trained in making and repairing wooden barrels and casks. Peter next moved to Brookville, where he worked at the Christ and Allgeier Brewery.

In 1872, Peter finally put down roots in the small German settlement of St. Marys, Pennsylvania, which boasted numerous breweries at the time. However, this was where he would outlast all the others, giving birth to a local legend and, in doing so, helping contribute to beer's universal acclaim.

After arriving in the town he would call home for the rest of his life, my great-great-grandfather first worked at the Windfelder Brewery. With fate and faith ever at his side, Peter eventually went to work for his future father-in-law's brewery. He worked his way up through the company to become the brewmaster. He also fell in love with and married the boss's daughter, my great-great-grandmother, Sabina.

By 1878, Peter's dream became a reality: he bought his father-in-law's brewery, becoming the company president. He now had his slice of the American pie.

Today, my great-great-grandfather's Straub Brewery, like those of his fellow nineteenth-century brewing alums, has spanned three different centuries and the threshold of a new millennium. Peter's brewery also bears the distinction of being an American Legacy Brewery, one of the oldest breweries in the country to still be owned and operated by its founding family, now into its seventh generation.

Aside from its award-winning beverages, my great-great-grandfather's brewery has contributed an iconic marker of its own to the history of beer, one that has drawn beer fans from around the world: The Eternal Tap. The most popular site at the brewery, The Eternal Tap is located just outside of the production area. Installed decades ago, it is a spot where visitors are invited to enjoy a complimentary taste of the house specialty or one of the seasonal brews. Originally, the beer was served in tin cups. Today, the tin cups have been replaced with glass mugs, as the traditional and seasonal Straub beers continue to perpetually flow and satisfy visitors.

This tale of a young man who sought and grabbed hold of his destiny, and whose blood I share, has long inspired me. I'm not skilled in ways that would make me beneficial on the production floor of his brewery today—that would just turn into something like the chaotic scene from *I Love Lucy* when Lucy and Ethel go to work at the chocolate factory—but instead, through projects like this cookbook, I get to both celebrate this tasty legacy and help other cooking and beer enthusiasts pay due homage to the almighty beer.

Today, with history, style, and charisma on its side, not to mention a fan base that numbers well into the hundreds of millions of the partying faithful, beer appears nonstop across the globe, headlining at bars, restaurants, casinos, campgrounds, homes, frat houses, and sold-out stadiums. It's also a true media bonanza, trending on social media and having starred in countless songs, books, movies, television shows, video games, and on billboards, often leaving its carbonated and fruity competition in the dust.

Beer has certainly weathered the test of time to earn its five-star accolades on the global stage, and has become inextricably woven into the tapestry of our daily existence. In doing so, it has repeatedly affirmed the famous folk lyric, "In Heaven, there is no beer…that's why we drink it here." Now those are words to live by!

The Ultimate
BEER LOVER'S PANTRY

When whipping up your favorite beer snacks and cocktails, it's helpful to have a pantry of basics nearby. "The Ultimate Beer Lover's Pantry" contains many of the standard ingredients that are either used frequently throughout the book in various recipes or have a starring role in a dish or cocktail that you will likely return to on a regular basis.

Also, while each food recipe in this book includes three suggested beer pairings and each cocktail recipe includes your choice of three suggested beers as an ingredient, they are just that—suggestions. This cookbook is meant to be an informative guide and a place for experimenting with the infinite beers, including homebrews, available today. Feel free to follow my suggestions, as well as go in as many other different directions as you'd like by substituting different beers to ensure that your cooking time is as fun and rewarding as the eating (and drinking!).

Last but not least, one of the goals of this book was to make the following recipes as easy and accessible to everyone as possible, regardless of dietary restrictions or allergies, and including those of us who have embraced a vegetarian or vegan lifestyle. Thus, where recipes call for traditional dairy products (such as milk, butter, sour cream, and cheeses) as well as other ingredients that are animal products or are known to contain animal products (such as Worcestershire sauce, mayonnaise, and eggs), I have linked those ingredients back to either delicious, plant-based DIY versions here in the pantry section that can easily be made at home or to plant-based alternatives that are easily found in stores or online. You'll find all of these recipes and suggested plant-based alternatives listed in the following section. From this starting place, the result is a collection of recipes—what I like to think of collectively as a party-in-a-book—that *anyone* anywhere can enjoy time and again.

🍴 Agar

Agar, or agar-agar, which comes in powder or flakes, is a natural vegetable gelatin additive made from various species of red algae. Often used to make things like jelly, custards, puddings, and desserts, it is especially prized within plant-based cooking for its high gelling capabilities, and because true gelatin is made from animal products. Agar actually has higher gelling properties than traditional gelatin, and it sets in just an hour at room temperature. Note that 1 tablespoon of agar flakes is equal to 1 teaspoon of agar powder.

While agar is available in most natural food stores and large supermarkets, it is also available online through such websites as VeganEssentials.com, VeganStore.com, Amazon.com, iHerb.com, EdenFoods.com, BarryFarm.com, agar-agar.org, and BulkFoods.com.

For other plant-based gelatin needs, Lieber's Unflavored Jel is recommended and is available online at VeganEssentials.com.

🍴 Agave Nectar

Made from the agave plant, which is most recognized for its role in producing tequila, agave nectar, sometimes also called agave syrup, is a sweetener that is often used instead of sugar or honey because of the similarities in taste. For more information about agave, visit AllAboutAgave.com.

Throughout the book, it is used in such recipes as Alehouse Agave & Chipotle Mixed Nuts (page 47), Agave-Roasted Peanuts (page 62), Agave Barbecue sauce (page 112), Running Wild Rice Soup (page 149), and various beer cocktails.

🍴 Alcohol

While beer is the indisputable star of this production, many other favorites on the bar circuit also make cameos throughout the book—some in the snack recipes and the majority in "Part 2: The Ultimate Beer Lover's Party Drinks," which includes chapters 6 to 10. To see what beers and other types of alcohol are used throughout the book, along with descriptions of each, see the "Beer Style Guide" on page 32 and the "Alcohol Glossary" on page 302. Also, to check out the plant-based status of various brands of alcohol, visit Barnivore.com.

Beans

It's always good to have different kinds of beans in the pantry. For our purposes here, the following beans are used throughout the book:

Black beans	Kidney beans
Chickpeas (garbanzo beans)	Lima beans
Green beans	Pinto beans

Beer

To see what beers are used throughout the book, along with descriptions of each, see the "Beer Style Guide" on page 32. This section also includes an entry about gluten-free beer (page 39), which can be substituted for any of the beers used throughout the book. Also, to check out the plant-based status of various brands of beer, visit Barnivore.com.

Berries

When it comes to berries, if possible, try going for what's in season and fresh from a local fruit stand or farmers market, or picked by you. The following is a list of the berries that are used throughout the book:

Blackberries	Cranberries
Blueberries	Raspberries
Capers	Strawberries

Also, various companies make berry-flavored, plant-based syrups, such as the Raspberry Chocolate Syrup by Santa Cruz Organic (Scojuice.com), which you can use. In stores, read the label carefully to determine whether the syrup contains any products you're not comfortable with.

Bread

As with any other products, when it comes to bread, read the ingredient labels carefully to determine if a certain brand of bread is suitable for your needs, or visit the brand's website. Sometimes, bread will contain sugar, milk, butter, gluten, honey, or other ingredients you may not wish to consume (or perhaps can't). In addition, you can also find many plant-based and gluten-free bread recipes online. For the recipes that follow, feel free to experiment with different bread types, including making your own, while still sticking close to the recipe.

A variety of different breads and bread-related products are used throughout the book, including:

Baguettes
Breadcrumbs
French bread
Hamburger buns
Italian bread

Panko (Japanese breadcrumbs)
Potato bread buns/rolls
Slider buns
White bread

⫻ Broth, Vegetable

Plant-based vegetable broth is widely available in stores and can easily be made at home, using recipes found online. As always, carefully read the ingredient labels.

⫻ Butter

See Margarine.

⫻ Cheese

The cheeses used in recipes throughout the book are Cheddar, cream cheese, and Parmesan. Nondairy, plant-based cheese is also pretty widely available in stores and online. Some reliable plant-based brands of cheese are listed in the "Store-Bought Plant-Based Cheese Resource Guide" on page 304. The following are easy, homemade recipes for plant-based Cheddar, cream cheese, and two nutty Parmesan variations, which are all from my cookbook *The Cheesy Vegan*, where you can find nearly a dozen recipes for plant-based cheeses of all kinds, along with related recipes:

Homemade Cheddar

Canola oil, for oiling a loaf pan
5 teaspoons agar powder or 5 tablespoons
   agar flakes
1 1/2 cups filtered or bottled water
1/2 cup cashews
1/3 cup nutritional yeast
1/2 cup sliced pimiento

3 to 4 tablespoons lemon juice, depending on
   how sharp you want the Cheddar
2 teaspoons onion powder
1/4 teaspoon garlic powder
1/2 teaspoon Dijon mustard
Port wine (optional)

Lightly oil a loaf pan measuring 3 1/2 x 7 1/2 or 4 1/2 x 8 1/2 inches. Whisk together the agar and water in a small saucepan over medium heat. Stir often until the mixture comes to a boil, then reduce the heat to simmer. Let the mixture bubble gently for 5 minutes, stirring often to dissolve the agar completely.

Meanwhile, measure the cashews, nutritional yeast, pimiento, lemon juice, onion powder, garlic powder, and mustard into a blender.

When the agar has boiled for 5 minutes, carefully and slowly pour it into the blender. Return the lid to the blender, and blend the mixture on high for about 1 minute. Stop the blender, scrape down the sides of the container with a rubber spatula, replace the lid, and blend on high again for another minute. The mixture should be very smooth and approximately the same orange color as standard dairy Cheddar cheese.

Pour the mixture into the prepared loaf pan, dribble with the port wine, if using, transfer to the refrigerator, and let chill until firm, at least 1 hour.

Serve sliced, or grate it to garnish or melt into your favorite dishes.

The cheese will keep tightly wrapped in the refrigerator for at least 1 week.

Yields about 2 cups

Variations:

Horseradish Cheddar: Before pouring the mixture into the loaf pan, stir in 2 tablespoons of prepared horseradish, or to taste.

Smoked Cheddar: Before pouring the mixture into the loaf pan, add 1/2 teaspoon liquid smoke, or to taste.

Extra-Sharp Cheddar: Before pouring the mixture into the loaf pan, add more lemon juice and mustard, to taste.

Homemade Cream Cheese

I cup firm silken tofu, pressed and drained (see instructions on page 28)	3 tablespoons freshly squeezed lemon juice
	I tablespoon sugar
2 tablespoons canola oil	1/2 teaspoon kosher salt

Combine all the ingredients in a blender or food processor, and blend until very smooth. Transfer to a glass bowl and refrigerate until well chilled, at least 1 hour.

The cheese will keep tightly wrapped in the refrigerator for 4 days.

Yields about I 1/2 cups

Homemade Parmesan Walnut

I cup raw walnuts, coarsely chopped
2 tablespoons nutritional yeast flakes

1/2 teaspoon ground sea salt, or to taste

Mix the walnuts, nutritional yeast, and salt together in a small bowl. Grind the mixture in a coffee grinder dedicated to ingredients other than coffee, working in batches, if necessary. Grind for about 8 to 10 seconds per batch. Don't overgrind the mixture.

Transfer the mixture to a tightly covered container and refrigerate.

The cheese will keep in a tightly covered container, refrigerated, for about 1 week, assuming the walnuts are fairly fresh.

Yields I I/4 cups

Homemade Parmesan Almond

I cup slivered almonds
5 tablespoons nutritional yeast
I teaspoon lemon zest

Salt and freshly ground white pepper, to taste

Combine all the ingredients in a blender or food processor. Pulse until the ingredients form crumbs the size of a half grain of rice or baby peas.

The cheese will keep in a tightly covered container, refrigerated, for 3 to 4 days.

Yields about I I/4 cups

Chocolate

Plant-based, nondairy chocolate is available from such websites as VeganEssentials .com, NaturalCandyStore.com, and Amazon.com. In stores, read the label carefully to determine whether the chocolate contains any dairy products; ideally, it has also been manufactured in a dedicated milk-free environment.

Also, Santa Cruz Organic Chocolate Syrup, which comes in various flavors, is perfect for any number of uses (Scojuice.com).

Cornstarch

Extracted from the endosperm of a corn kernel, cornstarch is basically the starch of the corn grain. In this book, like in other recipes, it is used as a thickening agent.

⚙ Cream, Irish

In case you don't want to use dairy-based Irish cream where it is called for, or desired, in the cocktail chapters, here is an easy, nondairy, homemade version:

DIY Irish Cream

I 3/4 cups coconut milk
I 3/4 cups vanilla almond milk
I teaspoon vanilla extract
I teaspoon coconut extract
I teaspoon almond extract

I tablespoon dark or light brown sugar
I teaspoon unsweetened cocoa powder
2 tablespoons cooled espresso
2 cups whiskey

Combine all the ingredients in a blender and mix, stopping and starting the machine until well-blended. Serve chilled in tall glass mugs or other glassware of your choice.

Yields approximately 4 cups

⚙ Cream, Whipped

Where whipped cream is called for, or desired, throughout the book, in such recipes as Strawberry & Ale Float (page 298), Vanilla Cream Ale Float (page 300), Coconut Ale Float (page 301), and Chocolate-Dipped Strawberries (page 185), here is an easy, nondairy, homemade version:

DIY Whipped Cream

I (15-ounce) can full-fat coconut milk
2 teaspoons vanilla extract

1/4 cup confectioners' sugar, or to taste

Carefully drain the water from the can of coconut milk, leaving only the creamy coconut fat (reserve the coconut water for other uses, such as adding it to cocktails to boost flavors). To drain the water from the can, either create a small opening in the can to allow the water to drain, or refrigerate the can for several hours or overnight and then scoop out the thick floating cream and discard the coconut water.

Combine the coconut fat, vanilla, and sugar in a medium-size bowl, whisking for about 2 minutes, or until the mixture is fluffy. Or, using the whisk attachment in an electric mixing bowl, whisk for about 20 to 30 seconds, or until fluffy. Use immediately or refrigerate for 1 to 4 hours before using.

Yields about 3 cups, depending on how long you whip the mixture

Egg Replacers

While many of my friends choose to use eggs in the following recipes, many other people either avoid or can't have eggs in their diet. Therefore, I offer options for egg replacements in all recipes in this book. Today, there are many options for removing eggs from dishes and replacing them with plant-based egg substitutions or replacers, which basically consist of a natural powder combination of starches and leavening ingredients.

While there are various plant-based egg replacers available, one go-to source is Ener-G brand's Egg Replacer (Ener-G.com). For this particular egg replacer, the conversion is: 1 egg = 1 1/2 teaspoons dry Egg Replacer plus 2 tablespoons water. Also, see Flaxseed on page 19.

A few recipes call specifically for an egg replacer for egg yolks. One go-to, plant-based brand is The Vegg (TheVegg.com). For this particular egg yolk replacer, the conversion is: 2 to 3 egg yolks = 1 teaspoon Vegg blended with 1/4 cup water.

Extra-Virgin Olive Oil

Extra-virgin olive oil is the most flavorful and highest quality of the olive oils, and it is used frequently throughout the book. Moreover, it isn't made using chemicals. Olive oils can range in price widely, but using a less expensive, moderately priced extra-virgin olive oil for the recipes in this book is fine.

For more information on all things olive oil, go to OliveOilSource.com.

Other oils used in the book include:

Canola oil

Coconut oil

Corn oil

Peanut oil

Sunflower oil

Vegetable oil

Flavorings

Vanilla extract is used in the book and will come in handy for other cooking as well.

Flaxseed

To use flaxseed to replace eggs, for each egg, process or blend 3 tablespoons filtered or bottled water with 1 tablespoon ground flaxseed until the mixture is smooth and thick. Let the mixture rest for a minute or two before adding it to your recipe.

⑂⑂ Flour

The flours used throughout the book include:

All-purpose flour
Rye flour
Self-rising flour

Unbleached flour
Wheat flour

⑂⑂ Fruit

For the fruit used throughout the book, try using whatever is in season and fresh from a local fruit stand or farmers market, or try using fruit that you pick yourself. The following is a list of the fruits that are used throughout the book:

Apples (including green and red apples, plus applesauce and apple juice)
Apricots
Avocados
Bananas
Berries (see Berries on page 14)
Cherries (maraschino)
Clementines
Coconut
Grapefruit (juice)
Grapes (green, purple, red)
Lemons (fruit, juice, zest) (see the note that follows this list)

Limes (fruit, juice, zest) (see the note that follows this list)
Mangoes
Nectarines
Olives (green, juice)
Oranges (fruit, juice, zest)
Papaya (fruit, juice)
Peaches
Pineapples (dried, fresh, juice)
Pumpkin (canned pureed plain)
Raisins (golden)

Note: To yield more juice from lemons and limes, try rolling the fruit on your counter with the palm of your hand to soften them. Or lightly puncture the lemons and limes and then microwave them for 1 to 2 minutes, depending on your microwave oven's wattage.

⑂⑂ Herbs and Spices

Herbs and spices really do make the world go around. A dash of this herb and a pinch of that spice can completely revive, refresh, and transform a dish right before your eyes. A well-stocked herb and spice rack is an ever-evolving thing, but it will come in just as handy for these recipes as for any other cooking. Herbs and spices raise the flavor profile of a dish and whatever other ingredients they're being mixed and matched with. They can also be fun to experiment with when you are trying to switch up a dish.

The herbs and spices used throughout the book include:

Herbs

- Basil (see the note about chiffonade that follows)
- Bay leaves
- Caraway seeds
- Chervil
- Chives
- Cilantro (the leaves of the coriander plant)
- Coriander (the seeds from the same plant that produces cilantro)
- Dill
- Fennel
- Marjoram
- Mint
- Oregano
- Parsley
- Rosemary
- Sage
- Tarragon
- Thyme

Spices and Seasonings

- Allspice
- Cardamom
- Chili powder
- Chipotle powder
- Cinnamon
- Cloves
- Cumin
- Curry powder
- Dry mustard
- Five-spice powder
- Garlic powder
- Ginger
- Italian seasoning
- Jalapeño powder
- Mace
- Nutmeg
- Old Bay Seasoning
- Onion powder
- Paprika (Hungarian, smoked Spanish)
- Pepper (black, cayenne, lemon, seasoned, white)
- Red pepper flakes
- Saffron
- Salt (celery, coarse, kosher, pickling, sea, seasoned)
- Turmeric

Note: A few recipes, such as Beer-Marinated Vegetable Medley (page 159), Alfredo's White Garlic Pub Pizza (page 190), and Grilled Tomato-Basil Sliders (page 204), call for basil leaves to be cut chiffonade-style. To do this, stack the basil leaves, roll them tightly from the top down, and then carefully slice the roll into thin strips.

⑅ Hot Sauce

Several of the recipes call for hot sauce. While Tabasco sauce will always be the original liquid fire, one of the quintessential go-to hot sauces is Frank's RedHot Cayenne Pepper Sauce (FranksRedHot.com). Sriracha Hot Chili Sauce (Huyfong.com) is also used in several recipes throughout the book.

⑅ Ice Cream

Ice cream is a central ingredient in the milkshakes and floats in chapter 10. Nondairy, plant-based ice creams and frozen desserts are becoming more readily available in stores, such as the So Delicious Dairy Free brand (SoDeliciousDairyFree.com). The following is a homemade, plant-based vanilla ice cream recipe that you can easily make and also adapt into chocolate and strawberry variations:

DIY Vanilla Ice Cream

2 (14 1/2-ounce) cans vanilla soy milk, vanilla almond milk, or light coconut milk

3/4 cup sugar

2 teaspoons vanilla extract

Pinch of salt

Combine all the ingredients in a large bowl, mixing well. Refrigerate for three hours to overnight. Freeze the mixture in an ice cream maker, and follow the manufacturer's directions.

Yields about 4 cups

Variations:

DIY Chocolate Ice Cream: Use chocolate soy or almond milk and add chocolate syrup, such as Santa Cruz Organic Chocolate Syrup (Scojuice.com), to taste.

DIY Strawberry Ice Cream: Add freshly pureed strawberries to taste.

⑅ Ketchup

Most ketchup is inherently plant-based, but it is important to still read the labels to make sure you are comfortable with the product you are buying. One online source for plant-based ketchup is the Annie's Naturals brand of organic ketchup (Annies.com).

Also, Pickapeppa Sauce, which is made using cane vinegar, is sometimes called "Jamaican Ketchup" and is used in the book to make the Worcestershire & Peace Marinade (page 162) and Grilled Cauliflower Burgers (page 202). For more information or to buy the sauce online, visit Pickapeppa.com.

𝖄𝖄 Liquid Smoke

Liquid smoke is an easy way to give dishes that down-home country touch. Produced through a procedure using real smoke from select wood chips, liquid smoke mimics the taste of food produced through a traditional smoking process. It comes in a variety of flavors, like hickory, mesquite, apple, and more. Liquid smoke can be strong, so be aware that a little goes a long way. In some cases, you can even apply the liquid smoke using a spray bottle for greater control. While liquid smoke is easily found in stores, one online source offering a variety of plant-based liquid smoke flavors is Colgin.com.

𝖄𝖄 Margarine

Where a recipe calls for margarine as a substitute for traditional butter, I suggest using the Earth Balance brand of buttery spreads (EarthBalanceNatural.com) or another nondairy, trans fat–free, non-hydrogenated vegan margarine of your choice. Also, the following are two plant-based, DIY margarines that can be used in the recipes throughout the book.

DIY Margarine

16 ounces coconut oil
1 1/2 cups canola or sunflower oil
1 cup full-fat coconut milk

2 tablespoons smooth Dijon mustard
1 tablespoon ground turmeric
2 teaspoons salt, or to taste

Attach a candy thermometer to the side of a sturdy, medium-size saucepan. Prepare an ice water bath in a vessel large enough to hold the saucepan.

Add the coconut oil, canola oil, coconut milk, mustard, turmeric, and salt to the saucepan, stirring well. Bring the mixture to 125°F over medium heat, then transfer the pan to the ice water bath, and continue to stir until the mixture firms up. Transfer the mixture to a container with a screw-on lid. Cover and refrigerate the mixture. The margarine will keep for about 2 weeks.

Yields about 4 cups

DIY Herbed Margarine

I cup (2 sticks) margarine, at room
   temperature

1/4 teaspoon salt

2 tablespoons beer of your choice, preferably
   the same beer you're pairing with the dish

I teaspoon chervil

2 tablespoons minced chives

I shallot, minced

I teaspoon dried thyme

I teaspoon dried marjoram

8 to 10 fresh basil leaves, finely chopped

I small clove garlic, crushed

1/4 teaspoon finely ground black pepper

Cream the margarine with the salt and beer in a medium-size bowl. Blend in the remaining ingredients. Let the mixture stand at room temperature for 1 hour.

Yields I 1/2 cups

⁗ Mayonnaise

For anyone looking for a plant-based alternative to store-bought mayonnaise, Vegenaise
is the recommended brand. Vegenaise is becoming more widely available in stores, but
it can also be purchased online at FollowYourHeart.com, which is the website of the
company that originally created it.

For a homemade mayo, the following version can be used in recipes throughout
this book:

DIY Mayonnaise

3/4 cup all-purpose flour

1/2 cup sugar

I cup water

1/2 cup cider vinegar

3/4 cup vegetable oil

2 tablespoons freshly squeezed lime juice

I teaspoon grated lime zest

2 teaspoons salt

1/2 teaspoon dry mustard, such as Colman's

3/4 cup soft tofu, pressed and drained, if
   desired (see instructions on page 28)

Stir together the flour, sugar, water, and vinegar in a medium-size saucepan. Cook
over medium-low heat, stirring often, until thick. Combine the vegetable oil, lime
juice, zest, salt, mustard, and tofu in a blender, and blend well. Add half of the hot
flour mixture to the blender and blend. Add the remaining flour mixture and blend
again. Use at room temperature or cooled in the refrigerator. Homemade vegan mayonnaise will keep in the refrigerator for about 4 to 5 days.

Yields about 2 cups

Milk

Nondairy milk is widely available in grocery stores. Recipes throughout the book call for soy and almond milks, as well as coconut milk. Soy, almond, and rice milks can be used interchangeably where milk is called for throughout the book.

Mustard

Prepared mustard is one of those fine line items that most often is plant-based, but you still need to read the labels to make sure you are comfortable with all the ingredients, which could include such things as refined sugar (see page 27). Also, homemade mustard can include such ingredients as mayonnaise and eggs.

Several recipes in the book call for dry mustard, in which case the Colman's brand (ColmansUSA.com) is suggested and widely available.

For plant-based Dijon mustard, which is widely available in stores, one go-to source is the Annie's Naturals brand of organic Dijon mustard (Annies.com).

Chinese mustard is used in the Far East Lager Marinade on page 163. Chinese mustard is a hot mustard that is becoming more widely available in grocery stores, as well as online at such places as Amazon.com. Colman's Mustard can be used as a substitute, if desired.

Nutritional Yeast

Also called "nooch," nutritional yeast is a mustard-colored yeast that is used for its cheesy and even nutty flavor, as well as its power punch of protein and vitamins. Available in flakes or powder form, it's especially effective when used in place of cheese in many dishes. Just to be clear, it's not brewer's yeast or any other kind of yeast. It's found in most health food stores and online at such places as VeganEssentials.com, VeganStore.com, and Amazon.com. For more information on nutritional yeast and other yeasts, visit RedStarYeast.com.

Nuts

Nuts help bring a wholesome earthiness to many dishes throughout the book. Each recipe will specify the type of nuts (for example, raw or toasted) needed. Easy instructions for toasting and roasting various nuts can be found in The Hot Spot Nut Bar on pages 58 to 63. The nuts that are most commonly used throughout the book include:

Almonds
Brazil nuts
Cashews
Macadamia nuts
Peanuts

Pecans
Pine nuts
Pistachios
Walnuts

Pasta

Be sure to read the labels of any pasta you buy to make sure all the ingredients are to your satisfaction. The pasta used in the book includes:

Chow mein noodles
Fusilli (corkscrew pasta)

Penne

Seeds

Seeds used throughout the book include:

Anise seeds
Caraway seeds
Poppy seeds
Pumpkin seeds

Rice (wild)
Sesame seeds
Sunflower seeds

Seitan

Seitan (pronounced "say-tan") is made from the gluten of wheat. Wheat flour dough is washed with water to dissolve the starch, leaving only the elastic gluten, which is high in protein. For anyone who still has a hankering for meat, seitan is particularly known for its ability to take on the texture and flavor of meat. In fact, some varieties of seitan are flavored to taste like chicken, beef, and so on. In this book, when seitan is used, it is the regular, unflavored seitan, but by all means, feel free to experiment. Be aware that seitan sometimes tends to crumble or break into small pieces, so handle it carefully, especially if you are grilling with it (a grill screen is recommended).

Seitan is becoming more widely available in stores, and can also be found online at such websites as VeganEssentials.com.

▌▌▌ Sour Cream

Nondairy sour cream, such as Tofutti Sour Supreme, is available online at such sites as Tofutti.com. FollowYourHeart.com also produces a tasty sour cream alternative. Or you can use this homemade version:

DIY Sour Cream

5 (1-inch) slices silken soft tofu, pressed and drained (see instructions on page 28)

1 tablespoon canola oil

4 teaspoons freshly squeezed lemon juice

2 teaspoons cider vinegar

1 teaspoon sugar

Salt, to taste

White pepper, to taste

Combine all the ingredients in a blender, and blend for 5 minutes, until creamy and very smooth. Refrigerate for 1 hour or more to thicken. This sour cream alternative keeps for about a week.

Yields 1 1/2 cups

▌▌▌ Soy Sauce

Wherever soy sauce is used throughout the book, a low-sodium version can be substituted if desired, and in some cases, it is actually called for. Also, Bragg Liquid Aminos is a natural, soybean-based alternative to traditional soy sauce that is gaining momentum. Check it out at Bragg.com.

▌▌▌ Sugar

Regular white, refined table sugar is often made using animal bone char and is avoided by those following a plant-based lifestyle. Likewise, not all confectioners' sugars are vegan-friendly. Therefore, where you see "sugar" or "confectioners' sugar" used in the recipes, you can use sugar such as the Florida Crystals brand (FloridaCrystals.com) or other sugar substitutes of your choice.

▌▌▌ Tahini

Tahini is a paste made from ground sesame seeds. While it is becoming more widely available in stores, tahini is also available online at VeganEssentials.com and Amazon.com.

₩₩ Tempeh

Like tofu, and originally hailing from Indonesia, tempeh (pronounced "tem-pay") is a soybean-based product, which is formed into a fermented soybean cake. Tempeh's utilization of the entire soybean and its fermentation process empower this treat with protein, vitamins, calcium, and dietary fiber. It has a firm texture and a nutty, mushroomlike, earthy flavor that make it a super star in the minds of foodies. Tempeh comes in a wide range of varieties and flavors; the recipes in this book were tested with regular, unflavored tempeh, but you should feel free to experiment with the other varieties and flavors of tempeh.

FYI: Tempeh can be a little temperamental, since it doesn't absorb flavors as swiftly as tofu or seitan. The secret is to simmer it in vegetable broth or water for about 10 to 15 minutes (to soften it and make it more absorbent), and then drain it.

₩₩ Tofu, Soft and Firm or Extra Firm

A worldwide favorite for about two thousand years running, tofu, also known as bean curd, is a soy product made from pressing soy milk curds into blocks. Tofu comes in soft/silken and firm/extra firm varieties. Tofu is high in protein, calcium, and iron, and its beauty is its amazing versatility. With little taste as is, tofu acts as a magical sponge, soaking up whatever flavors it is combined with, such as sweet or spicy seasonings, sauces, and marinades.

Pressing and Draining Tofu

Before using tofu, it's best to press and drain it to remove excess water. This will firm up the tofu even more.

Cut the tofu block into pieces, usually bite-size pieces or 3/4-inch slices. Cover a dish or slanted cutting board (with a catch pan at the bottom) with an absorbent dish towel or paper towels. Place a single layer of tofu pieces on the surface. Cover the tofu layer with another dish towel or paper towels. Top that layer with a heavy object, such as another plate with canned vegetables on top of it, another cutting board, or a weighty skillet. Allow the tofu to drain for at least 30 minutes to an hour.

For any unused tofu, do not press and drain it. Place it in a sealed container, cover with water, and refrigerate. Replace the water every day. Tofu keeps fresh for at least 3 to 4 days.

Freezing Tofu

Some people prefer to freeze tofu for a chewier texture. Doing this also helps the tofu to better absorb seasonings. To freeze, first cut the tofu as desired and drain it as instructed, getting as much of the water out as possible. Leftover water will form ice pockets in the tofu, leaving holes when thawed. Then, either wrap the tofu in plastic wrap or place it in a resealable plastic bag, and store it in the freezer for up to 5 or 6 months. After only a few days, the frozen tofu will assume a chewy texture. To thaw, simply put the tofu in the refrigerator overnight.

Tofu has a tendency to take on a yellowish hue when frozen, but this is natural and nothing to worry about.

∭ Vegetables

For the vegetables used throughout the book, try to use those that are in season and fresh from a local vegetable stand or farmers market, or from your own garden. The following is a list of the vegetables that are used throughout the book:

Artichokes
Arugula
Asparagus
Beets
Broccoli
Cabbage (green, red)
Carrots
Cauliflower
Celery
Corn (kernels)
Cucumbers
Edamame
Eggplant (white, purple)
Garlic (see the note that follows this list)
Kale
Leeks
Lettuce (radicchio, romaine)

Mushrooms (button, cremini, enoki, portobello, shiitake, white)
Okra (baby)
Onions (green onions/scallions, red, sweet, white, yellow)
Parsley root
Parsnips
Peas (green, wasabi)
Peppers (Anaheim chile peppers, banana peppers, chiles de árbol, chipotle peppers, green/red/yellow bell peppers, green chiles, habaneros [see the note that follows this list], jalapeños [see the note], pimientos, serrano chile peppers)

Potatoes (baking, russet, Yukon gold)
Shallots
Spinach
Squash (yellow summer)
Sweet Potatoes
Tomatillos
Tomatoes (cherry, pickled green, plum, sun-dried)
Yams
Zucchini

Note: Throughout the book where garlic cloves are listed as an ingredient, the instructions often state that the garlic should be crushed. Crushing garlic can be achieved manually with a garlic press, or crushed garlic is widely available in grocery stores. If using store-bought crushed garlic, 1/4 to 1/3 teaspoon of crushed garlic is equal to 1 clove of fresh garlic.

Note: If your skin is sensitive to hot peppers, such as jalapeños and habaneros, wear rubber gloves when you chop them. If handling hot peppers with bare hands, be sure to wash your hands immediately after you're finished, and before you touch your face or anything else.

⚏ Vinegars

Vinegars add zest to many dishes in this book and can range in flavors and uses. The most used varieties in the book include:

Apple cider vinegar
Balsamic vinegar
Cider vinegar
Malt vinegar
Red wine vinegar
White vinegar
White wine vinegar

⚏ Worcestershire Sauce

Traditional Worcestershire sauce is made using anchovies, and therefore not used by those following a plant-based lifestyle. One go-to source for plant-based Worcestershire sauce is the Annie's Naturals brand of organic Worcestershire sauce (Annies.com).

Also, here is an easy homemade version:

DIY Worcestershire Sauce

2 cups cider vinegar
1/2 cup soy sauce
1/4 cup light brown sugar
1 teaspoon ground ginger
1 teaspoon dry mustard
1 teaspoon onion powder
1 teaspoon garlic powder
1/2 teaspoon ground cinnamon
1/2 teaspoon freshly ground black pepper

Combine all the ingredients in a medium-size saucepan over medium-high heat. Bring to a boil, then reduce the heat to a simmer. Cook and reduce the mixture by half, about 20 minutes. Strain through a fine sieve, and let cool completely before using. The sauce will keep in a tightly covered container, refrigerated, for 2 to 3 months.

Yields about I cup

BEER STYLE GUIDE

W hether you're new to Beer Town or simply need a little refresher every once in a while about the basic nuances and flavor profiles of various beer styles, the following list covers the more than three dozen beer styles that are used through-out the book. As always, feel free to experiment with any other beer styles not specifically mentioned. Also, while I provide three suggested beer pairings with each food recipe in the book and three suggested beers to use as an ingredient in each of the drink recipes, those are only suggestions. I encourage you to have fun experimenting with the limitless pairing and cooking combinations that the following list offers.

All the beers in the world fall into two main categories: ales and lagers. This designation is based on the type of yeast used to ferment the beer. Generally, ales are fermented at temperatures around 65°F to 70°F, and aged for several weeks. In contrast, lagers are fermented colder, at 50°F to 60°F, and can be aged at cold temperatures from several weeks to several months. Based on these differences, ales usually have more pronounced and vibrant flavors, while lagers are usually known for their subtle flavors and smooth finish. I have also divided porters and stouts (which are ales), wheat beers (which are also ales), sake, and specialty beers into their own sections for easy reference.

🍺 Ales

Altbier: Translated as "old beer" and often referred to simply as Alt, Altbier is a dark, copper-colored German-style barley ale that is well-hopped and made from dark malts. Altbier is the most bitter of the German style beers (or *biers*).

Amber Ale: Sometimes called Red Ale because of the hues found in the range of light amber to copper among different brands, Amber Ale ranges from medium to high in hops and malt flavoring. It sometimes even tends to be sweet because of the caramel/toffee flavor that results from the crystal malts that are used. See also Irish Red Ale.

American Pale Ale (APA): A descendant of English Pale Ale, American Pale Ale uses homegrown ingredients, such as American hops. Boasting a medium to high hops flavor and low to medium, and even sometimes high, malt overtones, APA can lean to the relatively high bitter side. Some have even described noticeable toasty taste points. While the color ranges from golden to dark amber and this style is close in flavor to Amber Ale, APA isn't usually as dark or as malty as Amber Ale.

Barley Wine (or Barleywine): Originating in England and also offered in an American style, Barley Wine is a very strong ale. The main difference between the two countries' styles in creating this beverage is that the American style uses American-grown hops, which creates a naturally hoppier, bitterer flavor profile. Otherwise, the styles share several similarities, from the light amber to dark brown coloring to the overall toasty to caramel/toffee range of flavoring because of the malt, along with a noticeable fruitiness.

Belgian Abbey Dubbel: Dating back to the nineteenth century when Trappist monks first brewed the lightly hopped, strong reddish-brown ale, Abbey Dubbel consists of many complex flavor points, including nutty, chocolate, caramel, spicy, and often fruity flavors like raisin or plum, as well as the noticeable yeast flavor.

Belgian Abbey Tripel: A strong, yellow to deep golden pale ale with origins dating back to the Trappist monasteries of the nineteenth century, Abbey Tripel consists of an intricate flavor mix, including citrus, spices, and sugar, as well as the distinct presence of yeast and heavier hops and moderate malt as compared to Abbey Dubbel.

Belgian Ale: Ranging in color from golden to amber, Belgian Ale tends to be a style denoting the lighter ales available from Belgium.

Brown Ale: English in origin, the moderate to high malt presence in Brown Ale gives it a rich and somewhat sweet flavor profile that can include caramel, toffee, chocolate, and nutty taste points. While moderate at best, the hops factor in Brown Ale tends to present only a minimal bitterness in various brands, such as the American style, which generally contains more hops.

Cream Ale: A close cousin of the traditional pale lager, this American invention often boasts a bigger punch of flavor. Straw to pale golden, Cream Ale ranges from dry to sweet and is light bodied with a low malt and hops presence.

English Bitter: An English-style pale ale, English Bitter ranges from light yellow to a subtle copper color with a moderate to high hops flavor profile, and often with a noticeable fruitiness.

English Pale Ale: The name "English" here is more descriptive and in tribute to those pale ales produced outside of England that are inspired by the classic and original English Pale Ales like Bitter. With more maltiness and less hoppiness than American Pale Ales, and apart from the fact that each style utilizes homegrown ingredients, the two styles are otherwise mostly similar, right down to the golden to amber coloring.

Golden Ale: Close in style to a lager, this mellow yellow to rich golden-hued ale is often also called Blonde Ale. The low malt sweetness and moderate hops bitterness temper the overall flavor as compared to other ales.

India Pale Ale (IPA): India Pale Ale was born out of necessity in the 1790s when British brewers created this low-to-moderate-malt, high-hop, high-alcohol beer to withstand long ocean voyages to hot climates. Today, the bold and hops-heavy flavor profile, accentuated even more in American versions, has made IPA a favorite among modern beer lovers.

Irish Red Ale: Also known simply as Irish Ale or Red Ale, Irish Red Ale is a dark, reddish-amber to copper-colored ale. Low to moderate in hops flavoring with a focus on the malt, Irish Red Ale is low on bitterness and instead bears a sweet caramel and toasty malt taste. See also Amber Ale.

Kölsch:
Light to golden colored and native to Cologne, Germany, Kölsch is similar to Pale Lager, Pilsner, and Golden Ale. With its low malt flavor and moderate hoppiness, Kölsch often boasts a refreshing fruitiness.

Rye Beer:
Rye Beer, such as the iconic Roggenbier (which is higher in rye malt than most Rye Beers), denotes any ale wherein rye malt is used in place of some percentage of the standard barley malt. Rye malt lends a spicy and smoky flavor, much like the flavor of rye bread, and it is also used in smoked and wheat beers. Straw to deep amber colored, Rye Beer is usually low in hoppy bitterness.

Saison:
Earthy and spicy with a distinct fruitiness and heavy hops presence, Saison (which means "season") is known as a farmhouse ale and originated in the French-speaking region of Belgium. Traditionally, Saison is brewed during the cold months and served during the warmer months.

Scotch Ale:
Dark and strong with a copper to deep brown coloring, Scotch Ale is heavier in malt and lighter in hops, and can even boast a nutty flavor profile.

🍺 Lagers

Amber Lager:
With an emphasis on malt over hops, Amber Lager is a style used for many craft and specialty beers. American Amber Lager, for example, boasts an intense caramel and hops flavor profile. See also Vienna Lager.

American Dark Lager:
A heavier, darker version of a Pale Lager, American Dark Lager offers low to moderate hoppiness and a subtle sweetness.

Bock:
A strong lager with roasted flavor points, a caramel taste, and a hops accent, dark amber to brown Bock is most known for its rich maltiness.

Doppelbock: A rich and especially strong dark lager, the original Doppelbock was created by Munich, Germany's Brothers of St. Francis of Paola and called Salvator. Boasting a robust maltiness and minimal hops flavor, Doppelbock is known for its pervasive caramel aroma and subtle toastiness. The names of Doppelbocks today usually end with "-ator" as a tribute to the original.

Dunkel: German Dunkel (which means "dark") is a copper to brown, malty lager with low hops bitterness and sweet flavor points, such as chocolate and caramel, and nutty accents and breadiness.

India Pale Lager (IPL): A very recent twist on the traditional India Pale Ales, IPLs utilize the same malts and hops as IPAs but are cold fermented and aged with lager yeast for a smooth, refreshing finish. The result is a bold and high hops lager, often boasting a citrusy and mildly sweet flavor profile with notes of orange and other citrus fruits.

Maibock: Literally "May Bock" in German, this Bock has a lighter color than most Bocks, but the same higher strength. Maibock is a strong gold- to amber-colored lager with a smooth maltiness and a low accent of hops. American versions tend to show more hop character.

Oktoberfest: Golden to orange-red in color, Oktoberfest, also called Märzen (which means "March")—especially when darker in color and heavier in flavor—is a German beer noted for its sweet malt profile and medium hoppiness.

Pale Lager: Pale Lager is the most popular style of lager worldwide, and it is enjoyed for its refreshing, light body with light malt and hops character. Its color ranges from straw to mellow yellow to light gold. Pale Lager is made in two versions: all-malt, as was traditionally typical in Europe and is now common among America's craft brewers, and malt and cereal adjunct, which was developed by the German American lager brewers in the nineteenth century. In the United States, Pale Lager is also referred to as American-Style Lager or American-Style Light Lager.

Pilsner: The world's first pale lager, Pilsner gets its name from the city of Plzen in the Czech Republic, where it was first brewed. Pilsners fall into various categories of styles, including German, Bohemian/Czech, and American, which is often based on the German-style while using American-grown ingredients. Depending on the style, the range of hoppiness and maltiness can extend from medium to high.

Vienna Lager: Originating in its namesake, Vienna, Austria, amber-brown to copper-colored Vienna Lager is an amber lager that is mild on the sweet malt flavoring, sometimes offering a toastiness, with a slight hoppy bitterness. In North America, Vienna Lager is often referred to as pre-Prohibition Amber Lager.

Porters and Stouts (Ales)

Dry Stout: Also known as Irish Stout, deep brown to black Dry Stout is a descendant of English Porter and offers a flavor profile that includes notes of coffee and dark chocolate with moderate maltiness and moderate to high hoppiness.

Oatmeal Stout: English in origin, Oatmeal Stout is created by the addition of oats during the brewing process, which can heighten the bitterness of the beer, depending on the proportion added along with the hops used. Smooth and even sweet, Oatmeal Stout displays a number of flavors, including oatmeal, coffee, and chocolate, sometimes with a noticeable creaminess.

Porter: English in origin, light to dark brown Porter encompasses a range of flavors, including caramel, bitter chocolate, coffee, licorice, and a distinct roasted maltiness and strong hoppiness. Porter is often likened to stout, and early Porters are seen as predecessors to Stout.

Russian Imperial Stout: Also known simply as Imperial Stout, Russian Imperial Stout dates back to eighteenth-century England, where it was produced for the imperial court of Catherine II of Russia. Boasting a high alcohol content and ranging in color from deep brown to black, Russian Imperial Stout offers a complex and rich flavor mix, including coffee, chocolate, fruit, and caramel, along with a distinct toastiness and high hops bitterness.

Stout: Hailing from England, Stout is generally dark brown to black in color and boasts an intense roasted malt flavor reminiscent of dark chocolate, coffee, and even caramel. Low on sweetness and heavy on bitterness, Stout is closely associated with Porter.

Wheat Beers (Ales)

American Wheat Ale: Similar to German Hefeweizen, American Wheat Ale ranges in color from mellow yellow to golden to light amber, and is often garnished with a lemon slice or wedge. The generous wheat flavor from the wheat malt is balanced by a low to medium hops presence and spicy citrus accents produced by the yeast strain.

Belgian Witbier: Dating back four centuries, Belgian Witbier (which means "white") is a top-fermented barley and wheat ale that appears white and cloudy when cold, and ranges in color from straw to golden. Brewed with a gruit, which is a blend of spices and plants, including coriander, orange, and other spices, Belgian Witbier leans to the sweeter side of flavoring with low hops bitterness.

Dunkelweizen: Dunkelweizen is translated as "dark" (*dunkel*) and "wheat" (*weizen*). An unfiltered, copper to brown German wheat beer, Dunkelweizen contains a malty and diverse flavor range consisting of vanilla, bubblegum, clove, banana, and other flavorings.

German Hefeweizen: Hefeweizen is translated as "with yeast" (*hefe*) and "wheat" (*weizen*). This unfiltered, straw to deep golden German-style wheat beer offers low hops bitterness and sometimes a wheat bread flavoring, along with a taste range of bubblegum, banana, clove, and other flavors.

Sake

Native to Japan, sake is an alcoholic beverage created by fermenting rice. For that reason, it's often called rice wine. The brewing process used to create sake is actually more closely related to beer. Therefore, for our purposes here, at the very least (and without getting into the middle of the debate over whether sake is or is not wine), we are adopting sake as a beer and using it as both a pairing suggestion and as an ingredient for a few of the recipes in this book.

🍺 Other Specialty Beers

Chili Beer: Hot, spicy, and refreshing, Chili Beer can range in intensity from moderate to fiery, and is made using a variety of peppers based on desired taste.

Fruit Beer: Ranging greatly based on the fruits and berries used, some Fruit Beer flavors include orange, strawberry, blueberry, raspberry, cherry, pineapple, pumpkin, and apricot, with endless variations.

Herb/Spiced Beer: Ranging greatly based on the herbs and spices used, Herb and Spiced Beers are often holiday favorites, boasting strong and rich flavor profiles.

Rauchbier or Smoked Beer: Originating in Germany, Rauchbier (derived from the German *rauch*, which translates to "smoke"), or Smoked Beer, is created when a smoked malt is added to a base beer, such as an Oktoberfest or Bock. American craft brewers have reignited interest in Rauchbiers by using smoked malt and other ingredients to achieve the smoky effect in the beer they produce. The level and complexity of the smokiness and other flavors vary from beer to beer.

Gluten-Free Beer: Gluten is found in some of the main ingredients in most beers, such as wheat and barley. However, Gluten-Free Beer is becoming more readily available and can easily be paired with the recipes throughout this book. It can also be used as an ingredient when beer is called for in the recipes, especially the cocktail recipes.

SEASONAL BEER CHART

L ists like these are very fluid (pun *so* intended!) and can easily change according to whom you're asking. A number of beer styles were historically brewed for a particular season of the year. While examples of all beer styles are available year-round now, there still is some magic to enjoying certain styles in particular seasons.

Bottom line here: use this chart and its suggested pairings as you wish and as a general pathway to exploring the many brews that are out there. Therefore, my general rule of thumb is: drink what you want, when you want it!

Spring

Belgian Abbey Tripel	page 33
Cream Ale	page 34
Golden Ale	page 34
India Pale Ale	page 34
India Pale Lager	page 36
Maibock	page 36

Summer

American or English Pale Ale	pages 33 and 34, respectively
German Hefeweizen	page 38
Kölsch	page 35
Pale Lager	page 36
Pilsner	page 37
Saison	page 35

Fall

Belgian Abbey Dubbel	page 33
Brown Ale	page 34
Dunkel	page 36
Oktoberfest	page 36
Vienna Lager	page 37

Winter

Barley Wine	page 33
Doppelbock	page 36
Dunkelweizen	page 38
Russian Imperial Stout	page 37
Scotch Ale	page 35

Part I

The Ultimate

BEER LOVER'S
BAR SNACKS

Chapter 1

BREW HOUSE NUTS & STUFF

There's nothing like tossing back a handful of just about anything salted or seasoned followed by a swig of beer. Nuts, pretzels, chips, popcorn, and more have long enjoyed bar-top status alongside rounds of ice-cold brews. Here, these favorite bar snacks are reimagined and infused with lively new layers of flavor, and more suggested beer pairings than you can shake a big frosty mug at.

Everyone will go absolutely nuts when you serve bowls full of Cinnamon & Brown Sugar Bar Nuts with a nutty German Dunkel; Alehouse Agave & Chipotle Mixed Nuts with a toasty Vienna Lager; Glazed Maple Peanuts & Pistachios with a hoppy Amber Ale; Crack Me Up! Nut Brittle with a malty Stout; Beer Lover's Trail Mix with a complementary American Wheat Ale; Sizzling Sriracha Peanuts with a refreshingly fruity Kölsch; or your own personalized combinations and pairings from The Hot Spot Nut Bar.

Pretzels go from hot to refreshing in recipes for Hippie Cayenne Sourdough Pretzels and Dilly Lime Thyme Pretzels, especially when served with your choices of Oktoberfest, Pale Lager, German Hefeweizen, Golden Ale, and more.

Meanwhile, The Pub Crawl Popcorn Bar and The Tavern Chips Bar give new meaning to "Bet you can't eat (or drink) just one" for game days, friendly get-togethers, or when the munchies come knocking.

Or you can really get the brews—like Bock, Altbier, and Belgian Abbey Tripel—flowing with Jumping Chickpeas, Marinated Olives at the Tap, and Seasoned Baby Artichokes.

Cinnamon & Brown Sugar Bar Nuts

Doesn't get much better than a handful of bar nuts and an ice-cold brewski! A coating of brown sugar and cinnamon with nutmeg and cayenne pepper transforms your choice of nuts, cranberries, and golden raisins into a sweet opener for a classic Pale Lager, nutty German Dunkel, or a smooth Maibock.

 Pair with:
Pale Lager (page 36), Dunkel (page 36), Maibock (page 36)

1/4 cup brown sugar

1/2 teaspoon ground cinnamon

1/4 teaspoon freshly ground nutmeg

3/4 teaspoon cayenne pepper

Egg replacer equal to 1 egg (page 19)

3 1/2 cups pecans, almonds, unsalted peanuts, and/or walnuts

1/2 cup dried cranberries

1/4 cup golden raisins

Preheat the oven to 300°F. Line a baking sheet with parchment paper. Combine the brown sugar, cinnamon, nutmeg, and cayenne pepper in a small bowl. Combine the egg replacer with the nuts of your choice, cranberries, and raisins in a large bowl. Sprinkle the nut mixture with the sugar mixture, and toss to coat.

Spread the coated nuts onto the prepared baking sheet. Bake for 18 to 20 minutes, or until golden brown, stirring once. Cool completely. Store in an airtight container for up to a week.

Yields 4 cups

Alehouse Agave & Chipotle Mixed Nuts

Made from the same plant used to create tequila (!!!), sweet agave nectar and spicy chipotle powder get these nuts seasoned and ready for some serious fun with a few rounds of a moderately hoppy Pilsner, toasty Vienna Lager, or a good old-fashioned Amber Lager.

 Pair with:
Pilsner (page 37), Vienna Lager (page 37), Amber Lager (page 35)

---

2 tablespoons agave nectar

1 1/2 teaspoons dried chipotle powder

3/4 teaspoon ground cinnamon

1 1/2 cups pecans, almonds, unsalted peanuts, and/or walnuts

3/4 cup Wheat Chex or Chex Mix

2 tablespoons brown sugar

3/4 teaspoon seasoned salt, such as Lawry's

Preheat the oven to 325°F. Combine the agave, chipotle powder, and cinnamon in a medium-size skillet and heat the mixture over low heat until it's warmed through. Add the nuts of your choice, and stir to coat evenly. Line a baking sheet with parchment paper, and spread the nuts and Wheat Chex in a single layer on the sheet. Bake until the nuts are fragrant, 10 to 15 minutes, stirring once. Allow the nuts to cool slightly for 1 to 2 minutes.

Combine the brown sugar and seasoned salt in a medium-size bowl. Add the warm nuts and Chex, and toss to coat evenly. Spread out the nuts on a sheet of waxed paper, and let them dry completely. Once dry, store the nuts in an airtight container for up to a week.

Yields 2 1/4 cups

Spicy Friday Night Nuts

Tabasco, cinnamon, cloves, garlic powder, Old Bay, and other seasonings will let your guests know you mean business when it comes to turning every nutty bite into Friday night, no matter the day or occasion. The aromatic spice combo here nicely complements the medium hoppiness of a Kölsch, the sweet malty notes of an Oktoberfest, or even a stronger Bock.

 Pair with:
Kölsch (page 35), Oktoberfest (page 36), Bock (page 35)

1/2 cup (1 stick) unsalted margarine (use recipe on page 23 or store-bought margarine)

4 cups pecans, almonds, unsalted peanuts, and/or walnuts

2 tablespoons Worcestershire sauce (use recipe on page 30 or store-bought Worcestershire sauce)

2 teaspoons Tabasco sauce, or more to taste

1 tablespoon low-sodium soy sauce

1/2 teaspoon salt

1/2 teaspoon ground cinnamon

1/2 teaspoon ground allspice

1/2 teaspoon ground cloves

1/2 teaspoon garlic powder

1/2 teaspoon ground mace

1 teaspoon Old Bay Seasoning, or to taste

Place the margarine in a 2-quart microwave- and oven-safe pan. Melt either in the microwave or over medium heat on the stove, and then stir in the nuts of your choice. Add the remaining ingredients, mixing well. Microwave the mixture on high for 6 to 8 minutes, stirring every 3 minutes. For a toastier flavor, spread the mixture on a baking sheet, and run the sheet under a hot broiler for 4 to 6 minutes, stirring once. Serve warm or at room temperature. Store the nuts in an airtight container lined with paper towels for up to a week.

Yields 4 cups

Curried Cocktail Nuts & Pretzels

Traditionally used in Indian cooking, curry powder leads the flavor charge here to give these nuts and pretzels a zesty bite. High-hop, high-alcohol IPA, as well as a bold Maibock or toasty sweet Irish Red Ale, hold their own against this spirited mix by offering their own big taste.

 Pair with:
India Pale Ale (page 34), Maibock (page 36), Irish Red Ale (page 34)

1/2 teaspoon freshly ground nutmeg

1 tablespoon plus 1 teaspoon curry powder

2 teaspoons ground ginger

2 teaspoons ground allspice

2 teaspoons ground cinnamon

1 teaspoon ground mace

1 teaspoon dried mustard, such as Colman's

1 teaspoon ground cumin

1/2 teaspoon cayenne powder, or to taste

3/4 cup sugar

Egg replacer equal to 4 eggs (page 19)

1/2 cup butter-flavored oil, such as Orville
Redenbacher's Popping & Topping Buttery
Flavor Popping Oil

10 to 12 drops Frank's RedHot Cayenne Pepper
Sauce, or to taste, or for hotter mixed nuts,
use Tabasco sauce instead

4 cups pecans, almonds, unsalted peanuts,
Brazil nuts, and/or walnuts

2 cups bite-size pretzels

Heat the oven to 200°F. Fit one medium-size paper bag inside another to make the bag extra sturdy. Combine the nutmeg, curry powder, ginger, allspice, cinnamon, mace, mustard, cumin, cayenne powder, and sugar in the bag, shaking to mix well, then set aside.

Beat together the egg replacer, butter-flavored oil, and hot sauce in a medium-size bowl. Add the nuts of your choice to the egg mixture, about 1/4 cup at a time, stirring well to coat. Place half of the coated nuts in the spice bag, and shake well. Repeat with the rest of the nuts.

Cover a 15 x 10 x 1–inch baking sheet with aluminum foil, and lightly oil the foil. Spread the nuts on the foil in a single layer. Bake slowly for 2 1/2 hours. Turn off the oven and let the nuts cool there, then bring to room temperature, stir in the pretzels, and serve. Store the mixture in an airtight container for up to a week.

Yields 6 cups

Rosemary's Nuts!

Woodsy and fragrant thanks to a healthy dash of rosemary, and with a cayenne accent, these nuts pair well with a basic Pale Lager or a laid-back, lighter Belgian Ale or Golden Ale.

Pair with:
Pale Lager (page 36), Belgian Ale (page 34), Golden Ale (page 34)

2 pounds pecans, almonds, unsalted peanuts, and/or walnuts

3 tablespoons fresh rosemary, finely minced

1/2 teaspoon cayenne pepper

1 tablespoon brown sugar

2 teaspoons coarse salt

1 tablespoon unsalted margarine (use recipe on page 23 or store-bought margarine)

2 teaspoons molasses

Freshly squeezed juice of 1 lime

Preheat the oven to 350°F. Spread the nuts of your choice onto a baking sheet in a single layer, and place the sheet in the oven. Warm the nuts for 5 to 10 minutes. Be careful to watch them, as they can burn easily. Combine the remaining ingredients in a small saucepan over low heat. Stir until the margarine melts and the mixture is well combined. Remove the saucepan from the heat and remove the nuts from the oven.

Add the warm nuts to the saucepan or combine the nuts and the heated mixture in a medium-size bowl, and toss to coat evenly. Spread the nuts in a single layer on a sheet of waxed paper, and let them dry completely at room temperature. Once dry, store the nuts in an airtight container for up to a week.

Yields 2 cups

Glazed Maple Peanuts & Pistachios

Peanuts and pistachios are a nice, unexpected pairing for the maple glaze, which practically begs to be washed down with a heavier American Dark Lager, a mellow Golden Ale, or a hoppy Amber Ale.

Pair with:
American Dark Lager (page 35), Golden Ale (page 34), Amber Ale (page 33)

I cup unsalted peanuts and I cup shelled pistachios, or 2 cups unsalted peanuts or almonds

I tablespoon unsalted margarine (use recipe on page 23 or store-bought margarine)

Sea salt, to taste

1/4 cup maple syrup

2 to 3 tablespoons malt vinegar

Freshly squeezed juice of I lemon

Toast the nuts in a 10-inch skillet over medium heat until they are warm, tossing frequently, about 2 minutes. Be careful, as they can burn easily. Add the margarine, melting it and stirring it into the nuts thoroughly. Sprinkle on the sea salt to taste, and pour in the maple syrup, malt vinegar, and lemon juice. The mixture will bubble up quickly if the pan is hot enough; if it doesn't, increase the heat slightly. Stir rapidly, coating all of the nuts. Keep the mixture over the heat until the syrup has thickened and no longer puddles in the pan, about 3 to 4 minutes. Be careful not to let the syrup burn.

Spread the nuts in a single layer on a sheet of waxed paper, and let them dry completely at room temperature. Once dry, serve the nuts or store them in an airtight container for up to a week.

Yields 2 cups

Crack Me Up! Nut Brittle

This glazed brittle is all about indulging your nutty sweet tooth. And while the mixture calls for a hefty swig of white vermouth, the real buzz is all about pairing this nut brittle and pretzel mix with a malty Amber Lager, or the roasted maltiness of a Stout or Porter.

Pair with:
Amber Lager (page 35), Stout (page 38), Porter (page 37)

1 1/2 cups sugar	4 cups mixed nuts, such as pecans, almonds,
1 cup light corn syrup	unsalted peanuts, and/or walnuts
1/3 cup dry white vermouth	1 teaspoon vanilla extract
2 teaspoons margarine plus 2 tablespoons	1/2 teaspoon salt
margarine, divided (use recipe on page 23	2 to 3 cups chocolate-covered pretzels,
or store-bought margarine)	broken into bite-size pieces (chocolate-
	covered is optional; see note)

Note: *An online source for plant-based chocolate-covered pretzels is RoseCityChocolates.com.*

Preheat the oven to 325°F. Combine the sugar, corn syrup, and vermouth in a large heavy saucepan over medium heat. Cover and bring the mixture to a boil. Uncover and cook until a candy thermometer reads 290°F (soft-crack stage). Reduce the heat and keep the mixture at a low simmer, keeping the temperature just below 290°F until ready to use. Meanwhile, grease a 15 x 10 x 1–inch baking pan with the 2 teaspoons of margarine, and set aside.

Place the mixed nuts in a single layer on two ungreased 15 x 10 x 1–inch baking pans, and bake for 10 to 15 minutes. Remove the sugar mixture from the heat, and stir in the toasted nuts, vanilla, salt, and the remaining 2 tablespoons of margarine. When the margarine has melted, quickly spread the mixture into the greased baking pan. Cool completely, then break into pieces. Stir in the pretzels and serve.

Yields 2 1/2 pounds

Beer Lover's Trail Mix

Oh, the places you'll go with this hearty blend of peanuts, almonds, pistachios, macadamia nuts, sesame sticks, dried cherries, and more. Just be sure to have plenty of wheat beer—German Hefeweizen or American Wheat Ale—on hand, or a Belgian Abbey Dubbel with a nice nutty and fruity profile to make it a happy trail for sure.

Pair with:
German Hefeweizen (page 38), American Wheat Ale (page 38), Belgian Abbey Dubbel (page 33)

1 cup roasted peanuts (page 62)	1 cup dried cherries
1 cup toasted almonds (page 58)	1 cup dried cranberries
1 cup shelled and toasted pistachios (page 59)	3/4 cup chopped dried pineapple
1/2 cup macadamia nuts	1 cup white chocolate chips (page 17)
1 cup sesame sticks	

Combine all the ingredients in a large bowl. This recipe is easily doubled or tripled, and it keeps nicely for up to a week in a tightly covered container.

Yields 8 cups

⫸ Sizzling Sriracha Peanuts ⫷

Sriracha Hot Chili Sauce teams up with crushed jalapeños and liquid smoke to take dry-roasted peanuts to a whole new level of five-alarm awesomeness. But fear not: a chilled Kölsch, Oktoberfest, or Maibock will help keep this nutty blaze under control!

 Pair with:
Kölsch (page 35), Oktoberfest (page 36), Maibock (page 36)

---

2 pounds dry-roasted, salted peanuts

1/8 cup Sriracha Hot Chili Sauce

1/8 cup peanut oil

Freshly squeezed juice of 1 lime

1 teaspoon sugar (or 2 teaspoons prepared

sweet red pepper relish)

1/4 cup bottled crushed jalapeños, drained

8 droplets of liquid smoke

Other hot sauce(s) of your choice to fill the cup to the brim

---

Note: *You can control the heat in this zippy preparation by selecting bottled sauces with less spice, but this recipe is really for people who like very spicy food. I'd advise you to write down your approximate combinations for future reference, because people are going to want this recipe—believe me. Note that this recipe takes 3 days to make. The peanuts won't be done until they've marinated overnight and dried in the oven overnight.*

Pour the peanuts into a sealable plastic bag. Blend the remaining ingredients in a medium-size bowl. Stir the mixture thoroughly, and pour it over the peanuts in the bag. Seal the bag and squish it around to mix. Marinate overnight in the refrigerator, turning the bag a few times.

Preheat the oven to 250°F. Line a baking sheet or jelly roll pan with parchment paper. Spread the peanuts in a single layer on the sheet. Roast for 2 1/2 to 3 hours, stirring every half hour.

Turn the oven off, and let the peanuts rest in the oven overnight to dry out.

Store the peanuts in airtight containers lined with paper towels for up to a week.

Yields 2 pounds

Tangy-Sweet Tap House Mix

Sunflower seeds and wasabi peas bring a fresh look and flavor combo to this addicting spicy-sweet peanut and almond mix. And no need to be fussy about the beer pairing—a classic Amber Lager or Irish Red Ale, with their hints of caramel, work just as well as a malty American or English Pale Ale.

Pair with:
Amber Lager (page 35), Irish Red Ale (page 34),
American or English Pale Ale (pages 33 and 34, respectively)

3 tablespoons margarine (use recipe on page 23 or store-bought margarine)
1/4 cup sesame seeds
1/2 teaspoon crushed red pepper flakes
1/4 cup brown sugar
1 tablespoon low-sodium soy sauce, or to taste
1 tablespoon Sriracha Hot Chili Sauce

1 cup canned chow mein noodles
1 cup peanuts
3/4 cup toasted almonds (page 58)
1/4 cup toasted sunflower seeds (page 19)
3/4 cup golden raisins
3/4 cup wasabi peas

Line a baking sheet with parchment paper. Melt the margarine in a medium-size skillet over medium heat. Stir in the sesame seeds and crushed red pepper flakes, and cook, stirring constantly, until golden brown, about 3 minutes. Stir in the brown sugar, and when just dissolved, stir in the soy sauce and Sriracha sauce, then the chow mein noodles. Quickly spread the mixture on the prepared baking sheet, and let cool for 4 to 6 minutes.

When the chow mein mixture is dry and cool enough to handle, place it in a large bowl with the peanuts, almonds, sunflower seeds, raisins, and wasabi peas, and serve. Or store the mixture in airtight containers lined with paper towels for up to a week.

Yields about 3 1/2 cups

Hippie Cayenne Sourdough Pretzels

Worcestershire sauce, garlic and onion powders, molasses, and Frank's RedHot leave nothing to the imagination when it comes to these seasoned sourdough pretzels. Perfect for any occasion, from happy hour to a campfire, these fiery pretzels pair nicely with a lighter Pale Lager or Pilsner, or even a heavier Oktoberfest.

Pair with:
Pale Lager (page 36), Pilsner (page 37),
Oktoberfest (page 36)

I cup (2 sticks) margarine (use recipe on page 23 or store-bought margarine)

2 tablespoons Worcestershire sauce (use recipe on page 30 or store-bought Worcestershire sauce)

I tablespoon garlic powder

I tablespoon onion powder

I tablespoon dry mustard, such as Colman's, or to taste

2 teaspoons mace

Freshly squeezed juice of I lime

I (I-ounce) packet dry vegetable soup mix

2 dashes Frank's RedHot Cayenne Pepper Sauce or Tabasco sauce, or more to taste

I teaspoon molasses

8 droplets liquid smoke, or to taste

20 ounces sourdough pretzels

Preheat the oven to 250°F. Line a baking sheet with parchment paper. Melt the margarine in a medium-size saucepan over medium heat. Stir in the Worcestershire sauce, garlic powder, onion powder, dry mustard, mace, lime juice, vegetable soup mix, hot sauce, molasses, and liquid smoke. Heat until just bubbly.

Using tongs, dip the pretzels in the mixture, one at a time, coating them completely, and place them on the baking sheet. Let the pretzels rest for 15 minutes, then bake for 1 hour, stirring every 15 minutes. Turn off the oven, and let the pretzels cool there thoroughly, for 90 minutes or so. Serve the pretzels or store them in an airtight container lined with paper towels for up to a week.

Yields about 4 cups

Dilly Lime Thyme Pretzels

With their dill, thyme, and lemon-lime seasoning, these are the most refreshing pretzels on the planet. Paired with a wheat beer—like German Hefeweizen or American Wheat Ale—which corresponds nicely to the pretzel flavor, or a Golden Ale, these pretzels are always ready for a good time, day or night.

Pair with:
German Hefeweizen (page 38), American Wheat Ale (page 38), Golden Ale (page 34)

I teaspoon chopped fresh dill	I teaspoon onion powder
1/2 teaspoon chopped fresh thyme	I cup extra-virgin olive oil
I teaspoon lemon pepper seasoning	I (I-ounce) packet Ranch-style salad
Finely grated zest of 2 limes	dressing mix
2 teaspoons garlic powder	I (20- to 24-ounce) bag large pretzels

Preheat the oven to 350°F. Combine all the ingredients, except the pretzels, in a large bowl, mixing well. Add the pretzels, mixing well to coat. Spread the pretzels in a single layer on a parchment-lined baking sheet and bake for 10 minutes. Cool the pretzels before serving, or store them in an airtight container for up to a week.

Yields 3 to 4 cups

The Hot Spot Nut Bar

Toasted Pecans

The rich, toasted, and buttery notes of these pecans go hand-in-handful with a chilled Maibock, Dunkel, or favorite Pale Lager.

Pair with:
Maibock (page 36), Dunkel (page 36), Pale Lager (page 36)

Preheat the oven to 350°F. Lightly rub a rimmed baking sheet with canola oil, wiping away excess oil with paper towels. Spread 1 cup raw pecans in a single layer on the sheet, and toast them just until they release their pecan fragrance, about 5 to 6 minutes. Watch the nuts carefully as they bake, as pecans burn easily.

Toasted Almonds

Toasted, sweet almonds are a nice counterpoint to a bitterer American or English Pale Ale or English Bitter, or a sweeter and nutty Brown Ale.

Pair with:
American or English Pale Ale (pages 33 and 34, respectively), English Bitter (page 34), Brown Ale (page 34)

Preheat the oven to 350°F. Spread the desired amount of almonds in a single layer on an ungreased shallow baking pan. Bake for 10 to 15 minutes, stirring 3 to 4 times, until golden.

Toasted Walnuts

Toasted and even buttery tasting, these walnuts pair well with a richer, darker Doppelbock or Amber Lager, or an American or English Pale Ale with equally toasty notes.

Pair with:
Doppelbock (page 36), Amber Lager (page 35), American or English Pale Ale (pages 33 and 34, respectively)

Preheat the oven to 350°F. Arrange the desired amount of walnuts in a single layer on a baking sheet. Bake them for 8 to 10 minutes, until golden brown, carefully watching so they don't burn. Or toast the walnuts in a single layer in a skillet over medium heat for about 4 minutes, until golden brown, stirring often and being careful not to burn them.

Toasted Pistachios

Sweet with a salty aftertaste, the flavor of these toasted pistachios melds just as nicely with an Amber Lager or American or English Pale Ale as it does with a lighter Pale Lager.

Pair with:
Amber Lager (page 35), American or English Pale Ale (pages 33 and 34, respectively), Pale Lager (page 36)

Remove the desired amount of pistachios from their shells. Preheat the oven to 325°F. Arrange the pistachios in a single layer on a baking sheet. Bake them for 8 to 10 minutes, or until lightly golden, stirring every few minutes and carefully watching so they don't burn.

Toasted Pine Nuts

Toasted and sweet, these pine nuts are irresistible alongside a sweet caramel and toasty malt Irish Red Ale, or the intense roasted maltiness of a Stout or Porter.

Pair with:
Irish Red Ale (page 34), Stout (page 38), Porter (page 37)

Preheat a small dry skillet over medium heat. Add the desired amount of pine nuts. Toast the pine nuts, shaking very often, just until they begin to color, only a few minutes. Immediately transfer the pine nuts to a medium-size bowl, shaking every so often to keep the nuts from steaming or browning.

Toasted Seasoned Pumpkin Seeds (Pepitas)

Toasted and seasoned with your choice of herbs—thyme, oregano, cumin, coriander, cardamom, and/or cayenne—these pumpkin seeds are a salubrious snack that pairs well whether you're craving a medium malt and hops Pilsner or a richer Oktoberfest or American Dark Lager.

Pair with:
Pilsner (page 37), Oktoberfest (page 36),
American Dark Lager (page 35)

Preheat the oven to 250°F. Remove the seeds from the pumpkin(s) and pull as much of the strands and pulp away from them as you can. However, don't rinse the seeds. Or, use the desired amount of store-bought pumpkin seeds.

Stir the seeds with peanut oil or canola oil, about 1/2 cup for every 4 cups of seeds, in a roomy bowl. Add a nominal amount of kosher salt. Try adding a bit of thyme, oregano, cumin, coriander, cardamom, and/or cayenne, if you like.

Line a baking sheet (or multiple baking sheets, depending on the quantity of seeds you're toasting) with parchment paper. Spread the seeds in a single layer on the sheet. Toast slowly for about 1 hour, checking them every 10 to 15 minutes, and stirring if they're browning unevenly. Let the seeds come to room temperature, then serve, or store the toasted seeds in tightly sealed containers lined with paper towels.

Toasted Coconut

Sweet and tropical, this toasted coconut can either go solo or liven up various mixes. Be adventurous and pair it with that Oktoberfest, Doppelbock, or Belgian Abbey Dubbel you've always wanted to try.

Pair with:
Oktoberfest (page 36), Doppelbock (page 36),
Belgian Abbey Dubbel (page 33)

Place an empty small stainless steel skillet over medium heat for 4 to 5 minutes. Sprinkle 3/4 cup shredded coconut into the skillet. Shake the skillet every 10 seconds until the coconut has begun to brown lightly, about 1 to 2 minutes. Stir well, and immediately transfer the coconut to a medium-size bowl.

Toasted Sunflower Seeds

Earthy and salty, these sunflower seeds can't help but put a healthy glow and smile on your face, especially when partnered with a low-malt, medium-hops Kölsch, or a rich Amber Lager or Vienna Lager.

Pair with:
Kölsch (page 35), Amber Lager (page 35),
Vienna Lager (page 37)

Preheat the oven to 325°F. Spread the desired amount of sunflower seeds in a single layer on a baking sheet. Bake for 6 to 8 minutes, until golden brown. For a little added flavor, gently toss the seeds in enough extra-virgin olive oil and salt, or other seasonings of your choice, to coat before baking.

Simple-Roasted Peanuts, Sugar-Roasted Peanuts & Agave-Roasted Peanuts

Let's just put it all on the table from the get-go: peanuts go with just about every beer known to mankind! For this trio of simple-roasted, sugar-roasted, or agave-roasted peanuts, either choose your favorite go-to beer, or play around with some new Amber Lagers, Doppelbocks, and Oktoberfests.

Pair with:
Amber Lager (page 35), Doppelbock (page 36), Oktoberfest (page 36)

For the simple-roasted peanuts: Preheat the oven to 350°F. Place the desired amount of raw peanuts in a single layer on a shallow baking pan. Roast for 15 to 20 minutes, until golden brown. Because the peanuts will continue to roast when removed from the oven, remove them right before your desired doneness, then let them cool.

For the sugar-roasted peanuts: Preheat the oven to 325°F. Combine 2 cups unsalted peanuts, 1 cup sugar, and 1/2 cup water in a large saucepan. Bring the mixture to a boil, and cook over medium-high heat, stirring often, until the water is gone. Spread the peanuts in a single layer on a greased baking sheet. Bake for 45 minutes, or until nicely caramelized and even crispy, if desired.

For the agave-roasted peanuts: Preheat the oven to 325°F. Combine 1/2 cup agave nectar for each 1 1/4 cups of unsalted peanuts in a medium-size bowl, and stir well to coat the peanuts. Spread the peanuts in a single layer on a greased baking sheet. Bake for 45 minutes, or until nicely caramelized and even crispy, if desired.

Roasted Cashews

Subtle and sweet, these roasted cashews are the perfect opener for a round of Barley Wine, strong English Bitter, or fruity and heavy-hopped Saison.

 Pair with:
Barley Wine (page 33), English Bitter (page 34), Saison (page 35)

Preheat the oven to 350°F. Place the desired amount of raw cashews in a single layer on a shallow baking pan. Roast for 15 to 20 minutes, until golden brown. Because the cashews will continue to roast when removed from the oven, remove them right before the desired doneness, then let them cool.

Jumping Chickpeas

Garbanzo beans, known most fondly as chickpeas, get the jump on fun here with a peppy coating of paprika, cayenne pepper, caraway seeds, and Dijon, with a lemon-lime twist. Your guests will be popping these babies in their mouths all night long, especially when paired with quenching rounds of chilled Pilsner, Bock, or Vienna Lager.

Pair with:
Pilsner (page 37), Bock (page 35), Vienna Lager (page 37)

2 teaspoons smoked paprika	2 (15-ounce) cans chickpeas, rinsed, drained,
I teaspoon cayenne pepper	and patted very dry
I teaspoon caraway seeds, lightly toasted	Kosher salt, to taste
I tablespoon Dijon mustard, or to taste	2 teaspoons finely grated lime zest
6 tablespoons extra-virgin olive oil	2 teaspoons freshly squeezed lime juice

Combine the paprika, cayenne pepper, caraway seeds, and Dijon mustard in a small bowl. Heat the olive oil in a large skillet over medium-high heat. Add half the chickpeas to the skillet and sauté, stirring frequently, until golden and crispy, 10 to 15 minutes. Repeat with the remaining chickpeas.

Transfer the chickpeas to paper towels to drain briefly, and then place them in a medium-size bowl. Sprinkle the paprika mixture over them and toss to coat. Season to taste with the salt. Toss with the lime zest and juice, and serve.

Yields about 3 1/2 cups

Bartender's Chex Mix

Classic Chex Mix gets a zesty makeover with ground black peppercorns, lemon zest, garlic, and dill weed. A Pale Lager, an Oktoberfest, or a bold, hoppy IPL nicely completes the pairing, making this a duo any home bartender can be proud of.

Pair with:
Pale Lager (page 36), Oktoberfest (page 36), India Pale Lager (page 36)

14 ounces Wheat/Corn/Rice Chex, or just Wheat Chex

1 (1-ounce) packet Ranch-style salad dressing mix

1/2 teaspoon roughly ground black peppercorns

1 teaspoon lemon zest, finely minced

1/2 teaspoon minced garlic

1/2 teaspoon dill weed

2/3 cup butter-flavored popcorn oil, such as Orville Redenbacher's Popping & Topping Buttery Flavor Popping Oil

Combine all the ingredients in a large sealable plastic bag. Seal and shake well, then shake every few minutes for 20 minutes or so. Serve promptly.

Yields about 2 cups

Marinated Olives at the Tap

Something rather marvelous occurs when the collective flavor of green olives marinated in a blend of orange and lemon zests, garlic, crushed red pepper, red wine vinegar, parsley, fennel, and bell pepper meets an equally resolute Golden Ale, Belgian Abbey Tripel, or hoppy Altbier.

Pair with:
Golden Ale (page 34), Belgian Abbey Tripel (page 33), Altbier (page 33)

---

3 1/2 cups large green olives

Zest of 1 small orange, sliced into 1/4-inch strips

Zest of 1 lemon, sliced into 1/4-inch strips

2 tablespoons freshly squeezed lemon juice

1 small clove garlic, crushed

1/2 teaspoon crushed red pepper flakes

1 tablespoon red wine vinegar

2 tablespoons extra-virgin olive oil

2 tablespoons chopped fresh parsley leaves

1/4 cup finely diced fennel bulb

1/4 cup finely diced red or yellow bell pepper

Combine all the ingredients in a large bowl and mix well. Cover and refrigerate for at least 6 hours to overnight to let the flavors meld, stirring or shaking the bowl every hour or so. Serve at room temperature with toothpicks.

Yields about 4 cups

Seasoned Baby Artichokes

With a basic flavor profile along the lines of the Brussels sprouts to avocado spectrum, these seasoned artichokes are complemented and enhanced by a fruitier Kölsch or Saison, or a bold and buzz-worthy IPA.

 Pair with:
Kölsch (page 35), Saison (page 35), India Pale Ale (page 34)

4 baby artichokes, about 2 ounces each

Freshly squeezed juice of 1/2 lemon; reserve the other half for rubbing the artichokes

Freshly squeezed juice of 1/2 lime; reserve the other half for rubbing the artichokes

3/4 cup vegetable stock

1/4 cup extra-virgin olive oil

2 teaspoons balsamic vinegar, or to taste

Garlic powder, to taste

Onion powder, to taste

1/4 teaspoon coriander seeds, lightly toasted

1/4 teaspoon cardamom pods, lightly toasted and ground

1/2 teaspoon white peppercorns, lightly toasted and ground

1 teaspoon mustard seeds, lightly toasted

Kosher salt, to taste

Remove the round bottom leaves from the artichokes, trim the leaf tips, and cut the artichokes in half lengthwise. Remove any outer leaves that seem hard or sharp, and any stiff inner leaves that have crimson edges. Rub the cut surfaces with the reserved lemon and lime halves, rubbing them over all the outer surfaces of the artichokes. Combine the artichokes, lemon and lime juices, vegetable stock, olive oil, balsamic vinegar, garlic and onion powders, spices, and salt in a roomy microwavable casserole dish. Cover with plastic wrap. Microwave on high for 6 to 7 minutes, stirring 2 or 3 times. Remove from the microwave. Uncover, test the artichokes for doneness (a skewer should go through the artichoke easily), and turn the artichokes over. Recover and cook for 2 to 3 minutes longer, if needed, until fairly tender. Remove the artichokes from the microwave. Carefully pierce the plastic with a sharp knife in several places. Let the artichokes stand, covered, until cool. Serve the artichokes with the dipping sauce of your choice.

Yields 2 servings

The Tavern Chips Bar

When it comes to beer and chips, there's no time to mess around. Everyone will want to dig in ASAP! The DIY kale, tortilla, potato, sweet potato, salt and vinegar, and barbecue chips that follow are easy to whip up, and when paired with the suggested beers, they're all you need to feed a houseful of guests or a parking lot full of tailgaters, or to indulge yourself while playing couch potato. The tortilla and potato chips also work well with the various dips and spreads in chapter 3, such as The Party Salsa Bar (pages 123 to 127), The Hoppy Hummus Bar (page 131), Guac 'n' Roll (page 134), Leek & Lager Spread (page 138), Cheesy Black Bean Dip (page 139), and Spiked & Spicy Cheddar Spread (page 140).

Kale Chips

The strong, even bitter flavor profile of curly, leafy green kale tempered by the olive oil and seasoned salt results in fun and crispy chips that stand up nicely, note for note, to a light-bodied Cream Ale, smooth Amber Lager, or even a Rauchbier.

Pair with:
Cream Ale (page 34), Amber Lager (page 35), Rauchbier (page 39)

l bunch kale, leaves removed from hard stems and torn into bite-size pieces, washed and thoroughly dried	2 tablespoons extra-virgin olive oil I teaspoon seasoned salt, such as Lawry's

Preheat the oven to 350°F. Line a baking sheet with parchment paper. Place the kale in a large bowl. Drizzle the kale with the olive oil, and sprinkle with the seasoned salt. Arrange the kale in a single layer on the baking sheet. Bake until the edges are browned but not burned, 10 to 15 minutes.

Yields 4 to 6 servings

Tortilla Chips

These homemade tortilla chips will come in handy for dips like Guac 'n' Roll (page 134), salsa selections on pages 123 to 127, and Cheesy Black Bean Dip (page 139), or even the Taco Night Pizza (page 188). When flying solo, they're particularly nice alongside an icy Chili Beer, Pilsner, or Pale Lager.

Pair with:
Chili Beer (page 39), Pilsner (page 37), Pale Lager (page 36)

1 (10-count) package flour or corn tortillas	Extra-virgin olive oil, for coating the tortillas

Preheat the oven to 350°F. Lightly oil a baking sheet. Lightly coat one side of each tortilla with the olive oil. Stack the tortillas, greased side up, in an even pile. Cut the stack into eighths with a sharp knife. Separate the pieces and arrange them, greased side up, in a single layer on the baking sheet or multiple sheets.

Toast the chips in the oven for 10 to 12 minutes, or until they are crisp and just beginning to brown lightly; watch them closely so they don't burn.

Serve immediately or let cool, and store the tortilla chips in an airtight container for up to 3 days.

Yields 4 to 6 servings

Potato Chips with Sea Salt

Bet you can't eat just one! These homemade potato chips, seasoned with sea salt, are addicting in and of themselves, but they really meet their match when served as a chip and dip combo with Hoppy Hummus (page 131), Parmesan-Artichoke Dip (page 136), Plastered Pimiento Spread (page 137), Leek & Lager Spread (page 138), and Spiked & Spicy Cheddar Spread (page 140). If you're enjoying them as a stand-alone snack, experiment by pairing the chips with a newfound American or English Pale Ale, IPA, or Brown Ale, or else enjoy the chips with the respective pairing suggestions for the dips previously mentioned.

Pair with:
American or English Pale Ale (pages 33 and 34, respectively),
India Pale Ale (page 34), Brown Ale (page 34)

4 large baking potatoes, peeled and sliced 1/8-inch thick	1/4 cup canola oil Sea salt, to taste

Place racks in the top and bottom thirds of the oven, and preheat the oven to 400°F. Toss the potato slices with the oil until well coated in a large bowl. Mist 2 large baking sheets with cooking spray. Place the potato slices in single layers on both sheets. Bake until golden brown, switching the baking sheets from the top to bottom racks and turning front to back twice, 18 to 20 minutes total. Immediately sprinkle the chips with the sea salt, and cool on wire racks.

Once cooled, serve immediately, or store the potato chips in an airtight container for up to 3 days.

Yields 4 to 6 servings

Sweet Potato Chips

The classic potato chip gets a sweet twist here, yielding a festive chip that makes snack time a happy time indeed, especially when accompanied by a hearty Brown Ale or Porter, or a mellow Golden Ale that complements that classic sweet potato flavor.

Pair with:
Brown Ale (page 34), Porter (page 37), Golden Ale (page 34)

1 large (about 8-ounce) sweet potato, unpeeled, washed, and patted dry	Salt, to taste Freshly ground black pepper, to taste

Place racks in the top and bottom thirds of the oven, and preheat the oven to 200°F. Line 2 baking sheets with parchment paper, and set aside. Slice the sweet potato crosswise, as thin as possible. Arrange the slices on the baking sheets in a single layer, and keep them from touching. Sprinkle lightly with the salt and pepper.

Bake for 25 to 30 minutes. The slices will dehydrate and shrink. Turn the chips over, and rotate the baking sheets, if needed, for even cooking. Bake until the slices are crispy and the centers are still orange, not brown, 10 to 15 minutes longer. Transfer the baking sheets to cooling racks. The chips will get crispier as they cool.

Once cooled, serve immediately, or store the sweet potato chips in an airtight container for up to 3 days.

Yields I serving

Salt & Vinegar Chips

One of the world's favorite potato chip flavors now comes home to your kitchen in this easy-to-make version that nicely pairs its tanginess with a good English Bitter, IPA, or American or English Pale Ale.

Pair with:
English Bitter (page 34), India Pale Ale (page 34), American or English Pale Ale (pages 33 and 34, respectively)

2 medium (I to I I/2 pounds) Yukon gold potatoes, scrubbed (or peeled) and sliced into I/4-inch-thick bite-size rounds	Kosher salt, to taste
	Freshly ground black pepper, to taste
	Malt vinegar, to taste, for splashing the
I/4 cup extra-virgin olive oil	finished potatoes

Preheat the oven to 425°F. Place 2 nonstick baking sheets in the oven, and heat them for about 10 minutes. Toss the potatoes with the olive oil and salt and pepper in a large bowl.

Carefully remove the baking sheets from the oven, and quickly arrange the potato slices in a single layer on the sheets. Bake until the potato slices are golden on the bottom sides, about 25 to 30 minutes. Turn the potato slices over, and bake, watching closely, until they are golden brown all over, about 10 to 15 minutes longer. Remove the sheets from the oven, drizzle the chips lightly with the malt vinegar, and serve immediately.

Yields 2 servings

Barbecue Chips

The mere mention of barbecue chips sends the taste buds into a frenzy! A homemade bowl full of this seasoned classic pairs well with an equally classic Amber Lager or Pale Lager, or a slightly heavier American Dark Lager.

Pair with:
Amber Lager (page 35), Pale Lager (page 36), American Dark Lager (page 35)

1 teaspoon smoked Spanish paprika	1/8 teaspoon ground mustard
1 teaspoon garlic powder	Pinch of cayenne pepper
1/4 teaspoon sugar	1 to 2 large Yukon gold potatoes, scrubbed (or
1/2 teaspoon onion powder	peeled) and thinly sliced, about 1/8-inch thick
1/2 teaspoon chili powder	Vegetable oil, for deep-frying
1/4 teaspoons seasoned salt, such as Lawry's	

Combine the paprika, garlic powder, sugar, onion powder, chili powder, seasoned salt, mustard, and cayenne pepper in a small bowl. Soak the potato slices in a medium-size bowl with enough ice water to cover the slices for 30 minutes, then drain and pat dry with paper towels.

Heat about 2 inches of oil to 375°F in a large skillet. Fry the potato slices in batches for 2 minutes, or until golden brown, turning frequently or as needed. Using a slotted spoon, remove the slices and drain them on paper towels. Sprinkle with the seasoning mixture. Serve immediately, or store in an airtight container for up to a week.

Yields 1 to 2 servings

The Pub Crawl Popcorn Bar

For a brew-packed movie night or friendly get-together, the following smorgasbord of popcorn lets you take this favorite snack in any direction you want, from hot, spicy, or seasoned Italian-style to sweet and nutty. This is also your perfect opportunity to play around with beer and popcorn pairings, treating yourself to everything from classic Pale Lagers to those more adventurous Rauchbiers and Chili Beers you've always wanted to try.

Bayou Popcorn

For a truly Southern dive bar treat, pair this spirited popcorn with a Rauchbier, or let the spicy seasonings shine against a go-to Pale Lager or Pilsner.

 Pair with:
Rauchbier (page 39), Pale Lager (page 36), Pilsner (page 37)

I teaspoon paprika	I teaspoon lemon pepper
1/2 teaspoon chili powder	I teaspoon Old Bay Seasoning, or to taste
1/4 teaspoon seasoned salt, such as Lawry's	1/4 cup (1/2 stick) margarine, melted (use recipe on page 23 or store-bought
2 teaspoons onion powder	margarine)
I teaspoon garlic powder	
1/4 teaspoon cayenne pepper, or more to taste	I0 cups freshly popped, warm popcorn

Combine the paprika, chili powder, seasoned salt, onion and garlic powders, cayenne pepper, lemon pepper, and Old Bay Seasoning in a small bowl, mixing well. Combine the margarine and popcorn in a large bowl, mixing gently to coat. Add the seasoning mixture, tossing to mix. Serve immediately.

Yields I0 cups

Popcorn Italiano

Mangia, mangia! This Italian-inspired popcorn is tossed in a classic mixture of fresh basil and parsley, oregano, and garlic powder, and served with your choice of a chilled Golden Ale, Vienna Lager, or Maibock.

Pair with:
Golden Ale (page 34), Vienna Lager (page 37), Maibock (page 36)

1 tablespoon minced fresh basil leaves	1/4 teaspoon garlic powder, or to taste
1 tablespoon minced fresh parsley	2 tablespoons extra-virgin olive oil
1/2 teaspoon sea salt	3 to 4 cups freshly popped, warm popcorn
1/2 teaspoon oregano	

Combine the basil, parsley, sea salt, oregano, garlic powder, and olive oil in a medium-size bowl, mixing well. Place the warm popcorn in a large bowl, and then mix in the herb mixture, tossing gently to coat. Serve immediately.

Yields 3 to 4 cups

Jalapeño Popcorn

This bowl of sparks will light up any movie night or gab session around the pool or campfire. The popcorn and jalapeño duo can be further fueled by a Chili Beer pairing, or tempered and chased by a cold Kölsch or Amber Lager.

Pair with:
Chili Beer (page 39), Kölsch (page 35), Amber Lager (page 35)

1/4 cup vegetable or canola oil

1/2 cup canned sliced jalapeños with 1 to 2
    tablespoons of juice

1/4 cup popcorn kernels

Sea salt, to taste

Jalapeño powder, to taste

Heat the oil in a large saucepan over medium-high heat. Add the jalapeños and juice. Add the popcorn kernels, and gently mix to coat. Cover the pan and pop the kernels the way you would make regular popcorn. Sprinkle with the salt and/or jalapeño powder. Serve immediately.

Yields about 6 cups

South of the Border Popcorn

Taco seasoning, chives, and jalapeño powder give this popcorn deeply Southwestern roots. It makes sense to then pair it with a Chili Beer to carry through a theme, or a favorite Pale Lager or American Wheat Ale for sheer enjoyment.

Pair with:
Chili Beer (page 39), Pale Lager (page 36),
American Wheat Ale (page 38)

1/2 cup (1 stick) margarine (use recipe on
    page 23 or store-bought margarine)

1 tablespoon dry taco seasoning mix

1 tablespoon dried chopped chives

1 to 2 teaspoons jalapeño powder

Cayenne pepper, to taste

4 quarts freshly popped, warm popcorn

Melt the margarine in a small saucepan over low heat. Add the taco seasoning, chives, jalapeño powder, and cayenne pepper, blending well. Combine the warm popcorn and margarine mixture in a large serving bowl, tossing gently until well coated. Serve immediately.

Yields 4 quarts

Maple-Glazed Popcorn with Toasted Almonds

The real prize at the bottom of this bowl of maple-glazed popcorn and toasted almonds will be the satisfied smile on your face, and knowing you can make as many batches as you want. And the beat goes on when the sweet maple glaze is matched with a moderately hoppy and subtly sweet American Dark Lager, Oktoberfest, or Vienna Lager.

Pair with:
American Dark Lager (page 35), Oktoberfest (page 36), Vienna Lager (page 37)

2 cups light brown sugar

1 cup (2 sticks) margarine (use recipe on page 23 or store-bought margarine)

1/2 cup maple syrup

1/2 teaspoon baking soda

1/2 teaspoon salt, or to taste

1 teaspoon vanilla extract

1 cup toasted almonds and/or roasted peanuts (pages 58 and 62)

2 gallons freshly popped, warm popcorn

Preheat the oven to 250°F. Combine the brown sugar, margarine, and maple syrup in a large saucepan, bringing the mixture to a boil. Boil very gently for 5 to 6 minutes without stirring. Remove from the heat and add the baking soda, salt, vanilla, and almonds.

Place the popcorn in a large bowl. Pour the caramel mixture over the popcorn, tossing gently until well coated. Spread the popcorn in single layers on greased baking sheets. Bake slowly for 1 hour, stirring every 15 minutes or so. When cooled, serve or store in sealable plastic bags for up to a week.

Yields 2 gallons

Chapter 2
FRIDAY NIGHT BITES

F reedom's just another word for Friday night—when a full-throttle beer tap, cranked jukebox, good friends, and great eats all conspire to tell reality to take a hike, at least for a few hours! But you don't have to hit the bar just to have a little fun, especially if you don't feel like venturing far. The recipes and suggested beer pairings that follow bring the flavor and fun of bar-hopping at your favorite haunts home for you to indulge in anytime you want.

From the Jalapeño Corn Fritters with a smooth and hoppy Amber Lager, Beer-Battered Onion Rings with a rich, malty Bock, Deep-Fried Dills with a darker German Hefeweizen, and Deep-Fried Olives with a mellow Golden Ale, to your choice of selections and pairings from The Deep-Fried Veggie Basket—mushrooms, cauliflower, green beans, zucchini, eggplant, asparagus, and jalapeños—these recipes prove once and for all that true decadence comes deep-fried with a beer chaser.

Also, inspired by one of the bar circuit's most famous side dishes and snacks, The Roadhouse Fries Bar presents an easy and traditional recipe for any kind of French fries you could dream of: fries sprinkled with sea salt, garlic fries, sweet potato fries, and portobello fries with numerous pairing combinations using India Pale Ale, Belgian Abbey Dubbel, Brown Ale, Porter, American Wheat Ale, and many more.

Even more comfort by the mouthful is served up in the recipes for Garlicky Breadsticks with Pizza Sauce and a go-to Pale Lager, Crunchy Pickled Dills with a light-bodied Cream Ale, Cheesy Speakeasy Sticks with a hearty American or English Pale Ale, and Golden Cheddar Balls with a robust Dunkel or Doppelbock.

Jalapeño Corn Fritters

Just the name "corn fritter" conjures up fond images and aromas of the food and beer booths at the annual county fair or town festival. But with the addition of diced jalapeños and paired with a frisky Chili Beer, or even a calmer Pilsner or Amber Lager, these bites will be a hit anywhere you serve them.

Pair with:
Chili Beer (page 39), Pilsner (page 37), Amber Lager (page 35)

1 cup all-purpose flour	1 red bell pepper, minced
1 teaspoon salt	2 jalapeños or 1 jalapeño and 1 habanero,
1 tablespoon sugar	seeded and roughly diced
Egg replacer equal to 2 eggs, beaten (page 19)	Jalapeño powder, to taste (optional, for
1/2 cup soy or almond milk	added heat)
2 teaspoons baking powder	Canola oil, for frying 1/2 to 1 inch deep
1 (10-ounce) can or package frozen corn	
kernels, drained	

Sift together the flour, salt, and sugar in a large bowl. Stir in the egg replacer, milk, baking powder, corn, red bell pepper, jalapeños, and jalapeño powder, if using, letting the batter remain slightly lumpy. Heat 1/2 to 1 inch canola oil in a pan. Drop the batter by spoonfuls into the hot oil, and cook until golden brown, 3 to 5 minutes.

Yields 2 to 4 servings

Beer-Battered Onion Rings

Nothing—*I mean nothing*—transforms an onion ring into pure gold better and with more flavor than adding beer to the batter. While a good basic Pale Lager (page 36) is the standard when it comes to cooking beer-battered onion rings, go off the beaten path and use the same Porter, Bock, or Kölsch you're pairing them with for a refreshing new brew batter twist.

 Pair with:
Porter (page 37), Bock (page 35), Kölsch (page 35)

---

3 cups all-purpose flour
Egg replacer equal to 2 eggs (page 19)
1 cup beer of your choice, preferably the same beer you're pairing with the dish
1 tablespoon caraway seeds, lightly crushed

4 tablespoons margarine, melted (use recipe on page 23 or store-bought margarine)
Salt and/or seasoned salt, such as Lawry's, to taste
3 large onions, sliced into 1/4-inch rings
Canola or vegetable oil, for frying

Sift the flour into a large bowl. Whisk together the egg replacer, beer, caraway seeds, margarine, and salt in another large bowl. Set aside 1 cup of the flour for dipping the onion rings. Slowly stir the egg mixture into the remaining flour, mixing well. Allow the mixture to stand for 30 to 45 minutes.

Heat the oil to 375°F in a deep fryer. Coat each onion ring with the reserved flour, and then dip into the batter. Deep-fry the rings, a few at a time, until golden brown, 3 to 5 minutes. Don't crowd the rings or they won't brown properly. Drain on paper towels, and serve warm with ketchup or other sauces of your choice.

Yields 6 servings

The Deep-Fried Veggie Basket

Feel free to mix up your selection by throwing in some Deep-Fried Dills (page 92), Happy Hour Onion Petals (page 91), Deep-Fried Olives (page 94), or even a few Drunken Avocado Wedges (page 100). For a unique dipping sauce, try the Red-Hot Beer Sauce on page 119.

Deep-Fried Mushrooms

Deep-fried, using a simple onion and garlic batter, these button mushrooms make for a nice, casual pairing with a moderately sweet and nutty Brown Ale, staunch Porter, or Belgian Witbier.

Pair with:
Brown Ale (page 34), Porter (page 37), Belgian Witbier (page 38)

Vegetable oil, for deep frying	Egg replacer equal to I egg (page I9)
I cup all-purpose flour	I cup vegetable stock
I teaspoon garlic powder	I pound large button mushrooms, quartered
2 teaspoons onion powder	

Heat the vegetable oil to 350°F in a deep fryer or electric skillet. (Or heat the oil in a large, deep skillet over medium-high heat. Test to see if the oil is hot enough by frying a drop of batter. If it quickly sizzles and floats to the top, the oil is ready.)

Stir together the flour, garlic powder, and onion powder in a medium-size bowl. Mix in the egg replacer and vegetable stock until smooth. Dip the mushrooms into the batter, and then carefully place them, a few at a time, in the hot oil. Fry the mushrooms until golden brown, 3 to 5 minutes. Remove the mushrooms from the oil using a slotted spoon, and drain them on paper towels.

Yields 4 servings

Deep-Fried Cauliflower

The oregano-garlic-cayenne batter energizes the normally subtle flavor of the cauliflower and creates a tasty back-and-forth with the intricate notes of a German Hefeweizen, an earthy and spicy Saison, or the malty and diverse range of a Dunkelweizen.

Pair with:
German Hefeweizen (page 38), Saison (page 35),
Dunkelweizen (page 38)

Vegetable or canola oil, for deep frying

1/2 cup cornstarch

1/4 cup all-purpose flour

2 teaspoon baking powder

1 teaspoon oregano

1 clove garlic, crushed

1/2 teaspoon salt and/or seasoned salt, such as Lawry's

1/2 teaspoon garlic powder

1/4 teaspoon cayenne pepper

1/2 cup soy or almond milk

Egg replacer equal to 1 egg, beaten (page 19)

1 large head cauliflower, cut into bite-size florets

Heat the vegetable oil to 350°F in a deep fryer or electric skillet. (Or heat the oil in a large, deep skillet over medium-high heat. Test to see if the oil is hot enough by frying a drop of batter. If it quickly sizzles and floats to the top, the oil is ready.).

Combine the cornstarch, flour, baking powder, oregano, garlic, salt, garlic powder, and cayenne pepper in a large bowl. Add the milk and egg replacer, stirring until smooth. Dip the cauliflower florets in the batter, shake off any excess batter, and place the florets, a few at a time, in the hot oil. Fry until golden brown, 3 to 4 minutes. Remove the cauliflower from the oil with a slotted spoon and drain on paper towels.

Yields 4 to 6 servings

Deep-Fried Green Beans

The chili, garlic, and onion powders in this deep-fried batter work with the fresh green beans to create a surprisingly unique addition to a veggie basket, a versatile side dish, or even a stand-alone, pop-'em-in-your-mouth snack, which can be accompanied by soy sauce or another dipping sauce of your choice. For the pairing, go old school with Pale Lager or Amber Lager, or choose a distinct seasonal IPL.

Pair with:
Pale Lager (page 36), Amber Lager (page 35),
India Pale Lager (page 36)

Vegetable oil, for deep frying	2 cups seasoned breadcrumbs
I pound fresh green beans, trimmed	I teaspoon chili powder or jalapeño powder
1/2 cup water	I teaspoon garlic powder
Egg replacer equal to I egg (page 19)	I teaspoon onion powder
1/2 cup soy or almond milk	I cup all-purpose flour

Heat the vegetable oil to 350°F in a deep fryer or electric skillet. (Or heat the oil in a large, deep skillet over medium-high heat. Test to see if the oil is hot enough by frying a drop of batter. If it quickly sizzles and floats to the top, the oil is ready.)

Combine the green beans and water in a medium-size saucepan. Cover and bring to a boil. Cook until the beans are bright green, about 4 minutes. Drain and transfer to a bowl. Cover the beans with cold water and set aside.

Whisk together the egg replacer and milk in a medium-size bowl. Mix together the breadcrumbs, chili powder, garlic powder, and onion powder in a separate medium-size bowl. Drain the green beans and toss them with the flour to coat, shaking off the excess. Dip the beans into the egg mixture and then into the seasoned breadcrumbs, coating thoroughly.

Fry the beans in batches, making sure they are not touching. Cook until golden brown, 2 to 4 minutes. Remove the beans from the oil using a slotted spoon, and drain on paper towels.

Yields 2 to 4 servings

Deep-Fried Zucchini or Eggplant

The cook's choice of zucchini or eggplant here, preferably when the vegetable is in season, is especially adept at not only serving as a sound foundation for the spicy, deep-fried coating, but also at absorbing the flavor for maximum impact. The pepper, jalapeño, and parsley taste points in the batter play well with a moderately hopped Golden Ale, Pilsner, or Kölsch.

 Pair with:
Golden Ale (page 34), Pilsner (page 37), Kölsch (page 35)

1/2 cup all-purpose flour	Jalapeño powder or chili powder, to taste
1/4 cup cornstarch	(optional, for added heat)
1/2 teaspoon baking soda	3/4 cup ice water
1/4 teaspoon salt or seasoned salt, such as	2 tablespoons finely chopped fresh parsley
Lawry's	4 cups vegetable or canola oil, for frying
1/8 teaspoon freshly ground black pepper or	3 cups peeled zucchini or eggplant, cut into
cayenne pepper for added heat	2 x 1/4–inch sticks or bite-size pieces

Stir together the flour, cornstarch, baking soda, salt, pepper, and jalapeño powder, if using, in a medium-size bowl. Gradually stir in the water until smooth. Stir in the parsley. Cover and refrigerate for 1 hour.

Heat the oil to 375°F in a 3-quart pan or deep fryer. (Or heat the oil in a large, deep skillet over medium-high heat. Test to see if the oil is hot enough by frying a drop of batter. If it quickly sizzles and floats to the top, the oil is ready.) Dip the zucchini or eggplant into the batter. Fry the zucchini or eggplant in batches, making sure the pieces are not touching, and turning once, until golden brown and crisp, 2 to 4 minutes. Remove the zucchini or eggplant from the oil using a slotted spoon, and drain on paper towels.

Yields 4 servings

~Deep-Fried Asparagus~

The key to this deep-fried batter is using the same Golden Ale, Belgian Abbey Tripel, or India Pale Lager with which you are pairing the dish. All three of these suggestions harmonize with the distinct flavor of the vegetable and accompanying seasonings.

 Pair with:
Golden Ale (page 34), Belgian Abbey Tripel (page 33),
India Pale Lager (page 36)

Vegetable oil, for deep frying
I cup all-purpose flour
I teaspoon salt
1/2 teaspoon white pepper
I teaspoon garlic powder
Seasoned salt, such as Lawry's, to taste

I teaspoon Italian seasoning
2 ounces (1/4 cup) beer of your choice, at
   room temperature, preferably the same
   beer you're pairing with the dish
I 1/2 pounds asparagus, sliced into 2-inch
   pieces

Heat the vegetable oil to 350°F in a deep fryer or electric skillet. (Or heat the oil in a large, deep skillet over medium-high heat. Test to see if the oil is hot enough by frying a drop of batter. If it quickly sizzles and floats to the top, the oil is ready.)

Combine the flour, salt, pepper, garlic powder, seasoned salt, and Italian seasoning in a medium-size bowl, mixing well. Add the beer, stirring until the mixture is thick. Dip the asparagus in the batter, coating completely. Fry the asparagus in batches, making sure the pieces are not touching, and turning once, until golden brown, 2 to 3 minutes. Remove the asparagus from the oil using a slotted spoon, and drain on paper towels.

Yields 3 to 4 servings

⋙ Deep-Fried Jalapeños ⋘

To triple the flame factor when making these jalapeños in their cayenne-chili-garlic-onion-jalapeño powder batter, mix in an equally hot Chili Beer, or tame this dish a bit by making and pairing it with a Golden Ale or Vienna Lager.

 Pair with:
Chili Beer (page 39), Golden Ale (page 34),
Vienna Lager (page 37)

Vegetable or canola oil, for deep frying	I teaspoon onion powder
I cup all-purpose flour	1/2 teaspoon jalapeño powder, or to taste
I teaspoon salt and/or seasoned salt, such as Lawry's	Egg replacer equal to 2 eggs (page 19)
I teaspoon freshly ground black pepper	I cup beer of your choice, preferably the same beer you're pairing with the dish
1/2 teaspoon cayenne pepper	2 cups jalapeños, sliced crosswise into 1/4- to 1/2-inch discs
I teaspoon chili powder	
I teaspoon garlic powder	

Heat 1 to 2 inches of the vegetable oil to 365°F in a deep fryer or electric skillet. (Or heat the oil in a large, deep skillet over medium-high heat. Test to see if the oil is hot enough by frying a drop of batter. If it quickly sizzles and floats to the top, the oil is ready.)

Combine the flour, salt, black pepper, cayenne pepper, chili powder, garlic powder, onion powder, jalapeño powder, egg replacer, and beer in a large bowl. Mix until the batter is fairly smooth. Place about 6 of the jalapeño slices in the batter, and stir gently to coat them completely. Transfer the battered slices directly to the hot oil, and fry the jalapeños, making sure they don't touch, until golden brown and floating in the oil, about 6 minutes. Remove the jalapeños from the oil using a slotted spoon, and drain them on layers of paper towels.

Yields 2 to 4 servings

Bar Top Poppers

These baked and loaded jalapeños ooze with the flavors of cream cheese, red onion, chipotle peppers, walnuts, and pimiento, all of which harmonize nicely with a low-malt and low-hops Pale Lager, a darker Amber Lager, or the wheat malt of an American Wheat Ale.

Pair with:
Pale Lager (page 36), Amber Lager (page 35),
American Wheat Ale (page 38)

---

8 medium to large jalapeños

1 small red onion, cut into 1/2-inch chunks

4 to 6 ounces cream cheese, at room temperature (use recipe on page 16 or store-bought cream cheese)

3 canned chipotle peppers, roughly chopped

3 teaspoons adobo sauce from the canned chipotle peppers (optional)

8 toasted walnuts (page 59)

4 bottled pimientos, sliced lengthwise in half

Note: *If you want less spicy jalapeños, look for smooth peppers without many "striations," or wavy white lines, on the skins. But heat levels in jalapeños remain fairly unpredictable. Scraping the seeds out of the jalapeños and cutting off the white ribs on the inner skins will also tame the heat, at least somewhat. But then the chipotles and their adobo sauce will bring the voltage right back up again, so just make sure the beer is ice cold!*

Preheat the oven to 450°F. Stem the jalapeños and cut them in half lengthwise. Scrape out the seeds, but leave in the ribs for heat (see note, and also wear rubber gloves if your skin is sensitive to the jalapeños).

Mince the onion in a food processor. Scrape down the sides of the processor bowl and add the cream cheese in chunks, then the chipotle peppers and adobo, if using. Process until the mixture is well blended.

Spoon the cheese mixture into each jalapeño half. Arrange the halves on a parchment-lined baking sheet, 1 inch apart. Bake for 8 to 9 minutes, or until the filling is bubbly, watching closely. Let cool for a few minutes. Top each jalapeño half with a toasted walnut and a pimiento half, and serve.

Yields 16 stuffed jalapeño halves

The Roadhouse Fries Bar

Fries go with *everything*! The following recipes for French Fries, Garlic Fries, Sweet Potato Fries, and Portobello Fries offer you the perfect excuse to turn the world's favorite side dish into one big, heaping platter of indulgence by arranging them kaleidoscope-style on a large serving dish for parties (or just for yourself!). Or enjoy them each separately as a snack with the suggested beer pairings, or in tandem with selections from The Beer & Burgers Bar on pages 196 to 205.

French Fries

These homemade French fries, sprinkled to taste with sea salt, are the perfect match for a bold and hops-heavy IPA, or the complex flavor mixes of a Belgian Abbey Dubbel or Belgian Abbey Tripel.

 Pair with:
India Pale Ale (page 34), Belgian Abbey Dubbel (page 33), Belgian Abbey Tripel (page 33)

4 baking potatoes, peeled and cut into 1/4- to 1/2-inch-thick lengthwise strips, and patted very dry with paper towels	Canola oil, for frying Sea salt, to taste

Heat about 1 1/2 inches of the oil in a large, deep frying pan over medium-high heat until the oil is hot, about 6 to 7 minutes. Carefully add the potato strips, and cook them until they become golden, about 8 to 10 minutes, then flip them. Fry until the potato strips reach your desired color. Remove the French fries from the oil using a slotted spoon, and drain them on paper towels. Salt to taste while still hot, and serve with ketchup or other dips of your choice, or spritz the fries with distilled white vinegar.

Yields 4 servings

Garlic Fries

When these garlic-parsley-thyme fries are paired with a Pilsner, Amber Lager, or stronger Maibock, the fusion of flavors will set a whole new high bar for savory snacks.

Pair with:
Pilsner (page 37), Amber Lager (page 35),
Maibock (page 36)

I pound frozen French fries (or use the recipe for homemade French Fries on page 87)

I tablespoon extra-virgin olive oil

2 teaspoons finely minced garlic, or 2 to 3 medium cloves garlic, crushed

2 teaspoons finely minced fresh parsley

I teaspoon finely chopped fresh thyme

1/4 teaspoon black pepper

1/8 teaspoon salt or sea salt

If using frozen French fries, prepare them according to the package directions. Combine the remaining ingredients in a small bowl. Place the French fries in a large bowl, and toss the warm fries with the garlic mixture, mixing well. Serve immediately.

Yields 2 to 4 servings

Sweet Potato Fries

The mouthwatering experience of cinnamon and cloves, along with the natural sweetness of sweet potatoes, comes full circle when paired with a rich and strong Brown Ale, Porter, or Stout.

 Pair with:
Brown Ale (page 34), Porter (page 37), Stout (page 38)

1 cup all-purpose flour	4 sweet potatoes or yams, cut into 1/2-inch
2 teaspoons ground cinnamon	lengthwise strips
1/2 teaspoon ground cloves	1/4 cup extra-virgin olive oil
	Sea salt, to taste

Preheat the oven to 400°F. Stir together the flour, cinnamon, and cloves in a medium-size bowl until well mixed. Place the sweet potatoes in a large bowl, and toss together the potatoes with the flour mixture. Add the olive oil, continuing to toss gently to coat. Coat a baking sheet with nonstick cooking spray, and arrange the sweet potatoes in a single layer. Use multiple baking sheets if necessary. Bake the sweet potatoes for 15 to 20 minutes, or until golden brown on the bottom. Gently shake the sheets to loosen the potatoes, then turn the potatoes over and bake about 15 to 20 minutes longer, or until golden brown all over. Sprinkle lightly with sea salt, and serve immediately.

Yields 4 servings

⫸ Portobello Fries ⫷

These red pepper, garlic powder, and oregano–seasoned portobello fries are an all-out pamper-yourself (and your guests) treat that work well with a Rauchbier, American Wheat Ale, or German Hefeweizen.

 Pair with:
Rauchbier (page 39), American Wheat Ale (page 38), German Hefeweizen (page 38)

1/2 cup plain breadcrumbs

2 tablespoons grated Parmesan cheese (use recipe on page 17 or store-bought cheese)

1/4 cup finely chopped almonds

Pinch of red pepper flakes

1/8 teaspoon garlic powder

1/8 teaspoon oregano

Salt, to taste

Freshly ground black pepper, to taste

Egg replacer equal to 2 large eggs, beaten (page 19)

2 large portobello mushrooms, gills scraped away, caps sliced into 1/8-inch-thick lengthwise strips

Ketchup or seasoned tomato sauce, for serving

Preheat the oven to 425°F. Line a baking sheet with parchment paper or spray it with cooking spray. Stir together the breadcrumbs, Parmesan cheese, almonds, red pepper flakes, garlic powder, oregano, salt, and pepper in a medium-size bowl.

Prepare the egg replacer in a separate medium-size bowl. Dip the portobello slices in the egg replacer, and then toss them in the breadcrumb mixture, coating completely. Place the mushrooms on the baking sheet in a single layer, and bake for 10 to 15 minutes, checking on them after 8 minutes, and flipping them to ensure even baking. Serve warm, with the ketchup or tomato sauce in ramekins for dipping.

Yields 2 servings

⫸Happy Hour Onion Petals⫷

There are two secrets as to why your guests will beg you for this onion petals recipe: (1) the power-packed blend of seasonings and (2) the burst of flavor is sent soaring off the charts when matched with a Kölsch, Cream Ale, or Bock.

 Pair with:
Kölsch (page 35), Cream Ale (page 34), Bock (page 35)

Egg replacer equal to 1 egg (page 19)
1 cup soy or almond milk
1 cup all-purpose flour
1 teaspoon salt
2 teaspoons cayenne pepper
2 teaspoons smoked Spanish paprika
1/2 teaspoon garlic powder

1/2 teaspoon chili powder
1/4 teaspoon dried thyme
1/4 teaspoon dried oregano
1/8 teaspoon ground cumin
1 medium onion
Vegetable or canola oil, for deep frying

Combine the egg replacer and milk in a large bowl, and set aside.

Combine the flour, salt, cayenne pepper, paprika, garlic powder, chili powder, thyme, oregano, and cumin in a medium-size bowl, and set aside.

To prepare the onion, cut 3/4 to 1 inch off the top and bottom of the onion, and remove the skin. Cut the onion in half lengthwise, and cut each half, lengthwise, into 4 equal sections. Dip the onion petals in the milk mixture and then in the flour mixture, coating completely. Place them in a single layer on a baking sheet and refrigerate for 20 minutes to help the coating adhere.

Heat the vegetable oil to 350°F in a deep fryer or electric skillet. (Or heat the oil in a large, deep skillet over medium-high heat. Test to see if the oil is hot enough by frying a drop of batter. If it quickly sizzles and floats, the oil is ready.)

Fry the onion petals in the oil for 2 to 3 minutes, or until golden brown. Remove the petals from the oil using a slotted spoon, and drain them on paper towels.

Yields 2 servings

Deep-Fried Dills

Anytime I hit up my favorite bars, the first thing I go for is the deep-fried pickles, along with a German Hefeweizen, Pale Lager, or Oktoberfest. With this seasoned, DIY version, you won't even have to leave the house! I have to let you in on a little secret, though: these homemade golden pickle spears are surprisingly addictive. Luckily, the only known cure is now right at your fingertips.

 Pair with:
German Hefeweizen (page 38), Pale Lager (page 36), Oktoberfest (page 36)

24 dill pickle spears, chilled (use recipe on page 96 or store-bought pickles)

Egg replacer equal to 3 eggs (page 19)

Seasoned breading (recipe follows)

Canola oil, for frying

Beat the egg wash in a medium-size bowl, and place the seasoned breading in a separate bowl. Line a cookie sheet with waxed paper. Make sure that you are using only very cold dill pickle spears for this recipe. Dip each pickle into the egg wash, and then coat with the seasoned breading. Arrange the breaded pickles in a single layer on the cookie sheet. Chill for at least 30 minutes.

Heat 2 inches of the canola oil to 375°F in a deep skillet or deep fryer. Carefully add the pickle spears, in batches of 3 or 4, to the hot oil, and fry for 3 to 4 minutes, or until golden brown. Transfer to a few layers of paper towels to drain. Serve with a dipping sauce or dressing of your choice.

Yields 24 deep-fried pickle spears

Seasoned Breading

2 1/2 cups cornmeal

1 1/2 cups all-purpose flour

3 tablespoons finely grated lemon zest

2 tablespoons freshly ground black or white
    pepper

1/3 cup dried dill

1 teaspoon anise seeds

1 tablespoon crushed caraway seeds

1 tablespoon smoked Spanish paprika or
    regular Hungarian paprika

2 teaspoons garlic powder

1/2 teaspoon cayenne pepper

Whisk together all the ingredients in a large bowl until well combined.

Deep-Fried Olives

Served alone, or popped into The Deep-Fried Veggie Basket lineup on pages 80 to 85, these golden-battered olives will dazzle any palate they meet, especially when followed down the hatch by a Golden Ale, Vienna Lager, or Altbier.

Pair with:
Golden Ale (page 34), Vienna Lager (page 37),
Altbier (page 33)

---

1 tablespoon water

Egg replacer equal to 1 egg, beaten (page 19)

1/4 cup all-purpose flour

8 toasted walnuts, finely ground (page 59)

1/2 cup panko (Japanese breadcrumbs),
   ground into fine crumbs

1 cup vegetable or canola oil, for deep drying

12 large green olives, pitted and patted dry,
   and stuffed with pimentos, hummus (page
   131), or your preferred filling

Combine the water and egg replacer in a small bowl. Mix the flour with the walnuts in another small bowl. Place the panko in a third small bowl.

Heat the oil to 350°F in a deep fryer or electric skillet. (Or heat the oil to 350°F in a large, deep skillet over medium-high heat.)

Dip the olives in the flour mixture, coating them completely. Dip them, one at a time, in the egg wash, coating completely again. Roll each olive in the breadcrumbs, coating evenly.

Fry the olives until golden brown, turning once, 3 to 5 minutes. Remove the olives from the oil using a slotted spoon, and drain on paper towels.

Yields 12 deep-fried olives

Garlicky Breadsticks with Pizza Sauce

These garlicky breadsticks are so easy to make as a stand-alone snack, starter, or side that you'll find yourself making them morning, noon, and night. Luckily, it's always five o'clock somewhere, so an accompanying go-to Pale Lager, Amber Lager, or Pilsner makes sense anytime as well.

Pair with:
Pale Lager (page 36), Amber Lager (page 35), Pilsner (page 37)

---

4 cloves garlic, crushed

1/2 cup (1 stick) unsalted margarine, melted (use recipe on page 23 or store-bought margarine)

1 loaf Italian or French bread, halved lengthwise

1 to 2 teaspoons smoked Spanish paprika

Freshly ground black pepper, to taste

2 cups (or more) pizza sauce (use recipe on page 195 or store-bought pizza sauce)

Preheat the broiler. Mash the garlic into the melted margarine in a medium-size bowl. Stir well. Brush the bread halves with the margarine mixture, using it all up. Sprinkle lightly with the paprika and pepper to taste.

Broil the bread until golden brown, watching it very closely. It takes only about 90 seconds. Slice into inch-wide wedges and serve at once with the pizza sauce.

Yields 2 to 4 servings

⫸Crunchy Pickled Dills⫷

Few things rock a burger or sandwich platter more than the ultimate crunchy sidekick! Easy to make fresh at home, these pickles are a great treat anytime you're craving that dilly kick or looking for the perfect garnish to finish off a selection from The Beer & Burgers Bar on pages 196 to 205. Likewise, that distinct dill flavor profile is a nice match for a lighter wheat beer, such as a Belgian Witbier or American Wheat Ale, or a Cream Ale.

 Pair with:
Belgian Witbier (page 38), American Wheat Ale (page 38), Cream Ale (page 34)

---

3 3/4 cups water

3 3/4 cups white or cider vinegar

6 tablespoons pickling salt (see note)

2 1/4 pounds cucumbers (either about 36 small [4-inch] cucumbers or 8 to 10 larger cucumbers)

16 to 18 heads fresh dill, or 8 tablespoons dill seed

1 tablespoon golden mustard seeds, toasted

10 cloves garlic, lightly toasted

Note: *Pickling salt is a fine-grained salt, designed specifically for pickling and canning. One go-to version is Morton Canning & Pickling Salt (MortonSalt.com).*

For the brine: Combine the water, vinegar, and pickling salt in a large saucepan over medium-high heat. Heat until the mixture boils.

Remove the stems and cut a slice off each end of the cucumbers. Loosely pack the cucumbers in hot, clean 1-pint canning jars, leaving a good 1/2-inch headspace. Add 2 to 3 heads dill or 3 to 4 teaspoons dill seed, 1/2 teaspoon mustard seeds, and a garlic clove or two to each jar.

Place a wide-mouth plastic funnel in each jar, and ladle the hot brine over the cucumbers. Remove the funnel. Release trapped air bubbles in the jar by gently working a narrow rubber spatula around the jar's sides. Add additional brine, if needed, to maintain the 1/2-inch headspace. Wipe the jar rim carefully with a paper towel.

Position a prepared lid and screw band on the jar, and tighten according to the manufacturer's instructions. Place each jar into the boiling water of a water-bath canner as the jar is filled. The jars should not touch. Cover the canner. Process the filled jars in the boiling water for 10 minutes.

When the jars have cooled, press the center of each lid to check the seal. If the dip in the lid holds, the jar is sealed. If the lid bounces up and down, the jar isn't sealed. Unsealed jars should be stored in the refrigerator and used within 2 to 3 days. But let the sealed jars stand 1 week before using. Store up to 1 year in a cool, dry place.

Yields 6 pints (8 to 36 pickles, depending on the cucumbers used)

What a Jerky!

Without missing a single smoky-garlicky-spicy-maple beat, this is one perky new twist on traditional jerky that everyone can enjoy! And its ambitious seasoning mix is enhanced all the more when paired with a rich Brown Ale, dark and hoppy Altbier, or your favorite Pale Lager.

Pair with:
Brown Ale (page 34), Altbier (page 33), Pale Lager (page 36)

3 tablespoons low-sodium soy sauce

1 tablespoon maple syrup

1/4 teaspoon liquid smoke, or more to taste

1 teaspoon garlic powder

1 teaspoon onion powder

1/2 teaspoon freshly ground black pepper

3 tablespoons smoky barbecue sauce

1 to 2 canned chipotle peppers, finely chopped

1 to 2 teaspoons adobo sauce (the spicy liquid from the canned chipotles), or more to taste

2 teaspoons dark brown sugar

1 (14-ounce) package firm tofu, pressed and drained, cut into 1/4-inch slices (page 28)

Stir together all the ingredients, except the tofu, in a medium-size bowl. Dip the tofu in the sauce to coat completely. Place the tofu in a tightly sealed container (you can pour the remaining marinade sauce over it), refrigerate, and marinate for 2 to 4 hours.

Line an oven rack with heavy-duty aluminum foil, and place in the lowest position of the oven. Heat the oven to the lowest temperature, around 200°F. Arrange the marinated tofu slices on the foil. Bake for about 8 hours, checking and turning the tofu slices over every few hours. Tofu jerky is done when it is hard and uniformly dark in color.

Yields 4 servings

⁕~Hey, Edamame!~⁕

A fancy name for soybeans in a pod, edamame sprinkled with sea salt is a super easy, fresh snack that is becoming a favorite everywhere. But one *ginormous* advantage we have here in taking it to the next level is that we know to pair it with a chilled Pilsner, American Wheat Ale, or Belgian Witbier for maximum effect.

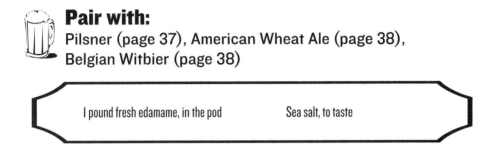

Pair with:
Pilsner (page 37), American Wheat Ale (page 38),
Belgian Witbier (page 38)

I pound fresh edamame, in the pod	Sea salt, to taste

Bring a large pot of water to a boil. Add the edamame and continue boiling until the beans are crisp-tender, about 10 minutes. To prevent overcooking, start checking for doneness after approximately 5 to 7 minutes: remove one edamame carefully, dip in cold water to cool, and then taste.

When the edamame is done to your liking, quickly immerse it in ice water to stop the cooking. Drain well and pat off the excess water with paper towels. Sprinkle with the salt.

To eat, hold the pod by the stem end, and slide the individual beans out by pressing the pod between your front teeth. Do not eat the pod.

Yields 4 to 6 servings

⚜︎~Drunken Avocado Wedges~⚜︎

Fresh avocadoes make an incredible addition to salads and sandwiches. Of course, they're also delicious in their most famous role—guacamole. But just wait until you deep-fry them using this beer batter seasoned with smoked Spanish paprika, garlic powder, and onion powder! Alone or as an unexpected surprise in The Deep-Fried Veggie Basket (pages 80 to 85), or even in a garden salad, these golden avocado wedges will be a hit with young and old alike. For continuity of flavor, in the batter, use the same Amber Lager, Irish Red Ale, or—for a really unique twist—Rauchbier with which you're pairing the wedges.

Pair with:
Amber Lager (page 35), Irish Red Ale (page 34),
Rauchbier (page 39)

I cup beer of your choice, preferably the same beer you're pairing with the dish
I cup all-purpose flour
I 1/2 teaspoons smoked Spanish paprika
2 to 3 teaspoons garlic powder
I teaspoon onion powder

2 ripe avocados, peeled and each cut into 6 wedges
Vegetable or canola oil, for deep frying
Salsa of your choice, for serving (use recipes on pages 123 to 127 or store-bought salsa)

Whisk together the beer, flour, paprika, garlic powder, and onion powder in a medium-size bowl. Let the mixture stand for at least 2 hours. Dip the avocado wedges in the batter, coating completely.

Heat at least 2 inches of the oil to 350° F in a deep fryer or electric skillet. (Or heat the oil in a large, deep skillet over medium-high heat. Test to see if the oil is hot enough by frying a drop of batter. If it quickly sizzles and floats to the top, the oil is ready.) Fry the avocado wedges in batches, making sure they are not touching, and turning once, until golden brown and crisp, about 3 minutes. Remove the avocado wedges from the oil using a slotted spoon, and drain them on paper towels. Serve the wedges with your choice of salsa.

Yields 2 ample servings

Cheesy Speakeasy Sticks

Using nutritional yeast is the perfect way to add a cheesy twist to everything from appetizers to entrées, without the dairy. Here, it spins its magic with garlic, tahini, rolled oats, dry mustard, and onion powder to help create deep-fried, cheesy-flavored sticks so flavorful that they practically dive into the pizza sauce themselves. Really, you could also call these Pizza Sticks. Serve them with a Pale Lager, or experiment with a heartier American Wheat Ale or American or English Pale Ale.

Pair with:
Pale Lager (page 36), American Wheat Ale (page 38),
American or English Pale Ale (pages 33 and 34, respectively)

2 cloves garlic	1/4 teaspoon dry mustard, such as Colman's
1 cup water	2 teaspoons onion powder
2 tablespoons freshly squeezed lemon juice	1/2 teaspoon kosher salt
2 tablespoons tahini (see note)	1 to 2 cups all-purpose flour, for dusting
1/4 cup nutritional yeast (see note)	Canola oil, for deep frying
3 tablespoons lightly ground toasted	4 to 6 cups pizza sauce (use recipe on page
rolled oats	195 or store-bought pizza sauce),
1 tablespoon cornstarch	for serving

Note: *The more tahini and nutritional yeast you use in this recipe, the cheesier the flavor will be.*

Toast the garlic cloves in a dry cast-iron skillet, tossing them often, until lightly browned, about 2 to 4 minutes. Remove the garlic from the skillet.

Combine the toasted garlic cloves, water, lemon juice, tahini, nutritional yeast, rolled oats, cornstarch, mustard, onion powder, and kosher salt in the bowl of a food processor. Process the ingredients until very smooth.

Using a rubber spatula, transfer the mixture to a roomy saucepan, and place over medium heat. Stir the mixture constantly, until it thickens, about 4 minutes after it comes to a low boil. Let the mixture cool.

When cool, form the mixture into stick shapes on a sheet of waxed paper. Dust the sticks with the flour.

Heat 1 to 2 inches of the oil to 350°F in a medium-size or large skillet. Fry the sticks, a few at a time, until golden brown, about 8 minutes, turning often. When browned, drain the sticks on paper towels. Serve warm with the pizza sauce.

Yields 4 to 6 servings

Golden Cheddar Balls

These cheesy-flavored little balls, with their sparks of Tabasco and onion and garlic powders, are perfect counterpoints to the low hop and robust maltiness of a Dunkel or Doppelbock, yet also work nicely one-on-one with an American Wheat Ale.

Pair with:
Dunkel (page 36), Doppelbock (page 36),
American Wheat Ale (page 38)

Canola oil, for oiling a loaf pan

5 teaspoons agar powder or 5 tablespoons agar flakes

1 1/2 cups filtered or bottled water

1/2 cup cashews

1/3 cup nutritional yeast

1/2 cup sliced pimiento

3 to 4 tablespoons freshly squeezed lemon juice, depending on how sharp you want it

2 tablespoons Tabasco sauce

2 teaspoons onion powder

1/4 teaspoon garlic powder

1/2 teaspoon mustard, such as Dijon mustard

3 to 4 cups plain breadcrumbs

Canola oil, for deep frying

Lightly oil a loaf pan measuring 3 1/2 x 7 1/2 or 4 1/2 x 8 1/2 inches. Whisk together the agar and water in a small saucepan over medium heat. Stir often until the mixture comes to a boil, then reduce the heat to simmer. Let the mixture bubble away gently for 5 minutes, stirring often to dissolve the agar completely.

Place the cashews, nutritional yeast, pimiento slices, lemon juice, Tabasco sauce, onion powder, garlic powder, and mustard into a blender.

When the agar has boiled for 5 minutes, let it cool slightly, then carefully and slowly pour it into the blender. Return the lid to the blender, hold a kitchen towel over the lid to keep the heat from blowing it off, and blend the mixture on high for about 1 minute. Stop the blender, scrape down the sides of the container with a rubber spatula, replace the lid, and blend on high again for another minute. The mixture should be very smooth and approximately the same orange color as standard Cheddar cheese.

Pour the mixture into the prepared loaf pan, transfer to the refrigerator, and let it chill until firm, at least 1 hour.

Form the mixture into balls the size of large marbles, toss them with the breadcrumbs, and let them rest for 10 minutes.

Heat an inch of the canola oil to 350°F in a medium-size to large skillet. When the cheese balls have rested, drop them, a few at a time, into the hot oil. Cook, turning often, until well browned, about 6 minutes. Drain on paper towels and serve warm.

Yields 4 to 6 servings

Chapter 3

GAME DAY SAUCES, SALSAS & DIPS

This chapter has "PARTY CENTRAL!" written all over it. No matter the occasion—tailgating, a backyard BBQ, a campfire, a holiday get-together, or a party for one or two on the couch—these recipes and their suggested beer pairings will fill your table or home bar with new and spirited takes on classic party bar snacks and dippers.

For starters, The Game Day Sauce Bar will take you in new directions of celebratory flavor that all your guests can enjoy, with such sauces as Blazing Saddles, East Meets West, Garlic Love Fest, Agave Barbecue, Rajun Cajun, Jalapeño Fire Sauce, and Peanut Butter Flame Sauce.

Your pregame, halftime, or party-all-the-time mind-set will get a boost when the homemade tortilla chips on page 69 meet up with selections from The Party Salsa Bar. Or score big time by serving the Guac 'n' Roll with its choice of scrumptious variations. And, use pretzels and the homemade potato chips or sweet potato chips on pages 69 and 70, respectively, to play ring around the tap with selections from The Hoppy Hummus Bar.

With their updated infusions and waves of flavor, classic dips—such as Parmesan-Artichoke Dip with a commanding Bock; Plastered Pimiento Spread with a dark, hoppy Altbier; Leek & Lager Spread with a brown, malty Dunkel; Cheesy Black Bean Dip with a toastier Vienna Lager; and Spiked & Spicy Cheddar Spread with a sweeter Brown Ale—will also get the party started from the first bite onward.

The Game Day Sauce Bar

Many of my friends use sauces like these for chicken wings and other meaty dishes, but I prefer to use baked, deep-fried, or grilled tofu (page 28), tempeh (page 28), or seitan (page 26). These protein- and vitamin-packed alternatives to meat act as extraordinary sponges, absorbing the full ingredient ranges of the sauces for maximum flavor and effect. Plus, because they help spotlight the flavor profiles of the sauces, the impact of the suggested beer pairings with each sauce is all the stronger.

Preparing the Tofu, Tempeh, and Seitan

Tofu, tempeh, and seitan are the ultimate blank canvases when it comes to sauces. They're just as delish climbing up a skewer with veggies for a snack or light meal as they are performing alone for a hearty main course.

For parties, consider preparing several of the sauces that follow. Then, either invite your guests to engage their inner culinary artist at a DIY sauce or kebab bar stocked with a variety of bite-size pieces of tofu, tempeh, and/or seitan plus vegetables, or surprise them with a smorgasbord of your own creations.

Unless otherwise noted, each of the sauces that follow works well with at least 8 ounces of unflavored tofu, tempeh, or seitan. Naturally, the sauce amounts can easily be doubled or tripled for larger parties. Some of the sauces with larger yields already work well for parties.

To bake tofu, tempeh, or seitan:

Preheat the oven to 350°F. Line a baking sheet with aluminum foil. Cut the tofu/tempeh/seitan into large but bite-size slices, and arrange them on the prepared baking sheet in rows (press and drain the tofu first—see page 28). Bake for 10 minutes, turning once, or until nicely tanned.

To deep-fry tofu, tempeh, or seitan:

Heat 1 or 2 inches of canola oil to 350°F in a large skillet. Cut the tofu/tempeh/seitan into large but bite-size slices, pat them dry, and fry them in batches until golden brown, about 8 to 20 minutes (press and drain the tofu first—see page 28).

To grill tofu, tempeh, or seitan:

All grills are different, so the cooking times for tofu, tempeh, and seitan may differ slightly from the following directions, depending on your grill and heat level. Therefore, the best rule of thumb is to always watch the food closely while grilling, turn it every few minutes, and follow your instincts. Also, depending on the size of your grill grate, you may want to use a grill screen, especially when grilling seitan. Grilling times over medium to high heat are roughly as follows:

* Tofu kebabs (press and drain the tofu first—see page 28): 8 to 10 minutes, or until the tofu is golden and crispy and the vegetables are tender. Turn every minute or two.
* Tofu slices (cut as desired, press and drain the tofu first—see page 28) alone: 8 to 10 minutes, or until golden and crispy. Turn once or twice.
* Tempeh kebabs: 8 to 10 minutes, or until browned and the vegetables are tender. Turn every minute or two.
* Tempeh slices (cut as desired) alone: 8 to 10 minutes, or until browned. Turn once or twice.
* Seitan kebabs: 8 to 10 minutes, or until browned and crispy and the vegetables are tender. Turn every minute or two.
* Seitan slices (cut as desired) alone: 8 to 10 minutes, or until browned and crispy. Turn once or twice.

Blazing Saddles

Nothing tempers a fiery sauce while still keeping the blaze going like an ice-cold one. Here, go classic with your favorite Pale Lagers, Amber Ales, or Amber Lagers.

Pair with:
Pale Lager (page 36), Amber Ale (page 33),
Amber Lager (page 35)

---

1 (23-ounce) bottle Frank's RedHot Cayenne Pepper Sauce

1/4 cup ketchup or your preferred thick tomato sauce, or to taste

6 tablespoons margarine (use recipe on page 23 or store-bought margarine)

2 tablespoons minced garlic, or to taste

1 1/2 tablespoon Worcestershire sauce (use recipe on page 30 or store-bought Worcestershire sauce)

1 tablespoon apple cider vinegar

1 to 2 tablespoons toasted sesame seeds

2 tablespoons light or dark brown sugar

Mix together the hot sauce and ketchup in a large bowl, then set aside. Melt the margarine in a large saucepan over medium heat. Stir in the garlic, and simmer until fragrant. Add the Worcestershire sauce, vinegar, sesame seeds, and brown sugar to the pan. Raise the heat and bring the mixture to a simmer, and cook for 2 minutes. Add the margarine mixture to the hot sauce mixture, stirring to combine. Toss with baked, deep-fried, or grilled tofu, tempeh, or seitan, and serve.

Yields about 4 cups

 Saucy Maple

The molasses and maple syrup in this sauce play best with a rich and sweet Brown Ale or the roasted maltiness and bitterness of a Porter or Stout.

 Pair with:
Brown Ale (page 34), Porter (page 37), Stout (page 38)

1 1/2 cups Frank's RedHot Cayenne Pepper Sauce	1 tablespoon ketchup
1/4 cup (1/2 stick) margarine (use recipe on page 23 or store-bought margarine)	2 tablespoons light molasses 1/2 cup maple syrup

Combine all the ingredients in a medium-size saucepan over medium heat. Cook until heated through, about 6 to 8 minutes. Adjust the seasonings to taste. Toss with baked, deep-fried, or grilled tofu, tempeh, or seitan, and serve.

Yields about 1 cup

East Meets West

Soy sauce, ginger, and garlic powder lend this sauce a Far East–inspired flare, with a few extra sparks thanks to the Frank's RedHot. For the pairing, choose either a traditional Sake or go Western-style with a Pale Lager or Pilsner.

Pair with:
Sake (page 38), Pale Lager (page 36), Pilsner (page 37)

1/4 cup soy sauce	2 tablespoons sugar
1/4 cup Frank's RedHot Cayenne Pepper Sauce	1 tablespoon cornstarch
1 tablespoon dry white vermouth or Sake	1/4 teaspoon ground ginger
1 tablespoon extra-virgin olive oil	1/8 teaspoon garlic powder

Combine all the ingredients in a small saucepan over medium heat. Add more vermouth if needed to smooth out the mixture. Heat until the mixture boils and thickens, 10 to 12 minutes. Remove from the heat. Toss with baked, deep-fried, or grilled tofu, tempeh, or seitan, and serve.

Yields 1/2 cup

Garlic Love Fest

There is one star in this sauce: GARLIC! While the potential is there to overwhelm the palate with too much of a good thing, a well-chosen Pale Lager, Maibock, or Vienna Lager will level the playing field so you can easily head into extra innings with this feast.

Pair with:
Pale Lager (page 36), Maibock (page 36), Vienna Lager (page 37)

1/4 cup (1/2 stick) margarine (use recipe on
    page 23 or store-bought margarine)
4 tablespoons extra-virgin olive oil
3 shallots, finely chopped
3 to 4 cloves garlic, crushed

I teaspoon garlic powder
1/2 teaspoon onion powder
7 ounces Frank's RedHot Cayenne Pepper
    Sauce

Melt the margarine in a small saucepan over medium heat. Add the olive oil, shallots, and garlic cloves, and simmer until tender, about 7 minutes. When you are ready to use the sauce, remove the pan from the heat. Immediately stir in the garlic and onion powders and hot sauce, and keep warm. Toss with baked, deep-fried, or grilled tofu, tempeh, or seitan, and serve.

Yields about 2/3 cup

Agave Barbecue

For a change from the classic honey barbecue, catch a new buzz by using agave and apricot nectars in this tangy-sweet BBQ sauce that begs to be paired with an ice-cold Amber Ale, Amber Lager, or IPA.

Pair with:
Amber Ale (page 33), Amber Lager (page 35), India Pale Ale (page 34)

---

4 cups barbecue sauce

1/4 cup agave nectar

2 tablespoons apricot nectar

1 teaspoon Tabasco sauce, or more to taste

1/4 cup tomato sauce of your choice, or ketchup

1/4 cup Dijon mustard

1/2 cup finely chopped yellow onion

Combine all the ingredients in a large saucepan over medium heat. Simmer for 5 minutes. Toss with baked, deep-fried, or grilled tofu, tempeh, or seitan, and serve.

Yields 5 cups

Barbecue Inferno

Once this boozy inferno of Worcestershire sauce, Dijon mustard, and your choice of Frank's RedHot or Tabasco begins, there's no turning back from an unforgettable meal. To add even more fuel to this palate fire, pair the sauce with a Chili Beer, or opt for the fire-and-ice approach by choosing a chilled Kölsch or American Dark Lager instead.

 Pair with:
Chili Beer (page 39), Kölsch (page 35),
American Dark Lager (page 35)

I cup ketchup	I 1/2 tablespoons Worcestershire sauce
I cup beer of your choice, preferably the same beer you're pairing with the dish	(use recipe on page 30 or store-bought Worcestershire sauce)
3/4 cup chopped onions	I 1/2 tablespoons Dijon mustard
1/4 cup white vinegar	1/8 teaspoon Frank's RedHot Cayenne Pepper
I teaspoon onion powder	Sauce or Tabasco sauce
I teaspoon garlic powder	1/2 teaspoon salt

Combine all the ingredients in a large saucepan, and bring to a boil. Reduce the heat and simmer, uncovered, for 25 minutes. Toss with baked, deep-fried, or grilled tofu, tempeh, or seitan, and serve.

Yields about 2 cups

Chile Barbecue

Make no mistake that the forecast for this sauce is extra *chile*! Tame this heat wave with an American or English Pale Lager or a malty Scotch Ale, or try a Pale Lager you've never tried before.

 Pair with:
American or English Pale Ale (pages 33 and 34, respectively),
Scotch Ale (page 35), Pale Lager (page 36)

2 (14-ounce) bottles ketchup

1 (12-ounce) bottle chile sauce or chile-ketchup

1/2 cup Dijon mustard

1 teaspoon dry mustard

1 teaspoon salt

1 1/2 cups brown sugar

2 tablespoons freshly ground black pepper

3/4 cup Worcestershire sauce (use recipe on page 30 or store-bought Worcestershire sauce)

1 tablespoon low-sodium soy sauce

12 ounces beer of your choice, preferably the same beer you're pairing with the dish

2 teaspoons minced garlic

Combine all the ingredients, except the garlic, in a large saucepan, mixing well. Simmer the mixture, uncovered, over medium heat for 30 minutes. Add the garlic right before using the sauce. Toss with baked, deep-fried, or grilled tofu, tempeh, or seitan, and serve.

Yields about 3 cups

Sweet & Sour

The garlic, lemon, orange, sugar, pineapple juice, and soy sauce in this Asian-inspired sauce all meld together for optimum effect. To pair this sauce, try tossing a spicy and smoky Rye Beer or hefty Maibock into the mix, or play it safe with a Pale Lager, which is a winning choice every time!

Pair with:
Rye Beer (page 35), Maibock (page 36), Pale Lager (page 36)

1/2 cup all-purpose flour

1/4 teaspoon garlic powder

1/4 teaspoon lemon pepper seasoning

1 teaspoon freshly grated lemon zest

1 teaspoon freshly grated orange zest

8 ounces tofu, pressed and drained (see instructions on page 28), tempeh, or seitan, cut into 1/2-inch pieces

3 tablespoons vegetable oil

3/4 cup sugar

1/2 cup white vinegar

1/4 cup unsweetened pineapple juice

1/4 cup ketchup

1 teaspoon soy sauce

Preheat the oven to 350°F. Combine the flour, garlic powder, lemon pepper seasoning, and lemon and orange zests in a shallow dish. Coat the tofu, tempeh, or seitan pieces with the flour mixture. Heat the oil in a 12-inch skillet. Add the coated tofu, tempeh, or seitan pieces, and cook until browned, turning occasionally, 6 to 8 minutes. Remove the pieces from the skillet, and arrange them in a shallow baking dish.

Combine the sugar, vinegar, pineapple juice, ketchup, and soy sauce in a medium-size saucepan over medium-high heat. Bring to a boil, stirring to dissolve the sugar. Pour over the coated tofu, tempeh, or seitan pieces. Bake, uncovered, for 6 to 8 minutes, turning pieces over after 4 minutes.

Yields 3 to 4 servings

Rajun Cajun

Cue "When the Saints Go Marching In" and dive into this jazzy New Orleans–inspired sauce that will leave your spice rack spinning and your guests chewing to the beat of a fantastic meal. For the brewski, go hot on the pairing with a Chili Beer, or cool things down with a Pilsner or Bock.

 Pair with:
Chili Beer (page 39), Pilsner (page 37), Bock (page 35)

Vegetable oil, for frying
8 ounces tofu, pressed and drained (see instructions on page 28), tempeh, or seitan, cut into bite-size pieces
2 tablespoons Frank's RedHot Cayenne Pepper Sauce
1/2 teaspoon dried thyme
1/2 teaspoon dried oregano
8 basil leaves, stacked and cut into chiffonade (page 22), then finely chopped

1 teaspoon garlic powder
1 teaspoon onion powder
1 teaspoon chili powder
1 tablespoon Dijon mustard
Salt, to taste
Freshly ground black pepper, to taste
1/2 cup (1 stick) margarine (use recipe on page 23 or store-bought margarine)

Add an inch or two of the oil to a large skillet. Heat the oil to about 375°F. Add the uncoated tofu, tempeh, or seitan, and cook until browned, turning once, about 6 to 8 minutes. Remove from the pan, and drain on paper towels.

Combine the remaining ingredients, except the margarine, in a medium-size bowl, mixing well.

Remove the oil from the frying pan. Add the margarine to the pan, and return to low heat. Add the dried tofu, tempeh, or seitan and the spice mixture, stirring until well coated. Serve warm.

Yields 4 to 6 servings

Jalapeño Fire Sauce

If you like it hot—really, *really* hot—you're about to get your wish. A jalapeño, an ample dose of Frank's RedHot, crushed red pepper flakes, and dry hot mustard will send you running for the nearest, coldest, tallest bottle of Oktoberfest, Pale Lager, or Vienna Lager you can find!

Pair with:
Oktoberfest (page 36), Pale Lager (page 36),
Vienna Lager (page 37)

---

1 jalapeño, finely chopped

1/2 cup Frank's RedHot Cayenne Pepper Sauce

2 tablespoons crushed red pepper flakes

2 teaspoons dry hot mustard, such as
   Colman's

1/2 cup (1 stick) melted margarine (use recipe
   on page 23 or store-bought margarine)

12 to 18 strips of baked, deep-fried, or grilled
   tofu, tempeh, or seitan

Combine the jalapeño, hot sauce, red pepper flakes, mustard, and margarine in a large bowl, mixing well. Toss with the tofu, tempeh, or seitan, and serve.

Yields 4 to 6 servings

Just Yell Fire!

When Sriracha, Frank's RedHot, *and* Tabasco join forces with a Chili Beer, you'll have no choice but to yell "FIRE!" and then eat some more. Just be sure you also have a cooler full of Pale Lager and Amber Lager nearby when it's time to put out the blaze and chill for a while.

Pair with:
Chili Beer (page 39), Pale Lager (page 36),
Amber Lager (page 35)

2 cups Sriracha Hot Chili Sauce	recipe on page 30 or store-bought
2/3 cup water	Worcestershire sauce)
2 cups brown sugar	1 tablespoon garlic powder
3/4 cup Frank's RedHot Cayenne Pepper Sauce	1 tablespoon chili powder
2 teaspoons Tabasco sauce, or to taste	8 to 10 ounces baked, grilled, or deep-fried tofu,
6 tablespoons Worcestershire sauce (use	tempeh, or seitan, cut into bite-size pieces

Whisk together the Sriracha, water, brown sugar, RedHot sauce, Tabasco sauce, Worcestershire sauce, garlic powder, and chili powder in a medium-size bowl. Toss with the tofu, tempeh, or seitan. Cook in a slow-cooker on very low for 3 to 4 hours or bake in a 350°F oven for 1 hour.

Yields 4 servings

Red-Hot Beer Sauce

This traditional hot sauce is easy to whip up in minutes, and even makes a nice alternative dipping sauce for the French Fries on page 87, Portobello Fries on page 90, or The Deep-Fried Veggie Basket selections on pages 80 to 85. The simplicity of the sauce also nicely complements the various flavor notes of an American or English Pale Ale, Amber Lager, or IPA.

 Pair with:
American or English Pale Ale (pages 33 and 34, respectively), Amber Lager (page 35), India Pale Ale (page 34)

---

1 (.7-ounce) packet powdered Italian dressing mix, such as Good Seasons

1/2 cup (1 stick) margarine (use recipe on page 23 or store-bought margarine)

2 cups Frank's RedHot Cayenne Pepper Sauce

6 tablespoons beer of your choice, or a bit more to taste, preferably the same beer you're pairing with the dish

---

Combine all the ingredients in a large bowl, mixing well. Toss with baked, deep-fried, or grilled tofu, tempeh, or seitan.

Yields 2 1/4 cups

Buttery Cayenne-Mustard Sauce

Smooth and tangy, the peppery mustard essence of this sauce is heightened when paired with a sweet Oktoberfest, malty Maibock, or a robust Doppelbock.

 Pair with:
Oktoberfest (page 36), Maibock (page 36), Doppelbock (page 36)

1/2 cup (I stick) unsalted margarine (use recipe on page 23 or store-bought margarine)

1/2 cup beer of your choice, preferably the same beer you're pairing with the dish

I teaspoon garlic powder

I teaspoon onion powder

I teaspoon cayenne pepper

I teaspoon ground mustard, such a Colman's, or 2 teaspoons Dijon mustard, smooth or grainy

I tablespoon Worcestershire sauce (use recipe on page 30 or store-bought Worcestershire sauce)

Melt the margarine in a medium-size saucepan, and allow it to start to simmer. Gradually add the beer. Add the garlic and onion powders, cayenne pepper, mustard, and Worcestershire sauce, mixing well. Boil the sauce for 2 minutes, and then remove it from the heat and let cool. Toss with baked, deep-fried, or grilled tofu, tempeh, or seitan.

Yields 3/4 cup

⇒ Slow as Molasses ⇐

This chile and molasses beer sauce, with its hickory-smoked accent, is meant to be made with and savored slowly alongside a Brown Ale, Porter, or fiery Chili Beer.

 Pair with:
Brown Ale (page 34), Porter (page 37), Chili Beer (page 39)

1 1/4 cups chile sauce	1 1/2 tablespoons chili powder
1 cup mild-flavored molasses	2 1/2 teaspoons soy sauce
3/4 cup beer of your choice, or more to adjust the liquid's thickness, preferably the same beer you're pairing with the dish	2 teaspoons Tabasco sauce, or more to taste
	1 1/2 teaspoons freshly squeezed lemon juice
	1 teaspoon hickory-flavored liquid smoke, or
2 tablespoons Dijon mustard	more to taste

Combine all the ingredients in a large saucepan, whisking well. Bring the mixture to a boil over medium heat, stirring constantly. Reduce the heat and simmer the mixture, uncovered, until it thickens and reduces to about 2 cups, stirring often, 8 to 10 minutes. Cool before using. Toss with baked, deep-fried, or grilled tofu, tempeh, or seitan.

Yields about 2 cups

Peanut Butter Flame Sauce

With the obvious flavor allusions to all those scrumptious and spicy Asian peanut sauces, you can take this sizzle-meets-sweet sauce in even more savory directions by pairing it with the rich and complex flavoring of a Belgian Abbey Dubbel, the low malt and subtle hoppiness of a Golden Ale, or a hopped-up, citrusy IPL.

 Pair with:
Belgian Abbey Dubbel (page 33), Golden Ale (page 34),
India Pale Lager (page 36)

I teaspoon cracked black pepper

I 1/2 teaspoons garlic powder

I teaspoon crushed red pepper

1/2 teaspoon onion powder

1/2 teaspoon salt

1/2 teaspoon Frank's RedHot Cayenne Pepper
Sauce

2 tablespoons Worcestershire sauce (use
recipe on page 30 or store-bought
Worcestershire sauce)

I to 2 tablespoons Sriracha Hot Chili Sauce

I (16- to 18-ounce) jar smooth peanut butter
(see note)

24 ounces beer of your choice, divided,
preferably the same beer you're pairing
with the dish

2 cups soy or almond milk

Note: *When buying peanut butter, be sure to read the ingredient label to make sure you are comfortable with all the ingredients.*

Combine all the ingredients, except 12 ounces of the beer and the milk, in a large saucepan, mixing well. Bring the mixture to a boil over medium-high heat. When the sauce thickens, turn the heat down to simmer the mixture. Add the remaining beer and continue to simmer the mixture, uncovered, until the sauce thickens, about 6 to 8 minutes, then slowly add the milk. Continue to simmer until the sauce thickens again, about 6 to 8 minutes. Toss the sauce with baked, deep-fried, or grilled tofu, tempeh, or seitan.

Yields 3 to 4 cups

> ## The Party Salsa Bar
> All you really need for tailgating season, or your next get-together, is a tableful of these five salsas, some homemade tortilla chips on page 69, and a giant cooler filled to the top with brewskis.

Tomato & Hot Pepper Salsa

The basic, everyday tomato salsa gets a flavor boost here from jalapeños and chile peppers, Sriracha, cilantro, oregano, and toasted cumin seeds. With all that going on, it's best to pair this fiery salsa with a very cold go-to Pale Lager, American Wheat Ale, or Amber Lager.

 Pair with:
Pale Lager (page 36), American Wheat Ale (page 38), Amber Lager (page 35)

1 to 1 1/2 pounds (2 to 3 medium-size) fresh tomatoes, finely diced

1/2 red onion, finely diced

1 jalapeño, ribs and seeds removed, finely diced

1 serrano chile peppers, ribs and seeds removed, finely diced, or more to taste

Freshly squeezed juice of 1 lime

1/4 cup Sriracha Hot Chili Sauce

1/2 cup chopped fresh cilantro

Salt, to taste

Freshly ground black pepper, to taste

2 teaspoons dried oregano, or to taste

1 teaspoon ground toasted cumin seeds, or to taste

Combine all the ingredients in a medium-size bowl. Taste and adjust seasonings according to personal preference. Let the mixture sit for 1 hour before serving.

Yields 3 to 4 cups

Chili Beer Salsa

It really is a no-brainer that a chili beer salsa would be made with one of the Chili Beers that are popping up everywhere. But if you can't take the heat, there's no need to leave the kitchen—just swap in a Pale Lager or Vienna Lager, and start eating and chugging!

Pair with:
Chili Beer (page 39), Pale Lager (page 36),
Vienna Lager (page 37)

5 dried chile peppers, such as ancho chiles	I clove garlic
I cup beer of your choice, at room temperature, preferably the same beer you're pairing with the dish	Freshly squeezed juice of I orange
	1/4 medium onion, chopped
	Salt, to taste

Toast the chile peppers in a small skillet over medium heat, cooking them until they blister. Stem the chiles and split them open. Remove the veins and seeds. Place the chile peppers in a small bowl. Soak the peppers in the beer for 20 to 30 minutes, or until very soft. Place the chile peppers, beer, garlic, and orange juice in a blender, and puree until the mixture is smooth. Stir in the chopped onion and add salt to taste.

Yields 2 cups

Black Bean & Corn Salsa

Earthy, sweet, and with a little sizzle, this black bean and corn salsa with bell peppers, red onion, and jalapeño is as eye-catching as it is full-on yummy. Add to that a pairing of Amber Lager, Maibock, or—to be really adventurous—Rauchbier, and you've got yourself a tasty conversation piece that will keep the party going all night long!

Pair with:
Amber Lager (page 35), Maibock (page 36), Rauchbier (page 39)

---

2 (16-ounce) cans black beans, drained and rinsed

1 (12-ounce) can white corn, drained and rinsed, or 1 (14-ounce) package frozen corn, thawed

1/4 cup chopped fresh cilantro

3/4 cup finely diced red, yellow, and/or green bell peppers

1 medium red onion, finely chopped

1 (14-ounce) can diced tomatoes, partially drained

1 jalapeño, finely chopped, or more to taste

1 tablespoon canola oil

3 tablespoons freshly squeezed lime juice

1 teaspoon salt

1 teaspoon garlic powder

Combine the black beans, corn, cilantro, peppers, onion, tomatoes, and jalapeño in a large bowl, mixing well. Drizzle the oil and lime juice over top, then add the salt and garlic powder. Stir. Refrigerate, covered, for 3 hours to overnight.

Yields about 2 cups

Fruit Salad Salsa

The beauty of this chunky fruit salad salsa is that it can be a totally new dish every time you make it if you mix up the fruit you use or choose fruit that is in season and available at your local farmers market or roadside stand. The fruity sweetness is balanced with a fresh jalapeño and green onions, and topped off with a complementary Fruit Beer, Kölsch, or American Wheat Ale.

Pair with:
Fruit Beer (page 39), Kölsch (page 35),
American Wheat Ale (page 38)

2 to 3 cups fruit mixture of your choice, such as mango, peach, pineapple, clementine, orange, nectarine, strawberries, or papaya, chopped into 1/2-inch pieces	1/2 bunch fresh cilantro, leaves only, finely chopped
1 red bell pepper, chopped into 1/2-inch pieces	1 jalapeño, seeded and diced, or more to taste
	4 green onions, white and light green parts diced
	Freshly squeezed juice of 1 lime

Combine all the ingredients in a large bowl, mixing well. Cover tightly and refrigerate for at least 30 minutes, or until ready to use (the sooner, the better).

Yields about 2 1/2 cups

Under the Apple Tree Salsa

The concept behind this salsa is simple: start with fresh apples and then add everything that pairs well with them, like jalapeños and chiles on the hot side of the spectrum, and walnuts, ginger, and cinnamon on the sweet, cozy side. And on the refreshing side—a few rounds of Golden Ale, Pilsner, or Maibock.

 Pair with:
Golden Ale (page 34), Pilsner (page 37), Maibock (page 36)

---

2 to 3 tart apples, such as Granny
   Smith, cubed

4 tablespoons freshly squeezed lime juice

I jalapeño, seeded and sliced

I Anaheim chile, seeded and sliced

I small onion, finely chopped

2 tablespoons coarsely chopped fresh cilantro

3/4 cup chopped lightly toasted walnuts
   (page 59)

2 tablespoons fresh ginger, peeled and minced

I teaspoon ground cinnamon, or to taste

1/4 teaspoon kosher salt, or slightly more
   to taste

Stir together the apples and lime juice in a large bowl. Mix in the jalapeño and chile. Stir in the onion, cilantro, walnuts, ginger, cinnamon, and salt. Mix thoroughly.

Yields about 2 cups

The Dipping Mustard Trio

Get a big container of pretzels and settle in with one or all of these dipping mustards, which were practically custom-made to be paired with an ice-cold beer.

Hot or Mild Mustard

Whether you opt for the hot or the mild variations here, the real magic happens when the distinctive flavor points of dry mustard, cider vinegar, and sugar meet the sweet malt and moderate hop profile of an Oktoberfest, the sweet notes of a Dunkel, or the potent maltiness of a Doppelbock.

 Pair with:
Oktoberfest (page 36), Dunkel (page 36),
Doppelbock (page 36)

Hot:	Mild:
1 cup dry mustard, preferably Colman's	1/2 cup dry mustard, preferably Colman's
1 cup cider vinegar or white vinegar	1/2 cup cider vinegar or white vinegar
Egg replacer equal to 2 egg yolks (page 19)	1/2 cup water
1 cup sugar	Egg replacer equal to 2 egg yolks (page 19)
2 teaspoons cornstarch, dissolved in 2 teaspoons water	1 cup sugar
	3 teaspoons cornstarch, dissolved in 3 teaspoons water

Place the mustard and vinegar in a large bowl. Dissolve the mustard in the vinegar, whipping with a fork or whisk until smooth. Add the remaining ingredients, stirring well. Transfer the mustard mixture to a double boiler and cook over medium heat, stirring constantly, until the mustard reaches the desired thickness, at least 10 minutes. (If needed, add more cornstarch to reach the desired thickness). Let cool enough to handle. Pour the mustard into 1 or 2 glass jars with screw-on lids. Then cover and keep refrigerated.

Yields about 1 1/2 cups

Horseradish Mustard

Horseradish, with touches of turmeric and white wine vinegar, transforms this dipping mustard into a mind-blowing experience that requires the balancing forces of a good solid Oktoberfest, Pilsner, or Pale Lager to help you keep both feet on the ground.

 Pair with:
Oktoberfest (page 36), Pilsner (page 37),
Pale Lager (page 36)

2 vegetable bouillon cubes

1 1/2 cups hot water

4 teaspoons cornstarch, or more if needed for
    desired thickness

4 teaspoons sugar

4 teaspoons dry mustard, preferably Colman's

2 teaspoons ground turmeric

1/4 cup white wine vinegar

4 teaspoons prepared horseradish

Egg replacer equal to 2 egg yolks, lightly
    beaten (page 19)

Place the bouillon cubes in a small bowl. Add the hot water and dissolve the bouillon cubes. Blend the cornstarch, sugar, mustard, turmeric, vinegar, and horseradish in a small saucepan. Place over low heat, and slowly whisk in the dissolved bouillon. Cook, stirring, until thickened and bubbly, about 8 minutes. Place the egg replacer in a bowl. Stir 2 tablespoons of the bouillon mixture into the egg replacer, then pour the egg replacer mixture slowly into the saucepan. Cook, stirring constantly, for about 1 minute. (If needed, add more cornstarch to reach the desired thickness.) Let cool enough to handle, then transfer to 1 or 2 glass jars with screw-on lids, and keep refrigerated.

Yields 1 1/2 cups

Sweet Beer Mustard

This tipsy-sweet mustard is a unique blending of molasses, turmeric, dried peaches, and candied ginger that has a nice edge, especially when made and paired with Brown Ale, Porter, or Dry Stout.

Pair with:
Brown Ale (page 34), Porter (page 37), Dry Stout (page 37)

2/3 cup beer of your choice, preferably the same beer you're pairing with the dish

1 cup dry mustard, preferably Colman's

1/4 cup molasses

1/4 teaspoon salt

1/8 teaspoon ground turmeric

1/2 cup minced dried peaches or apricots

1 tablespoon minced candied ginger

Whisk together the beer and mustard in a medium-size bowl. Set aside for 30 minutes. Stir in the remaining ingredients. Spoon the mustard into 3/4-pint jars, screw on the lids, and refrigerate until thickened, at least 2 hours.

Yields about 3 cups

The Hoppy Hummus Bar

The magic of hummus is its ability to be enjoyed either as a traditional blend of chickpeas, tahini, and garlic, such as in the Hoppy Hummus below, or as a launching point for countless variations, such as the Spicy-Hot Hummus, Pumpkin Patch Hummus, Garden Veggie Hummus, Smoky Hangout Hummus, Extra Garlicky Hummus, Roasted Red Pepper Hummus, and Pine Nut Hummus that follow. Not to mention its range of respective beer pairing suggestions, from your go-to Pale Lager or Pilsner to IPA, Altbier, or Belgian Abbey Dubbel. To serve, choose a selection of pretzels, vegetables, or the homemade potato chips on page 69, or spread your hummus of choice on a favorite sandwich as a surprisingly flavorful topping.

Hoppy Hummus

Pair with:
Pale Lager (page 36), Pilsner (page 37),
American or English Pale Ale (pages 33 and 34, respectively)

2 cloves garlic

1 (15-ounce) can chickpeas (garbanzo beans), half the canning liquid reserved

1/4 cup freshly squeezed lemon juice

2 tablespoons tahini

1 teaspoon salt

2 tablespoons extra-virgin olive oil

Freshly ground black or white pepper, to taste

Place the garlic cloves in a blender and chop. Add the chickpeas and canning liquid, lemon juice, tahini, and salt. Blend until creamy and well mixed. Transfer the mixture to a serving bowl. Pour the olive oil over the hummus, and sprinkle with pepper.

Yields about 2 1/2 cups

Variations:

Spicy-Hot Hummus

 Pair with
India Pale Ale (page 34)

Add 1 tablespoon Tabasco sauce and/or 1 finely chopped jalapeño to the other ingredients before blending.

Pumpkin Patch Hummus

 Pair with
American or English Pale Ale (pages 33 and 34, respectively)

Add 1/3 cup canned pureed plain pumpkin (*not* pumpkin pie filling) to the other ingredients before blending.

Garden Veggie Hummus

 Pair with
American Wheat Ale (page 38)

Finely chop your choice of vegetable combination—red/yellow/green bell peppers, white onion, red onion, raw asparagus, cucumbers, carrots, and/or celery—to equal about 1/2 to 2 cups as desired, and stir into the finished hummus.

Smoky Hangout Hummus

 Pair with
Altbier (page 33)

Add 2 teaspoons liquid smoke, or to taste, to the other ingredients before blending.

Extra Garlicky Hummus

 Pair with
Golden Ale (page 34)

Add 2 (or more) crushed garlic cloves to the other ingredients before blending, or mix them into the finished hummus.

Roasted Red Pepper Hummus

 Pair with
Belgian Abbey Dubbel (page 33)

Roast 1 red pepper under a hot broiler or on a hot gas burner, turning until blackened all over. Place in a paper bag to cool. Rub off the blackened skin with paper towels. Stem, seed, and finely chop the pepper, and stir it into the finished hummus.

Pine Nut Hummus

 Pair with
Amber Lager (page 35)

Add 1 to 3 tablespoons of lightly toasted pine nuts (page 60), or more or less according to taste, to the other ingredients before blending, and also reserve some pine nuts to garnish the finished hummus.

Guac 'n' Roll

There is not a party on the planet that is complete without a good, classic guacamole on the table. To liven up this traditional recipe, pump up the volume with a Rauchbier in addition to a Pilsner and Golden Ale. Likewise, really get your party groove on and prepare a tableful of guacamoles, such as the Garlicky Guacamole, Smoky Saloon Guacamole, Spicy-Hot Guacamole, and Garden Veggie Guacamole variations, with their related beer pairings that follow, along with the homemade tortilla chips on page 69.

Pair with:
Rauchbier (page 39), Pilsner (page 37), Golden Ale (page 34)

2 (about 6 ounces each) ripe avocados, halved and pitted	2 tablespoons chopped plum tomato
3 tablespoons chopped fresh cilantro	2 tablespoons freshly squeezed lime juice, or a bit more to taste
2 tablespoons minced red onion	1/2 teaspoon kosher salt, or more to taste

Scoop the avocado flesh into a large bowl. Mash the flesh with a fork into a coarse paste. Stir in the cilantro, onion, tomato, and lime juice. Season with the salt. Add more lime juice and/or salt to taste. Be careful, as the lime juice can really take over.

Yields about 1 1/2 cups

Variations:

Garlicky Guacamole

 Pair with
Golden Ale (page 34)

Stir 2 (or more) crushed garlic cloves into the finished guacamole, and stir well.

Smoky Saloon Guacamole

 Pair with
Altbier (page 33)

Stir 2 teaspoons liquid smoke, or to taste, into the finished guacamole, and stir well.

Spicy-Hot Guacamole

 Pair with
Pilsner (page 37)

Stir 2 teaspoons Tabasco sauce, or to taste, into the finished guacamole, and stir well.

Garden Veggie Guacamole

 Pair with
Cream Ale (page 34)

Finely chop your choice of vegetable combination—red/yellow/green bell peppers, white onion, red onion, carrots, and/or celery—to equal about 1/2 to 1 cup as desired, and mix into the finished guacamole, stir well.

Parmesan-Artichoke Dip

While this artichoke dip may take a little extra time to prepare—especially when you use the homemade Parmesan, sour cream, and mayonnaise—the resulting master-piece will secure your title as host or hostess with the most, hands down. As for the Pilsner, Amber Lager, and Bock it's paired with, they're just an excuse (not that you need one) to hop up on the bar and dance!

Pair with:
Pilsner (page 37), Amber Lager (page 35), Bock (page 35)

1/2 cup mayonnaise (use recipe on page 24 or store-bought mayo)

1/2 cup sour cream (use recipe on page 27 or store-bought sour cream)

3/4 cup grated Parmesan cheese (use recipe on page 17 or store-bought cheese)

1 to 2 teaspoons Dijon mustard

1/2 teaspoon white pepper

1 (14-ounce) can artichoke hearts, drained and coarsely chopped

1 cup coarsely chopped fresh spinach leaves

1/2 cup finely chopped red onion

1 to 2 jalapeños, seeded and finely minced

Note: *Plan to prepare this dip several hours before serving.*

Combine the mayonnaise, sour cream, all but 2 tablespoons of the Parmesan cheese, mustard, and pepper in a large bowl. Stir in the artichoke hearts, spinach, onion, and jalapeño. Transfer the mixture to a 1-quart casserole dish, cover, and chill for at least 3 hours.

Preheat the oven to 350°F. Bake the mixture, covered, for 30 to 40 minutes, or until thoroughly heated. Sprinkle the top of the mixture with the reserved 2 tablespoons of Parmesan cheese. Bake, uncovered, for 5 minutes longer, or until the mixture is bubbling nicely. Serve with toast points, crackers, the homemade tortilla chips on page 69, or the homemade potato chips on page 69.

Yields about 2 1/2 cups

Plastered Pimiento Spread

While this pimiento-onion-oregano-thyme spread doesn't call for it, I'm not opposed to adding a teaspoon or two of the paired Oktoberfest, Altbier, or Doppelbock to the mix. But that'll be our little secret.

 Pair with:
Oktoberfest (page 36), Altbier (page 33), Doppelbock (page 36)

I cup finely minced red onion

2 tablespoons flat-leaf parsley or cilantro

Freshly ground black or white pepper, to taste

I teaspoon dried oregano

I teaspoon dried thyme

4 tablespoons extra-virgin olive oil

4 teaspoons red wine vinegar

2 (6 I/2-ounce) jars whole pimientos, drained and roughly chopped

Note: *Plan to prepare this spread several hours before serving and keep refrigerated to let the flavors blend before chasing it with an ice-cold one.*

Place the onion in a medium-size bowl. Place the parsley in a food processor, and finely mince the herb. Add the pepper, oregano, thyme, olive oil, and vinegar, and puree the mixture. Add the pimientos and pulse just a few times, to keep a slightly chunky texture.

Pour the mixture into the bowl with the onion, and stir to blend. Refrigerate for several hours to overnight. Bring to room temperature before serving. Spread the mixture over 2 thin toasted slices of a good baguette or crackers, or use as a dip for pretzels or the homemade potato chips on page 69.

Yields about 2 cups

Leek & Lager Spread

Leeks and Cheddar cheese together in one place is almost too good to be true. As a spread for crackers, or as a dip for pretzels, the homemade potato chips on page 69, or veggies, this mixture is always a hit with guests, especially when the sharp and mild Cheddar and oniony leek are augmented by a malty, brown Dunkel, the roasted notes of a Bock, or the malt-over-hops smoothness of a classic Amber Lager.

 Pair with:
Dunkel (page 36), Bock (page 35), Amber Lager (page 35)

I pound sharp Cheddar cheese, shredded
　(use recipe on page 15 or store-bought
　cheese)
I pound mild Cheddar cheese, shredded
　(use recipe on page 15 or store-bought
　cheese)
3 tablespoons ketchup
I tablespoon Dijon mustard
2 tablespoons mayonnaise (use recipe on
　page 24 or store-bought mayo)

I tablespoon Worcestershire sauce (use
　recipe on page 30 or store-bought
　Worcestershire sauce)
I leek, white part only, minced
I clove garlic, crushed
1/2 teaspoon Frank's RedHot Cayenne Pepper
　Sauce
1 1/2 to 2 cups beer of your choice, flat,
　preferably the same beer you're pairing
　with the dish

Note: *Plan to prepare this spread 1 to 3 days before serving and keep refrigerated to let the flavors blend before chasing it with an ice-cold one.*

Blend all the ingredients, except the beer, in an electric mixer at high speed or in a food processor fitted with a chopping blade, mixing until the mixture is smooth. With the motor running, pour the beer into the mixture in a slow, steady stream until the mixture reaches your desired thickness. Pack the mixture into a covered container, and refrigerate for 1 to 3 days to blend and mellow the flavors.

Yields 5 1/2 cups

⫸Cheesy Black Bean Dip⫷

There are a couple ways you can play this Cheddar cheese and black bean dip: either let the soft hops and sweet malt profiles of the Vienna Lager or Cream Ale accent the overall mixture as both an ingredient and pairing partner, or fire it up with a spicy Chili Beer. You pick!

Pair with:
Vienna Lager (page 37), Cream Ale (page 34), Chili Beer (page 39)

---

1 (8-ounce) package cream cheese, softened (use recipe on page 16 or store-bought cream cheese)

8 ounces Cheddar cheese, cubed (use recipe on page 15 or store-bought cheese)

1/3 cup beer of your choice, preferably the same beer you're pairing with the dish

1 cup canned black beans, drained and rinsed

1/2 cup sliced green onions

1/2 cup chopped fresh tomatoes, or 1/2 cup diced canned tomatoes

1 to 2 teaspoons ground toasted cumin seeds

2 jalapeños, seeded and minced

Tortilla chips, for serving (use recipe on page 69 or store-bought chips)

2 to 3 cups sour cream, at room temperature, for serving (use recipe on page 27 or store-bought sour cream)

Combine the cream cheese, Cheddar cheese, and beer in a medium-size saucepan. Place over low heat, and mix well until the cheeses are melted. Add the black beans, green onions, tomatoes, cumin, and jalapeños, mixing well. Serve warm with the tortilla chips and a ramekin or two of sour cream.

Yields 3 1/2 cups

Spiked & Spicy Cheddar Spread

Simply put, this spread is beer cheese at its very best, especially when you use the homemade Cheddar cheese along with an equally tenacious IPA, Brown Ale, or Stout. Serve with your favorite crackers, pretzels, or the homemade potato chips on page 69.

Pair with:
India Pale Ale (page 34), Brown Ale (page 34), Stout (page 38)

12 ounces beer of your choice, flat, preferably the same beer you're pairing with the dish

1 1/2 pounds Cheddar cheese, cubed and at room temperature (use recipe on page 15 or store-bought cheese)

2 tablespoons Worcestershire sauce (use recipe on page 30 or store-bought Worcestershire sauce)

1 clove garlic, crushed, or to taste

4 drops Frank's RedHot Cayenne Pepper Sauce, or to taste

Kosher salt, to taste

Freshly ground black pepper, to taste

Note: *Plan to prepare this spread several hours before serving and keep refrigerated to let the flavors blend before chasing it with an ice-cold one.*

Pour the beer into a blender or food processor. Add the cheese, Worcestershire sauce, garlic, and hot pepper sauce. Blend the ingredients to a coarse puree. Season with the salt and pepper. Pack the spread into a container, cover, and refrigerate for 8 hours to overnight to let the flavors blend.

Yields about 3 cups

Chapter 4

BARROOM TAPAS

Sometimes, when you're cozying up to the bar for a snack, planning a light meal for a few friends, or even when you're in couch-potato mode, you want to savor your favorite beer or a new seasonal or craft brew you've been wanting to try with something more than just chips and nuts. The following recipes and their suggested beer pairings provide you with countless mix-and-match options—hearty snacks, light meals for any time of day, or unique sides to pair with larger meals.

For recharged classic bar tapas, check out the Potato Skins Stuffed with Chiles, Tomatoes & Green Onions with a roasted malt and high-hops Stout; Tipsy Stuffed Tomatoes with a fruit-accented Kölsch; Bruschetta Brewski with a low malt, mildly hopped-up Golden Ale; and Patatas Bravo! Bravo! with a spicy Chili Beer.

Offerings for a light breakfast or brunch include Apple Tree Pancakes with a dark and strong Doppelbock or Tanked Banana Pancakes with a toasty Barley Wine.

Lunch catches a buzz with The Boozy Soup & Stew Bar and The Beer Lover's Salad Bar. You can also go old school at noontime (or for a midnight snack) with the Greasy Spoon Grilled Cheese Sandwiches.

Dinner gets energized with a selection of dishes that can work as a light meal, a starter, or a side, including Avocado & Onion Quesadillas with a Pilsner; Taproom Tacos with a Chili Beer; Screwy Pasta & Vegetables with Cheesy Beer Sauce and an India Pale Ale; Eggplant & Portobello Pasta with a Vienna Lager; The Slaw Platter; and The Mash Up! Platter. Or bring out the inner culinary artist in you and all your guests with The DIY Kebab Bar.

Potato Skins Stuffed with Chiles, Tomatoes & Green Onions

Snack time is calling and it wants THESE loaded potato skins! And nothing goes better with the attention-grabbing green onion–tomato–jalapeño–chile–pine nut filling than a vibrant Stout or, for the particularly fearless, a Chili Beer. But then again, Pale Lager always does the trick too.

Pair with:
Stout (page 38), Chili Beer (page 39), Pale Lager (page 36)

---

5 russet potatoes, roughly the same size

Salt, to taste

Freshly ground black pepper, to taste

1/2 cup chopped green onions

1 cup canned diced tomatoes, drained

1/4 cup toasted pine nuts (page 60)

Diced seeded jalapeños to taste, or a nonspicy green bell pepper, if preferred

1 to 2 teaspoons minced serrano chile peppers (optional)

1 cup sour cream (use recipe on page 27 or store-bought sour cream)

Preheat the oven to 350°F. Pierce the potatoes all over with a sharp fork. On a baking sheet, bake the potatoes until tender, 45 minutes to 1 hour. Remove the potatoes from the oven, and increase the heat to 400°F.

When the potatoes have cooled enough for you to handle, cut them in half lengthwise and scoop out most of the potato flesh with a spoon. Keep the potato flesh for another use. Salt and pepper the potato skins.

Divide the green onions, tomatoes, pine nuts, and peppers among the 10 potato halves, and arrange the potato halves on a baking sheet. Bake for 10 minutes, or until the filling is bubbly. Serve with the sour cream on the side for guests to scoop onto their potatoes.

Yields 10 potato halves

Avocado & Onion Quesadillas

The avocado blends nicely with the flavors of the green onions, Cheddar cheese, jalapeños, and salsa to deliver a new, mouthwatering favorite at halftime or anytime. And with all that flavor on the plate, a go-to Pale Lager, Amber Lager, or Pilsner in a frosted mug is a nice, relaxing complement to the dish.

Pair with:
Pale Lager (page 36), Amber Lager (page 35),
Pilsner (page 37)

---

4 (8-inch) flour tortillas

I ripe avocado, halved lengthwise and pitted

2 green onions, chopped

1/2 cup grated Cheddar cheese (use recipe on page 15 or store-bought cheese)

1/2 cup chopped red bell pepper

I jalapeño, seeded and minced

2 cups salsa (use recipes on pages 123 to 127 or store-bought) (optional)

Heat an empty 10-inch cast-iron skillet over medium-high heat. Scrape the avocado flesh from the skin and into a small bowl, mash the avocado with a fork, and then spread it over two of the tortillas. Sprinkle the green onions, Cheddar cheese, pepper, and jalapeño over the avocado. Cover each with another tortilla.

Cook the quesadillas in the hot cast-iron skillet for 2 minutes. Carefully turn and cook for another 2 minutes. Using a pizza cutter, cut each quesadilla into 6 pieces. Serve with the salsa, if desired.

Yields 2 to 4 servings

Taproom Tacos with Green Sauce

Bring Taco Night home with this edible piñata of marinated tofu, tomatillos, serrano chile peppers, avocado, cilantro, and more, all tucked inside simple corn tortillas. Taking your taste buds south of the border has never been so adventurous and so much fun, especially when the follow-up act is a Pale Lager, Amber Lager, or sizzling hot Chili Beer!

 Pair with:
Pale Lager (page 36), Amber Lager (page 35),
Chili Beer (page 39)

1/8 cup freshly squeezed lemon juice	3 tomatillos, husked and rinsed
1/8 cup pineapple juice	1 serrano chile pepper, stemmed
1/8 cup sherry	1 ripe avocado, chopped
1/8 cup low-sodium soy sauce	1/4 cup sour cream (optional) (use recipe on
2 teaspoons freshly ground black pepper	page 27 or store-bought sour cream)
2 whole chiles de árbol, crushed (optional)	2 tablespoons chopped fresh cilantro
1 clove garlic, crushed	Salt, to taste
Zest of 1 lemon	3 tablespoons canola or vegetable oil, divided
Zest of 1 small orange	1 red bell pepper, thickly sliced
12 ounces extra-firm tofu, pressed, drained,	1 yellow onion, thickly sliced
and sliced into 1/2-inch cubes (page 28)	12 warm soft corn tortillas

Combine the fruit juices, sherry, soy sauce, pepper, the optional chiles de árbol, garlic, and zests in a large bowl. Add the tofu cubes, and toss to coat. Cover and marinate in the refrigerator for 2 hours.

Meanwhile, make the green sauce: Bring a large pot of water to a boil. Add the tomatillos and serrano chile, and cook until tender, 8 to 10 minutes. Drain and transfer to a blender. Add the avocados, and blend the mixture until smooth. Transfer to a large bowl, and stir in the sour cream, if using, cilantro, and salt. Cover with plastic wrap pressed against the surface of the mixture and refrigerate.

Heat 2 tablespoons of the oil over medium-high heat in a medium-size skillet. Add the red pepper, onion, and salt to taste. Cook, stirring occasionally, until the vegetables are softened and beginning to blacken around the edges, 8 to 10 minutes. Transfer to a plate and set aside.

Wipe out the skillet. Heat the remaining tablespoon of oil in the skillet over medium-high heat. Stir-fry the tofu cubes for about 4 minutes, until lightly browned and heated through. Transfer to a platter, along with any accumulated juices, and gently stir in the pepper and onions. Serve with the tortillas and the green sauce at room temperature.

Yields 3 to 4 servings

Tipsy Stuffed Tomatoes

Not only do you get to drink the beer here, but you get to cook with it too. The sweet malt and low bitterness of a Golden Ale, a medium- to high-hops Pilsner, or the fruitiness of a Kölsch all work with the acidic juiciness of the tomatoes, as well as all the other flavor points in the corn–shallot–bell pepper–Cheddar cheese filling.

Pair with:
Golden Ale (page 34), Pilsner (page 37), Kölsch (page 35)

---

8 large (or 10 to 12 medium) tomatoes

12 ounces whole corn kernels, drained

2 medium shallots, finely chopped

1 small to medium green bell pepper, finely chopped

8 ounces sharp Cheddar cheese, grated (use recipe on page 15 or store-bought cheese)

3 cups fresh breadcrumbs

2 cups plus 1/2 cup beer of your choice, preferably the same beer you're pairing with the dish, divided

Salt, to taste

Freshly ground black pepper, to taste

Seasoned salt, such as Lawry's, to taste

Preheat the oven to 350°F. Slice off the tops of the tomatoes and scoop out the seeds and inside pulp, leaving about 1/4 inch of flesh around the interior circumference.

Combine the remaining ingredients in a large bowl, using the 2 cups of beer, mixing well. Lightly season the insides of the tomatoes with the salt, pepper, and seasoned salt. Scoop the cheese mixture into the hollowed tomatoes. Using the remaining 1/2 cup of beer, drizzle or brush it over the tops of the stuffed tomatoes. Bake the tomatoes for 15 to 20 minutes.

Yields 8 to 12 servings

The Boozy Soup & Stew Bar

Consider yourself warned! Once you add beer to your soups and stews, and discover the infusion of flavor that occurs, there is no turning back.

Blitzed Bean Soup

Beans and beer have always been a foolproof match in the kitchen. For this bean and beer soup, experiment by mixing and matching different types of beans, and then using a heavier, dark beer, such as Stout, American Dark Lager, or Amber Lager, as both an ingredient and for the pairing.

Pair with:
Stout (page 38), American Dark Lager (page 35), Amber Lager (page 35)

2 (15-ounce) cans pinto, black beans, or other beans of your choice, drained and rinsed
3/4 cup beer of your choice, preferably the same beer you're pairing with the dish
2 cups vegetable stock
1/2 medium yellow onion, sliced
3 cloves garlic, crushed
1/2 cup chopped fresh cilantro
1 jalapeño, thinly sliced
1 1/2 to 2 cups sour cream, for serving (optional) (use recipe on page 27 or store-bought sour cream)

Combine all the ingredients in a large pot over medium-high heat, mixing well. When the mixture comes to a boil, lower the heat to low and simmer, uncovered, for 30 minutes. Serve in warm bowls with a dollop of sour cream on top of each serving.

Yields 6 servings

Buzzed Broccoli & Cheese Soup

You may think you know broccoli and cheese soup, but I bet you've never seen it buzzed quite like this one! Just as the earthy, and sometimes bitter, flavor profile of the broccoli is countered by the tanginess of the Cheddar, choose a beer that works with both of these costars to take the soup to a whole new level. Here, a rich and minimally bitter Brown Ale, dark malt Altbier, or amber to brown Bock with a rich maltiness are all strong enough to do the job without stealing the show completely.

Pair with:
Brown Ale (page 34), Altbier (page 33), Bock (page 35)

---

2 (14-ounce) cans vegetable stock

1 small onion, chopped

1/2 teaspoon garlic powder

1/4 teaspoon white pepper

Seasoned salt, such as Lawry's, to taste

Cayenne pepper, to taste

1 pound broccoli florets, chopped, divided

3/4 cup (1 1/2-sticks) margarine (use recipe on page 23 or store-bought margarine)

3/4 cup all-purpose flour

4 cups soy or almond milk

1 1/2 to 2 pounds Cheddar cheese, cubed or shredded (use recipe on page 15 or store-bought cheese)

2 ounces beer of your choice, or more to taste, preferably the same beer you're pairing with the dish

4 bottled pimientos, chopped (optional)

Combine the vegetable stock and onion in a large pot, bringing the mixture to a boil. Add the seasonings and 1/2 of the broccoli, bringing the mixture to a boil again. Lower the heat and let the mixture simmer.

Meanwhile, make the roux: Melt the margarine in a medium-size skillet, and gradually whisk in the flour. Cook, stirring constantly, until the mixture thickens, about 8 minutes. Stir the roux into the soup, and whisk to blend.

Combine the milk and cheese in a medium-size saucepan over medium-high heat, continually stirring until the cheese melts. Blend the cheese mixture into the soup mixture, mixing well, then stir in the beer. Add the remaining broccoli, continuing to stir. Cook for 10 to 12 minutes, or until completely heated through. Stir in the chopped pimientos, if using, for a more colorful soup. Serve warm.

Yields 8 to 10 servings

Running Wild Rice Soup

With a grainy and even nutty flavor profile, wild rice is both beautiful and delicious! For this effortless soup, fresh onions, shallots, garlic, carrots, and bell pepper help coax even more flavor from the wild rice, while the agave nectar adds a sweet touch. The addition of Pale Lager, Porter, or Kölsch then helps this gang of ingredients circle back around to that down-home, earthy flavor you'll crave again and again.

 Pair with:
Pale Lager (page 36), Porter (page 37), Kölsch (page 35)

1/4 cup extra-virgin olive oil

1 medium yellow onion, finely chopped

1 medium red onion, finely chopped

8 green onions, finely chopped

8 shallots, finely chopped

5 cloves garlic, crushed

3 cups finely chopped carrots

1 medium red bell pepper, finely chopped

8 cups vegetable stock

1/3 cup agave nectar

18 ounces (2 1/4 cups) beer of your choice, preferably the same beer you're pairing with the dish

3 cups cooked wild rice

Salt, to taste

Freshly ground black pepper, to taste

Combine the olive oil, onions, shallots, and garlic in a medium-size skillet over medium-high heat, sautéing until the mixture is browned, 6 to 8 minutes.

Combine the onion mixture with the carrots, pepper, vegetable stock, and agave in a large pot, mixing well. Bring the mixture to a boil. Add the beer, stirring well. Add the rice, and simmer the mixture, uncovered, for about 10 minutes, or until heated through. Season with the salt and pepper.

Yields 6 servings

Cheddar & Beer Bisque

Cheddar and beer are a union that is about as old as time itself. But for this warm and cozy bisque, Cheddar and a hearty dose of Brown Ale, Altbier, or Maibock takes a standard on the soup circuit from ordinary to extraordinary!

Pair with:
Brown Ale (page 34), Altbier (page 33), Maibock (page 36)

1/4 cup (1/2 stick) margarine (use recipe on page 23 or store-bought margarine)

1 small onion, finely chopped

2 small carrots, finely chopped

1/2 cup celery, finely chopped

1/3 cup all-purpose flour

3 cups soy or almond milk

1 cup beer of your choice, preferably the same beer you're pairing with the dish

2 1/2 cups grated sharp Cheddar cheese (use recipe on page 15 or store-bought cheese)

Egg replacer equal to 4 egg yolks, lightly beaten (page 19)

Salt, to taste

Freshly ground white pepper, to taste

Sour cream (optional) (use recipe on page 27 or store-bought sour cream)

1/4 cup finely chopped fresh chives, or to taste

Melt the margarine in a large pot over medium-high heat. Add the onion, carrots, and celery, sautéing the vegetables until they are golden, 4 to 6 minutes. Stir in the flour and cook for 3 to 4 minutes. Slowly stir in the milk and beer. Lower the heat, and cook the mixture, stirring constantly, until slightly thickened. Add the Cheddar cheese, stirring until the cheese has melted.

Place the egg replacer in a large bowl. Slowly beat 1 cup of the soup mixture into the egg replacer using a whisk or electric mixer. Pour the egg mixture into the soup pot, and heat until desired doneness. Add the salt and white pepper to taste. Garnish each serving with a dollop of the sour cream, if using, and a generous sprinkling of chives.

Yields 4 servings

Soused Black Bean Chili

For that burst of brew in and out of the chili pot, you can go lighter with a Pale Lager or really make a statement by using a stronger Porter or Oktoberfest.

 Pair with:
Pale Lager (page 36), Porter (page 37), Oktoberfest (page 36)

2 tablespoons extra-virgin olive oil

1 small onion, diced

3 cloves garlic, crushed

1 jalapeño, seeded and finely diced

1 chile pepper, seeded and finely diced

1 (15-ounce) can black beans with their canning juices

3 plum tomatoes, cut into eighths

1/2 cup tomato paste

1/4 cup roasted cashews, lightly crushed (page 63)

1 teaspoon ground toasted cumin seeds

1 teaspoon chili powder

1/2 teaspoon ground cinnamon

1/4 teaspoon cayenne pepper

1/4 teaspoon red pepper flakes

1 to 2 pinches of ground cloves

1 cup beer of your choice, preferably the same beer you're pairing with the dish

1/2 cup frozen corn kernels, or more to taste, thawed

2 heads broccoli, steamed, florets cut into bite-size pieces, stems cut into 1/4-inch-thick coins (optional)

Combine the olive oil, onion, and garlic in a medium-size to large pot, and sauté until the onions become translucent, about 4 minutes. Add the jalapeño and chile pepper, and sauté for a few more minutes, until the jalapeño is softened. Add the beans, tomatoes, tomato paste, cashews, cumin, chili powder, cinnamon, cayenne pepper, red pepper flakes, cloves, and beer, and mix well. Bring the mixture to a boil. Continue to boil the mixture, stirring frequently, for approximately 30 to 35 minutes, or until most of the liquid has evaporated. Add the corn about 12 to 15 minutes before the mixture is ready to be served.

Yields 4 to 6 servings

~Dive Bar Veggie Stew~

Make the most of halftime, anytime, and *your* time by easily throwing together this generous beer stew that truly is the gift that keeps on giving.

Pair with:
English Bitter (page 34), Bock (page 35),
American or English Pale Ale (pages 33 and 34, respectively)

---

1 (15-ounce) can black beans, drained

2 (15-ounce) cans pink kidney beans, drained

2 cups frozen baby lima beans, drained

32 ounces, or more as needed, V8 juice (preferably the Spicy Hot V8 juice) or vegetable juice of your choice

1 (7-ounce) can chopped green chiles, mild or hot

Minced jalapeños, to taste (optional)

2 (16-ounce) bags frozen stir-fry vegetables, thawed

1 small head green or red cabbage, chopped

1/2 cup chopped fresh chives

2 tablespoons minute tapioca

2 tablespoons pearl barley

1/2 stalk celery, cut as desired

10 large carrots, cut into coins

1 to 2 large red, yellow, or green bell peppers, cut into bite-size pieces

1 cup frozen corn kernels, thawed

1/2 pound shiitake mushrooms, stems discarded, caps sliced into 1-inch pieces

4 sprigs fresh parsley, if using parsnips

4 cloves garlic, crushed

Seasoned salt, such as Lawry's, to taste

Garlic powder, to taste

2 teaspoons maple syrup

2 tablespoons fresh orange juice

12 ounces beer of your choice, or more to taste, preferably the same beer you're pairing with the dish

1 cup frozen or fresh baby okra, thawed and sliced (optional)

Combine all the ingredients, except the beer and okra, if using, in a large pot. Bring to a low boil and cook, covered, over medium to medium-low heat for 2 1/2 to 3 hours, until the vegetables are tender. Slowly pour the beer into the pot about 30 to 45 minutes before serving, and add the thawed okra at the end of cooking. If necessary, keep at a low simmer, but try to serve a few minutes after adding the okra so that it doesn't lose its texture and become slimy. If planning to freeze leftovers for future meals, or to give to friends and neighbors, omit the okra.

Yields 12 to 15 servings

The Beer Lover's Salad Bar

Spinach, Romaine & Radicchio Salad with Beer Dressing

Whether you're one of the dudes or ladies who lunch bar-side, you simply want to add a little spark to your noontime eats, or you want to use this dish as an opening dinner course, this leafy salad with carrots, cauliflower, broccoli, and mushrooms on top has you covered. The real dazzler here, however, is the tangy beer dressing that sets a whole new standard for salad bars everywhere. For a fresh and new salad every time, switch it up with your choice of Pilsners, American Wheat Ales, and Belgian Witbiers for the dressing and pairing.

Pair with:
Pilsner (page 37), American Wheat Ale (page 38), Belgian Witbier (page 38)

For the salad:
3 carrots, cut into 1-inch pieces
1 cup cauliflower florets
1 cup broccoli florets
1/2 cup fresh mushrooms, thinly sliced
1 firmly packed cup spinach, stemmed and patted dry
1 firmly packed cup romaine, torn into bite-size pieces
1/2 firmly packed cup radicchio, torn into bite-size pieces
1 to 2 cups nuts of your choice from The Hot Spot Nut Bar, for garnishing (pages 58 to 63) (optional)

For the dressing:
1/2 cup mayonnaise (use recipe on page 24 or store-bought mayo)
1/4 cup Dijon mustard
3 tablespoons pickle relish (optional)
1/4 cup beer of your choice, preferable the same beer you're pairing with the dish
1 tablespoon prepared horseradish
2 drops Frank's RedHot Cayenne Pepper Sauce, or to taste (optional)

Bring 6 cups of water to boil in a medium-size saucepan. Place the carrots, cauliflower, and broccoli into the boiling water. Lower the heat to medium and simmer for 5 minutes. With a slotted spoon, transfer the vegetables to paper towels to drain. Combine the carrots, cauliflower, broccoli, mushrooms, spinach, romaine, and radicchio in a large serving bowl.

To make the dressing: Combine the mayonnaise, mustard, pickle relish, beer, and horseradish in a medium-size bowl, mixing well. Stir in the hot pepper sauce, if using. Spoon the dressing over the vegetables, and toss well. Garnish with nuts of your choice, if desired. Serve at once.

Yields 4 to 6 servings

Mixed Greens with Spicy Beer Dressing

This spicy beer dressing, which can always be upped a notch or two by using a Chili Beer or held hot and steady with an American Wheat Ale or Pale Lager, works on any combo of mixed greens and veggies you can dream up. Add the finishing touch with a sprinkled selection of nuts from The Hot Spot Nut Bar (pages 58 to 63).

Pair with:
Chili Beer (page 39), American Wheat Ale (page 38), Pale Lager (page 36)

Suggested mixed greens and vegetables:

Baby spinach, radicchio, romaine, and/or mixed greens

Asparagus spears (steamed or sautéed)

Brussels sprouts (steamed or sautéed)

Onion, chopped

Mushrooms, cut as desired

Broccoli, cut as desired

Cauliflower, cut as desired

Carrots, cut as desired

Avocado slices or chunks

Red, green, or yellow bell peppers, chopped

Cherry tomatoes

For the dressing:

1 1/2 cups canola oil

1 cup beer of your choice, preferably the same beer you're pairing with the dish

1 tablespoon Worcestershire sauce (use recipe on page 30 or store-bought Worcestershire sauce)

2 (10 3/4-ounce) cans condensed tomato soup

1 small onion, grated

1 clove garlic, crushed

1 tablespoon sugar

2 tablespoons salt

1 tablespoon prepared horseradish

Tabasco sauce, to taste

To make the dressing: Combine all the ingredients in a medium-size bowl, mixing well. Chill the mixture until you are ready to serve it over a salad of mixed greens and vegetables of your choice. Whisk the mixture well just before serving.

Yields 5 cups

The Slaw Platter

To serve, consider making two or all three of the following slaws, and arrange one scoop of each on a single rectangular plate to create a snack platter for 1 to 2 people.

Cabbage Slaw

The cabbage in this beer slaw is a fitting backdrop for the bell pepper, onion, celery seeds, toasted caraway seeds, and a pairing pal.

Pair with:
Oktoberfest (page 36), German Hefeweizen (page 38), Belgian Witbier (page 38)

8 cups shredded green cabbage

1/2 medium-size green or red bell pepper, or a combination, chopped

1 1/2 tablespoons minced onion

1 cup mayonnaise (use recipe on page 24 or store-bought mayo)

1/4 cup sour cream, or to taste (use recipe on page 27 or store-bought sour cream)

1/4 cup beer of your choice, preferably the same beer you're pairing with the dish

1 teaspoon celery seeds

1/2 teaspoon toasted caraway seeds

1/2 teaspoon salt

1/4 teaspoon freshly ground black pepper

Note: *Grind the celery and toasted caraway seeds if you like, but I prefer them whole.*

Combine the cabbage, bell pepper, and onion in a large bowl. Combine the mayonnaise, sour cream, beer, celery and caraway seeds, salt, and pepper in a small bowl. Pour the mayonnaise mixture over the cabbage mixture, and toss to coat well. Refrigerate the slaw for at least 30 to 45 minutes before serving.

Yields 12 servings

Broccoli Slaw

Broccoli, red onion, and red cabbage are accented by the toasted sunflower and mustard seeds in this simple, tasty slaw that corresponds nicely to the flavor points in a Pilsner, American Wheat Ale, or Amber Lager.

 Pair with:
Pilsner (page 37), American Wheat Ale (page 38), Amber Lager (page 35)

I large head red cabbage, chopped into bite-size or matchstick slices

I 1/2 cups broccoli florets, chopped into bite-size or matchstick slices

I medium-size red onion, chopped into bite-size or matchstick slices

1/2 cup toasted sunflower seeds (page 19)

3 to 4 tablespoons toasted mustard seeds

1/2 cup sugar

I cup mayonnaise (use recipe on page 24 or store-bought mayo)

I tablespoon cider vinegar

Toss the vegetables with the sunflower seeds in a large bowl. Whisk together the mustard seeds, sugar, mayonnaise, and vinegar in a medium-size bowl just before serving. Pour the mayonnaise mixture over the slaw, and toss to coat well.

Yields 6 to 8 servings

Carrot Slaw

Bursting with color and zing, this refreshing carrot slaw is best suited for a round of Pale Lager, American Wheat Ale, or Belgian Witbier.

Pair with:
Pale Lager (page 36), American Wheat Ale (page 38), Belgian Witbier (page 38)

5 tablespoons Dijon mustard

1/4 cup extra-virgin olive oil

1/4 cup finely chopped fresh parsley or cilantro

3 tablespoons minced fresh chives

3 tablespoons red wine vinegar

3 lightly packed teaspoons orange zest

1 1/2 teaspoons kosher salt

2 pounds carrots, grated into narrow strips with a food processor or box grater (about 5 or 6 cups)

Freshly ground black pepper, to taste

Whisk together all the ingredients, except the carrots and black pepper, in a large bowl, mixing until evenly blended. Add the carrots, and toss until well coated. Season with the pepper. Let the mixture marinate at least 30 minutes to 1 hour before serving, either chilled or at room temperature.

Yields 4 servings

Beer-Marinated Vegetable Medley

Served alone as a zesty snack or as a side, this garden of veggies really springs to life after a night in the beer and herb marinade. With the range of flavors happening in this medley, from the veggies themselves to the spices and herbs, choose a lighter beer, such as a Golden Ale, Pilsner, or Pale Lager, to mix in and pair with the dish.

Pair with:
Golden Ale (page 34), Pilsner (page 37), Pale Lager (page 36)

I medium cucumber, thinly sliced

I medium green or red bell pepper, or a combination, cut into strips

I medium zucchini or yellow summer squash, peeled and cut into bite-size pieces

I cup cauliflower florets

I cup broccoli florets

I cup halved fresh mushrooms

I cup cherry tomatoes, halved if desired

1/2 cup beer of your choice, preferably the same beer you're pairing with the dish

1/4 cup extra-virgin olive oil

2 tablespoons balsamic vinegar

5 fresh basil leaves, cut into chiffonade (page 22)

3/4 teaspoon dill seed or dill weed

1/2 teaspoon salt

I teaspoon smooth Dijon mustard

2 dashes seasoned pepper, such as Lawry's, or more to taste

Seasoned salt, such as Lawry's, to taste

Garlic powder, to taste

Combine all the vegetables in a large storage container. Combine the beer and remaining ingredients in a medium-size bowl, mixing well. Pour the beer marinade over the vegetables, stirring to coat well. Cover and chill for at least 6 hours to overnight. Serve at room temperature.

Yields 4 to 8 servings

The DIY Kebab Bar

Many of my friends use marinades like these with chicken, beef, and fish, but you can also use baked, deep-fried, or grilled tofu (page 28), tempeh (page 28), or seitan (page 26). These protein- and vitamin-packed alternatives to meat are my ingredients of choice because they act as extraordinary sponges, absorbing the full ingredient ranges of the marinades for maximum flavor and effect.

For parties, consider preparing several of the marinades that follow. Then either invite your guests to engage their inner culinary artist at the DIY Kebab Bar stocked with a variety of bite-size, marinated tofu, tempeh, and/or seitan pieces, along with vegetables, or surprise them with a smorgasbord of your own creations.

Unless otherwise noted, each of the marinades that follow works well with at least 8 ounces of unflavored tofu, tempeh, or seitan. Naturally, the marinade amounts can easily be doubled or tripled for larger parties. Some of the marinades with larger yields already work well for parties.

For instructions on baking, deep-frying, or grilling tofu, tempeh, and seitan, go to page 106. Also, for instructions on pressing and draining tofu, go to page 28.

Cayenne & Horseradish Beer Marinade

Marinade power brokers like cayenne pepper and horseradish, with all the additional herbs and spices in this marinade, work with everything from a calmer Pale Lager to a stronger, more definitive Stout or Maibock.

Pair with:

Pale Lager (page 36), Stout (page 38), Maibock (page 36)

24 ounces beer of your choice, preferably the same beer you're pairing with the dish

2 teaspoons salt

1/2 cup extra-virgin olive oil

1 teaspoon ground cayenne pepper, or to taste

1 tablespoon wine vinegar

1 tablespoon dry white vermouth

1 tablespoon prepared horseradish

1 teaspoon onion powder

1 teaspoon garlic powder

1/2 teaspoon mace

1/2 teaspoon sage

1 teaspoon five-spice powder

Freshly squeezed juice of 1 lime (about 3 tablespoons)

Whisk together all the ingredients in a large bowl, mixing well.

Yields 8 cups

Worcestershire & Peace Marinade

Worcestershire sauce, especially when you use the unique homemade version, goes flavor note for note with a Brown Ale, Porter, or Dunkel to provide a deep, rich experience with every bite.

Pair with:
Brown Ale (page 34), Porter (page 37), Dunkel (page 36)

---

1 cup Worcestershire sauce (use recipe on page 30 or store-bought Worcestershire sauce)

24 ounces beer of your choice, preferably the same beer you're pairing with the dish

2 teaspoons vegetable oil

3 tablespoons freshly squeezed lemon juice

1 teaspoon liquid smoke

1 cup low-sodium soy sauce

1 teaspoon garlic powder, or to taste

1 teaspoon onion powder

1 teaspoon Frank's RedHot Cayenne Pepper Sauce

1 tablespoon Pickapeppa Sauce (page 22, see "Ketchup")

1 tablespoon apple cider vinegar

Combine all the ingredients in a medium-size bowl, mixing well.

Yields 5 cups

Far East Lager Marinade

Choices, choices, choices! If you're the kind of person who likes to carry through a theme, then opt for Sake in this Far East–inspired beer marinade. Otherwise, a go-to Pale Lager works nicely, or add an extra spark with a Chili Beer.

 Pair with:
Sake (page 38), Pale Lager (page 36), Chili Beer (page 39)

12 ounces beer of your choice, preferably the same beer you're pairing with the dish
1 cup low-sodium soy sauce
2 tablespoons Sriracha Hot Chili Sauce
2 teaspoons Chinese mustard, or more to taste (page 25)
1/4 cup vegetable oil
2 tablespoons finely minced onion
2 teaspoons garlic powder
2 tablespoons sugar
2 tablespoons vinegar
1/2 teaspoon ground ginger
1/2 teaspoon ground cinnamon
Juice from 2 limes

Combine all the ingredients in a food processor, mixing well.

Yields 3 cups

Brown Sugar & Spice Marinade

Brown sugar and spice, and everything nice! Brown Ale, Porter, and Stout, with their varying and distinctive flavor notes reminiscent of coffee, chocolate, caramel, and their even nutty overtones, make them a no-brainer for preparing and pairing here.

Pair with:
Brown Ale (page 34), Porter (page 37), Stout (page 38)

4 cups beer of your choice, preferably the
   same beer you're pairing with the dish
2 cups dark brown sugar
1 tablespoon molasses
2 teaspoons hoisin sauce
1 cup cider vinegar

1 tablespoon chili powder
1 teaspoon ground cumin
1 teaspoon dry mustard
2 teaspoons hot red pepper flakes
Tabasco sauce, to taste

Combine all the ingredients in a medium-size saucepan, mixing well. Bring the mixture to a boil, whisking often. Remove it from the heat and let cool before using.

Yields about 7 cups

Tomato & Beer Marinade

Something electric happens when the acidic juice of tomatoes meets the malt and hops duo in beer, such as a favorite Pale Lager or Golden Ale, or a Belgian Abbey Tripel, with its citrus and spicy flavor mix. Now add to that some thyme, Worcestershire sauce, Frank's RedHot, Sriracha, and bay leaves, and you have a secret marinade that will leave your guests begging for more.

Pair with:
Pale Lager (page 36), Golden Ale (page 34),
Belgian Abbey Tripel (page 33)

I cup beer of your choice, preferably the same beer you're pairing with the dish

I cup vegetable stock

I teaspoon chopped fresh thyme leaves

3 tomatoes, peeled, seeded, and diced, or 2 (14-ounce) cans diced tomatoes, drained

2 teaspoons Worcestershire sauce (use recipe on page 30 or store-bought Worcestershire sauce)

I teaspoon Frank's RedHot Cayenne Pepper Sauce, or more to taste

Sriracha Hot Chili Sauce, to taste

2 teaspoons minced jalapeño (optional)

3 dried bay leaves

3/4 teaspoon cracked black peppercorns

1/4 cup chopped fresh parsley

Combine all the ingredients in a medium-size bowl, mixing well. Be sure to remove the bay leaves before serving the marinated dish.

Yields 3 cups

Southwestern Red Wine & Lager Marinade

Who ever said wine and beer snobs can't get along? Time for some marinade diplomacy with this red wine and beer partnership that guarantees a peaceful meal every time, when made and paired with Pale Lager, Amber Lager, or Pilsner.

Pair with:
Pale Lager (page 36), Amber Lager (page 35), Pilsner (page 37)

2 cups dry red wine of your choice

12 ounces beer of your choice, preferably the
   same beer you're pairing with the dish

1 small red onion, thinly sliced

Freshly squeezed juice of 6 limes

Zest of 3 limes

1/4 cup chopped fresh cilantro

1/2 teaspoon kosher salt

1/4 teaspoon freshly ground black pepper

1/4 teaspoon red pepper flakes

1/4 teaspoon chili powder

1/4 teaspoon ground cumin

1/4 teaspoon ground mace

Combine all the ingredients in a medium-size bowl, whisking well with a fork.

Yields 4 cups

Brew & BBQ Marinade

Beer has always been the ultimate BBQ sidekick, but now it's an important part of the mix. For this buzzed barbecue sauce, go with either a Pale Lager or a stronger Brown Ale or Porter to balance with the classic ingredients like ketchup, brown sugar, mustard, and the various spices.

 Pair with:
Pale Lager (page 36), Brown Ale (page 34), Porter (page 37)

2 1/2 cups ketchup
9 ounces beer of your choice, preferably the
    same beer you're pairing with the dish
3/4 cup dark brown sugar
3/4 cup freshly squeezed lemon juice
1 1/2 cups chili sauce
1/2 cup smooth Dijon mustard
1 1/2 cups red wine vinegar
1 tablespoon lightly toasted celery seeds
1 1/2 cups water
4 tablespoons Worcestershire sauce (use
recipe on page 30 or store-bought
    Worcestershire sauce)
2 tablespoons low-sodium soy sauce
2 tablespoons steak sauce, such as A-1 Steak
    Sauce, which, despite the name, is vegan
2 cloves garlic, crushed
2 tablespoons chili powder
2 tablespoons jalapeño powder, or to taste
Frank's RedHot Cayenne Pepper Sauce, to
    taste
Freshly ground black pepper, to taste

Whisk together all the ingredients in a large bowl, mixing well.

Yields 10 cups

Screwy Pasta & Vegetables with Cheesy Beer Sauce

Now you can add a brewski or two to pasta night when you add a rich Brown Ale, smooth Amber Lager, or high-octane IPA to supercharge the Cheddar sauce for this corkscrew pasta and veggie feast.

Pair with:
Brown Ale (page 34), Amber Lager (page 35), India Pale Ale (page 34)

---

2 tablespoons margarine (use recipe on page 23 or store-bought margarine)

2 medium carrots, sliced

1 small zucchini, peeled and chopped

1 small onion, chopped

1 cup fresh mushrooms, trimmed and quartered

2 tablespoons all-purpose flour

1 cup soy or almond milk

1/4 cup beer of your choice, plus additional to achieve desired texture, preferably the same beer you're pairing with the dish

3/4 cup shredded Cheddar cheese (use recipe on page 15 or store-bought cheese)

Salt, to taste

Freshly ground black pepper, to taste

8 ounces dried or fresh tricolored fusilli (corkscrew pasta), cooked according to the manufacturer's instructions and kept warm

---

Melt the margarine in a medium-size saucepan over medium heat. Add the carrots, zucchini, onion, and mushrooms, mixing well. Sauté the mixture until the vegetables are tender, about 8 minutes. Stir in the flour. Slowly add the milk. Continue to cook, stirring constantly, until the mixture is thickened and bubbly, then cook it for 1 more minute. Pour in the beer, mixing well, and heat the mixture thoroughly. Remove from the heat.

Add the Cheddar cheese about 1/4 cup at a time, mixing well until the cheese is melted. Add more beer if necessary to reach your desired texture. Season with the salt and pepper. Pour the cheese sauce over each serving of pasta, and serve promptly.

Yields 6 to 8 servings

Eggplant & Portobello Pasta

Class up pasta night by adding sautéed eggplant and portobellos to your penne pasta, along with a nice dose and pairing of a slightly toasty Vienna Lager, mellow Golden Ale, or classic American Wheat Ale.

 Pair with:
Vienna Lager (page 37), Golden Ale (page 34),
American Wheat Ale (page 38)

1/2 cup extra-virgin olive oil

4 to 6 portobello mushroom caps, gills scraped, sliced into bite-size pieces

1 medium white eggplant, peeled and diced

Salt, to taste

Freshly ground black pepper, to taste

1 cup beer of your choice, preferably the same beer you're pairing with the dish

1/2 teaspoon dried rosemary

1 cup frozen peas, thawed

1 pound penne pasta, cooked according to the manufacturer's directions and kept warm

4 to 5 cups Parmesan cheese, grated (use recipe on page 17 or store-bought cheese)

Heat the olive oil in a medium-size skillet over medium heat. Add the mushroom pieces and sauté for 3 minutes, stirring often. Add the eggplant, and season with the salt and pepper. Stir often and cook for approximately 8 to 10 minutes, or until the eggplant cubes become tender. Add the beer and rosemary, bringing the mixture to a boil. Cook until the liquid is reduced by half, about 6 to 8 minutes. Add the peas and simmer the mixture, covered, for 2 minutes. Stir in the pasta, cooking for approximately 30 seconds, or until the pasta is warmed through. Garnish each serving with the Parmesan cheese.

Yields 6 to 8 servings

Greasy Spoon Grilled Cheese Sandwiches

Number one comfort sandwich the world over! Now, with the addition of a home-made Cheddar, five lively variations, and numerous beer pairing options, you're about to take comfort food to a whole new realm of scrumptious. Also, feel free to swap out the white bread for homemade slices.

Pair with:
Pale Lager (page 36), Amber Lager (page 35),
Rauchbier (page 39)

3 to 4 tablespoons margarine (use recipe on page 23 or store-bought margarine)

4 slices white bread

4 slices Cheddar cheese (use recipe on page 15 or store-bought cheese)

Heat a medium-size cast-iron skillet over medium heat. Liberally spread the margarine on one side of each bread slice. When the skillet is nice and hot, place two slices of the bread, buttered sides down, in the skillet, place two slices of Cheddar cheese on each bread slice, then top each with a bread slice, buttered side up. Grill until lightly browned, 2 to 3 minutes. Flip the sandwiches over, and grill until the cheese is melted and the bread is golden brown, about 3 minutes longer. Serve warm.

Yields 2 sandwiches

Variations:

Dilly Grilled Cheese Sandwiches

Pair with
Oktoberfest (page 36)

Add sliced dill pickles (use the recipe on page 96 or store-bought pickles), to taste, either before adding the top slices of bread or before serving, depending on preference. Also, serve a whole dill pickle or two on the side.

Red-Hot Grilled Cheese Sandwiches

 **Pair with**
Chili Beer (page 39)

Add jalapeños and hot sauce (preferably Sriracha Hot Chili Sauce), to taste, either before adding the top slices of bread or before serving, depending on preference.

Mushroom Lover's Grilled Cheese Sandwiches

 **Pair with**
Porter (page 37)

Add 1 or more types of mushrooms (see mushroom suggestions on page 29), to taste, before adding the top slices of bread.

Grilled Cheese & Tomato Sandwiches

 **Pair with**
German Hefeweizen (page 38)

Add tomato slices, mayonnaise (use recipe on page 24 or store-bought mayo), and maybe lettuce or spinach, to taste, either before adding the top slices of bread or before serving, depending on preference. To prevent the lettuce or spinach from wilting, add just before serving.

Uppity Grilled Cheese Sandwiches

 **Pair with**
Brown Ale (page 34)

Use cream cheese (use the recipe on page 16 or store-bought cream cheese), sliced roasted tomatoes, sliced portobello mushrooms, and Dijon mustard, to taste. Add these ingredients either before adding the top slices of bread or before serving, depending on preference.

The Beer Lover's Artisanal Cheese Platter

The meeting of two culinary icons! It's time for beer to share top billing with the world's ultimate comfort food. Different styles of cheese pair well with different styles of beer, each tempting and coaxing forth the distinct flavor notes of the other. Fortunately, today, with the growing popularity of nondairy cheeses, every one of us can enjoy cheese with our favorite brewskis.

While many of my friends may use traditional dairy cheeses with the following pairing combinations, for those of you who are interested in avoiding dairy, I invite you to either make your own nondairy cheeses, using the countless recipes available online and in my cookbook, *The Cheesy Vegan*, or seek out store-bought favorites, using the "Store-Bought Plant-Based Cheese Resource Guide" on page 304. You could also start by experimenting with the homemade Cheddar and cream cheese recipes on pages 15 and 16.

American

Pair with
Brown Ale (page 34),
Pale Lager (page 36), or
Pilsner (page 37)

Blue

Pair with
India Pale Ale (page 34),
English Bitter (page 34),
or Russian Imperial Stout
(page 37)

Brie

Pair with
Fruit Beer (page 39),
American or English Pale
Ale (pages 33 and 34,
respectively), or Stout
(page 38)

Cheddar (Mild)

Pair with
Amber Lager (page 35),
Pilsner (page 37), or Pale
Lager (page 36)

Cheddar (Sharp)

Pair with
Bock (page 35),
American Wheat Ale
(page 38), or Porter
(page 37)

Cream

Pair with
Fruit Beer (page 39),
Amber Lager (page 35),
or Irish Red Ale
(page 34)

Feta

Pair with
American Wheat Ale
(page 38), Fruit Beer
(page 39), or Pilsner (page
37)

Monterey Jack

Pair with
Brown Ale (page 34),
Pilsner (page 37), or Pale
Lager (page 36)

Mozzarella

Pair with
Fruit Beer (page 39),
Pilsner (page 37), or
American Wheat Ale
(page 38)

Muenster

Pair with
Belgian Ale (page 34),
American or English Pale
Ale (pages 33 and 34,
respectively), or Stout
(page 38)

Smoked

Pair with
Rauchbier (page 39),
Pale Lager (page 36),
or Amber Lager (page
35)

Swiss

Pair with
Maibock (page 36),
American Dark Lager
(page 35), or American
Wheat Ale (page 38)

Bruschetta Brewski

This jam-packed veggie bruschetta boasts an accent of Golden Ale, Kölsch, or Pilsner for an ideal appetizer, party starter, or indulgent couch potato snack!

Pair with:
Golden Ale (page 34), Kölsch (page 35), Pilsner (page 37)

---

4 medium tomatoes, peeled, seeded, and very coarsely chopped

2 teaspoons kosher salt

1 teaspoon sugar

12 slices crusty French bread, each slice about 3 inches in diameter

1 clove garlic, halved

3 tablespoons extra-virgin olive oil

2 teaspoons balsamic vinegar

2 teaspoons beer of your choice, preferably the same beer you're pairing with the dish

1 small red onion, minced

1 small red bell pepper, minced

2 teaspoons fresh thyme leaves, or 1 teaspoon dried thyme

2 teaspoons capers, or to taste

1 teaspoon chopped fresh oregano leaves, or 1/2 teaspoon dried oregano

Freshly ground black pepper, to taste

Grated Parmesan cheese, to taste (optional) (use recipe on page 17 or store-bought cheese)

Toss the tomatoes with the salt and sugar in a large bowl. Transfer the tomatoes to a large colander set over a bowl, and let the tomatoes drain for 30 to 40 minutes.

Toast the bread slices on both sides under a hot broiler, watching carefully. Rub the top of each slice with the garlic clove halves, then lightly brush the top of each slice with the olive oil.

Gently press down on the drained tomatoes with a large spoon to extract even more juices. Transfer the tomatoes to another large bowl, and toss with the balsamic vinegar, beer, onion, pepper, thyme, capers, and oregano. Season with the pepper. Spoon the tomato mixture in small mounds on top of the toasts, sprinkle the Parmesan cheese, if using, over the tops of the toasts, and serve at once.

Yields 12 slices

Patatas Bravo! Bravo!

This classic Spanish tapa, with its fierce mixture of traditional ingredients, goes dive bar chic when paired with a Belgian Ale, American Wheat Beer, or Chili Beer.

Pair with:
Belgian Ale (page 34), American Wheat Ale (page 38), Chili Beer (page 39)

12 small potatoes, slightly larger than bite-size, unpeeled

2 tablespoons extra-virgin olive oil

I tablespoon white wine vinegar

2 pinches hot smoked Spanish paprika, or more to taste

I teaspoon garlic powder

I teaspoon chili powder

1/4 cup mayonnaise (use recipe on page 24 or store-bought mayo)

Sea salt, to taste

Bring a large pan of salted water to a boil. Add the potatoes, and cook for 15 to 20 minutes, until tender but not falling apart. Drain, rinse, and let cool, then slice the potatoes in half. Transfer to a serving plate or tray.

Mix together the olive oil, vinegar, paprika, garlic powder, and chili powder in a small bowl. Dribble the mixture over the potatoes, then drizzle with the mayonnaise. Season with the sea salt to taste, and serve hot with festive toothpicks.

Yields 2 to 4 servings

The Mash Up! Platter

For fun lunches or ultimate comfort tapas, arrange a scoop of two or more of these mashes on a single rectangular plate to create a platter for 1 to 2 people to enjoy.

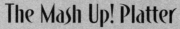

Yukon Gold Mash

The buttery Yukon golds are a nice base for the swigs of a vibrant IPA, Chili Beer, or Altbier.

Pair with:
India Pale Ale (page 34), Chili Beer (page 39), Altbier (page 33)

---

3 to 4 medium-large Yukon gold potatoes, peeled and cut into roughly 1-inch pieces

4 to 6 tablespoons margarine, at room temperature (use recipe on page 23 or store-bought margarine)

Salt, to taste

Freshly ground black or white pepper, to taste

1/2 cup (or more) soy or almond milk, warmed (optional)

Place the potatoes in a large saucepan, and cover the potatoes with water. Bring to a boil over medium-high heat, then lower the heat and simmer until the potatoes are tender, about 12 to 15 minutes. Drain the potatoes and let them cool for a few minutes, then pass them through a ricer into a large bowl, or mash them in a large bowl with a potato masher. Add the margarine, and stir it into the hot mashed potatoes until melted. Season with the salt and pepper. Add the milk, if using, to bring the mashed potatoes to your desired consistency.

Yields 4 to 5 servings

Cauliflower Mash

Cauliflower mash is an incredible alternative to traditional mashed potatoes. The subtle flavor of the cauliflower, along with the other ingredients, offers the eater an even more intense burst of flavor from a rich Brown Ale, Porter, or Stout pairing.

 Pair with:
Brown Ale (page 34), Porter (page 37), Stout (page 38)

I head cauliflower, florets chopped into bite-size pieces

1/2 cup sour cream (use recipe on page 27 or store-bought sour cream)

3/4 teaspoon salt

1/2 teaspoon pepper

2 tablespoons margarine (use recipe on page 23 or store-bought margarine)

1/4 cup grated Parmesan cheese (use recipe on page 17 or store-bought cheese)

2 teaspoons toasted cumin seeds

I tablespoon chives, chopped for garnishing, or more to taste

Place the cauliflower florets in a medium-size saucepan, and cover the cauliflower with water. Bring to a boil, and cook for about 8 to 10 minutes, or until the florets are tender. Drain the florets. Combine the cauliflower with the sour cream, salt, pepper, and margarine in a large bowl, mashing with a fork until the mixture reaches your desired consistency. Add the Parmesan cheese and the cumin seeds, and mix well. Garnish with the chives.

Yields 4 to 6 servings

Carrot Mash

The brown sugar, sherry, and molasses lend this carrot mash a sweet, glazed effect, which is then balanced by a hoppy Barley Wine or Bock, or complemented by a sweeter and even nutty Dunkel.

Pair with:
Barley Wine (page 33), Bock (page 35), Dunkel (page 36)

2 pounds carrots, peeled, topped, and halved if large, but otherwise left whole

I cup sour cream (use recipe on page 27 or store-bought sour cream)

I tablespoon light brown sugar

2 tablespoons dry sherry

2 teaspoons light molasses

3 tablespoons margarine, melted (use recipe on page 23 or store-bought margarine)

Preheat the oven to 350°F. Place the carrots in a large saucepan, cover the carrots with water, and cover the pan. Bring to a boil, lower the heat, and simmer until the carrots are tender, about 8 minutes, but testing for tenderness after 6 minutes. Drain well and place the carrots in a large bowl. Mash the carrots using a handheld masher until fairly smooth. Add the remaining ingredients, mixing well. Transfer to a casserole dish and bake for 20 minutes.

Yields 4 to 6 servings

Sweet Potato Mash

This is one scrumptious way to enjoy a holiday favorite—sweet potatoes—anytime the craving hits you. As a counterpoint to the sweet maple flavoring of the mash, pair it with a sturdy and rich Brown Ale, Stout, or Oktoberfest.

 Pair with:
Brown Ale (page 34), Stout (page 38), Oktoberfest (page 36)

6 sweet potatoes, peeled and cubed

3/4 cup soy or almond milk, or more or less to taste

1/2 cup margarine, or to taste, melted (use recipe on page 23 or store-bought margarine)

3/4 cup maple syrup, or to taste

Place the sweet potatoes in a large saucepan. Cover the sweet potatoes with water, and cover the pan. Bring to a boil, and simmer for about 25 to 30 minutes, or until tender. Drain the potatoes and place in a large bowl. Blend the sweet potatoes using an electric mixer set on low. Slowly add the milk, about 1/2 cup at a time, blending to smooth. Use more or less milk to reach your desired consistency. Add the margarine and maple syrup. Blend until smooth. Serve warm.

Yields 6 to 8 servings

Jalapeño Potato Mash

To say that the jalapeño takes charge in this otherwise classic mashed potato dish is an understatement for sure. You can either add fuel to the fire by pairing it with a Chili Beer, or err on the side of caution and kick back with a go-to Pale Lager or Vienna Lager.

Pair with:
Chili Beer (page 39), Pale Lager (page 36), Vienna Lager (page 37)

2 1/2 pounds Yukon gold potatoes, peeled and cut into large dice

1/2 cup margarine, cubed (use recipe on page 23 or store-bought margarine)

1/2 to 3/4 cup soy or almond milk, or slightly more, as needed to blend

1 jalapeño, roasted, peeled, and pureed (see note)

Salt, to taste

Freshly ground black pepper, to taste

Note: *To roast and peel a jalapeño, place it under a hot broiler or over a gas flame. Roast, turning the pepper as it browns, until it's blackened all over, 3 to 5 minutes. Let cool slightly, then rub off the jalapeño's skin with a paper towel. Stem the jalapeño, and puree it with a mortar and pestle, rolling pin, or blender.*

Place the potatoes in a large saucepan of water with a dash of salt. Bring to a boil. Reduce the heat to a simmer, and cook the potatoes until tender, about 10 to 15 minutes. Drain well, and place the potatoes in a large bowl. Mash the margarine into the potatoes using a handheld masher. Add the milk and continue to mash, using enough milk to reach your desired consistency. Mix the pureed jalapeño into the potato mixture until well combined. Season with the salt and pepper.

Yields 6 servings

Garlic Mash

To all the garlic lovers out there, this mash is my gift of comfort to you. For the pairing, a lighter Belgian Ale or Pale Lager, as well as a darker Amber Lager, all play nice with the garlic without getting in its way.

Pair with:
Belgian Ale (page 34), Pale Lager (page 36),
Amber Lager (page 35)

---

6 cloves garlic

1/4 cup extra-virgin olive oil

7 baking potatoes, peeled and cut into 1-inch cubes

1/2 cup soy or almond milk, or slightly more, as needed to blend

1/4 cup grated Parmesan cheese (use recipe on page 17 or store-bought cheese)

2 tablespoons margarine (use recipe on page 23 or store-bought margarine)

Salt, to taste

Freshly ground black pepper, to taste

Note: *Stick blenders can make mashed potatoes sticky if you overblend them, so test the potatoes as soon as they're mashed before you blend further.*

Preheat the oven to 350°F. Place the garlic cloves in a small baking dish, drizzle with the olive oil, and cover with foil. Bake for 45 minutes, or until golden brown.

Place the potatoes in a large pot. Cover the potato cubes with water, add a few teaspoons of salt, and bring to a boil. Cook until tender but still somewhat firm, about 8 to 10 minutes. Drain the potato cubes, and place them in a large bowl. Add the garlic, milk, Parmesan cheese, and margarine. Season with the salt and pepper. Using a stick blender or potato masher, blend the potato mixture to your desired consistency.

Yields 8 to 10 servings

⫸Bloody Mary Mash⫷

Brunch (or snack time) just got a new superstar added to the menu. With all the sizzle and pizzazz you've come to expect of the iconic thirst quencher this dish is inspired by, this Bloody Mary Mash, paired with a favorite Pilsner, Brown Ale, or Pale Lager, will put a smile on every guest's face the minute it hits the table.

 Pair with:
Pilsner (page 37), Brown Ale (page 34), Pale Lager (page 36)

---

3 cups mashed Yukon gold potatoes (page 176)

1 tablespoon Worcestershire sauce (use recipe on page 30 or store-bought Worcestershire sauce)

2 teaspoons freshly squeezed lemon juice

2 teaspoons freshly squeezed lime juice

2 teaspoons Tabasco or Sriracha Hot Chili Sauce, or to taste

1/2 cup V8 juice (preferably the Spicy Hot V8 juice) or tomato juice, possibly more to achieve desired texture

1 teaspoon vodka

1 tablespoon prepared horseradish

1 teaspoon celery salt, or to taste

Freshly ground black pepper, to taste

1 celery stalk, with leaves, for garnishing

Place the mashed potatoes in a large microwave-safe bowl. Add the Worcestershire sauce, lemon and lime juices, Tabasco sauce, V8 juice, vodka, horseradish, celery salt, and black pepper. Whip the mixture together with a fork. Microwave the mash until fairly hot (timing will vary according to your oven's wattage). Insert the celery stalk into the mash at the side of the bowl as a garnish, and serve at once.

Yields 4 to 5 servings

Apple Tree Pancakes

Not that you need one, but here's your ideal excuse to enjoy beer at breakfast or brunch: apple, cinnamon, and brown sugar pancakes, intensified by the addition of Brown Ale, Oktoberfest, or Doppelbock.

Pair with:
Brown Ale (page 34), Oktoberfest (page 36),
Doppelbock (page 36)

I cup all-purpose flour, sifted

1/3 cup sugar plus 1/2 teaspoon sugar, divided

1/4 teaspoon salt

I cup beer of your choice, room temperature, preferably the same beer you're pairing with the dish

Egg replacer equal to 4 eggs (page 19)

1/4 cup light brown sugar

I 1/2 teaspoons ground cinnamon

1/2 teaspoon ground cloves

2 green apples, peeled

1/2 small lemon

3 tablespoons margarine, melted (use recipe on page 23 or store-bought margarine)

I tablespoon vegetable oil

Preheat the oven to 350°F. Sift together the flour, 1 1/2 teaspoons of the sugar, and the salt in a large bowl. Add the beer, mixing until the batter is smooth. Beat in the egg replacer, 1/4 cup at a time. Combine the remaining sugar, brown sugar, cinnamon, and cloves in a small bowl, mixing well. Reserve 2 teaspoons of this mixture.

Slice the apples into medium-thin slices. Squeeze the lemon over the slices to keep them from browning. Place the apples on a board. Coat the apples with the sugar and cinnamon mixture in the small bowl. Heat the margarine and vegetable oil in a medium-size skillet. Pour the melted margarine and vegetable oil into a casserole dish. Pour half the batter into the casserole dish, and top with all the apple slices. Pour the rest of the batter over the apples. Place the dish on the middle oven rack, and bake for 1 hour, or until the pancake is puffy and golden. To serve, cut into bite-size pancakes and garnish with the remaining sugar and cinnamon mixture.

Yields 4 to 6 servings

⫸ Tanked Banana Pancakes ⫷

For everyday breakfasts, special weekend brunches, or even when made smaller for anytime tapas, these boozy banana pancakes offer a sweet and fruity twist matched by the distinctive edge of a Brown Ale, Doppelbock, or Barley Wine.

Pair with:
Brown Ale (page 34), Doppelbock (page 36),
Barley Wine (page 33)

1 cup all-purpose flour	12 ounces beer of your choice, preferably the same beer you're pairing with the dish
1 teaspoon baking powder	
1/2 teaspoon baking soda	2 ripe bananas, well mashed
1/2 teaspoon salt	Margarine, to taste (use recipe on page 23 or store-bought margarine)
Egg replacer to equal 2 eggs (page 19)	
3 tablespoons corn oil	4 to 5 cups berries of your choice, for serving
1 tablespoon light molasses	Syrup of choice, for serving

Combine the flour, baking powder, baking soda, and salt in a medium-size bowl, mixing well. Combine the egg replacer, corn oil, and molasses in a separate medium-size bowl, mixing well. Add the egg mixture and the beer to the flour mixture, then add the mashed bananas, mixing lightly.

Heat a griddle to 350°F, or use a lightly oiled, medium-size skillet over medium-high heat. Spoon 2 tablespoons of the batter onto the griddle or skillet, spreading the batter into a 2- to 3-inch circle with the back of the spoon. Heat the pancake until it is browned on one side, and then flip and brown the other side. Continue to make pancakes with the rest of the batter. Serve the pancakes with the margarine, berries, and syrup of choice.

Yields 8 to 10 servings

Chocolate-Dipped Strawberries

These deep-fried strawberries, dipped in whipped cream and chocolate—and paired with a smooth and sweet Oatmeal Stout, toasty Barley Wine, or malty Dunkelweizen— are the ultimate way to end (or even start) a great night.

Pair with:
Oatmeal Stout (page 37), Barley Wine (page 33), Dunkelweizen (page 38)

1 ounce active dry yeast

9 ounces beer of your choice, preferably the same beer you're pairing with the dish

Pinch of salt

Pinch of sugar

1 teaspoon white wine vinegar

6 ounces all-purpose flour, with extra for coating, divided

Vegetable oil, for deep frying

1 pound strawberries, hulled and halved

Confectioners' sugar, for coating the strawberries

Whipped cream (use recipe on page 18 or store-bought whipped cream)

2 to 4 cups chocolate, melted (page 17)

Place the yeast in a large bowl. Pour the beer into the bowl, and dissolve the yeast in the beer. Add the salt, sugar, and vinegar, mixing well. Sift the 6 ounces of flour into the mixture, and, using a whisk or electric beater, beat until it is creamy. Refrigerate the mixture for 20 to 30 minutes.

Heat the vegetable oil to 350°F in a deep fryer or electric skillet. (Or heat the oil in a large, deep skillet over medium-high heat. Test to see if the oil is hot enough by frying a drop of batter. If it quickly sizzles and floats to the top, the oil is ready.)

Dip the strawberries into the remaining flour. Then coat the strawberries with the beer batter. Carefully drop the strawberries into the hot oil, and fry them until they are golden. Remove the strawberries using a slotted spoon, and drain them on paper towels. Coat the strawberries with the confectioners' sugar. Serve the strawberries with the whipped cream and dipping chocolate.

Yields 8 servings

Chocolate-Dipped Bananas

Deep-fried bananas, dipped in chocolate and paired with a traditional Stout, toasty and hop-heavy Russian Imperial Stout, or German Hefeweizen, reconfirm that there is such a thing as bite-size comfort!

 Pair with:
Stout (page 38), Russian Imperial Stout (page 37), German Hefeweizen (page 38)

---

2 cups all-purpose flour

1 pint beer of your choice, preferably the same beer you're pairing with the dish

4 bananas, ripe but firm, peeled and cut crosswise into 3 pieces

Vegetable oil, for deep frying

Freshly squeezed juice of 2 lemons

1/2 cup agave nectar

2 to 3 cups chocolate, melted (page 17)

Mix the flour and beer in a medium-size bowl, blending until smooth. Coat the bananas with the beer batter. Heat the vegetable oil to 350°F in a deep fryer or electric skillet. (Or heat the oil in a large, deep skillet over medium-high heat. Test to see if the oil is hot enough by frying a drop of batter. If it quickly sizzles and floats to the top, the oil is ready.) Add the battered bananas to the oil, cooking until they are golden and crispy, about 6 to 9 minutes. (Timing will vary according to the temperature of the bananas, but bear in mind that they'll continue to cook after they're removed from the hot oil.) Remove the bananas from the oil using a slotted spoon, and sprinkle them lightly with the lemon juice and agave. Serve them with the melted chocolate for dipping.

Yields 4 servings

Chapter 5
LAST CALL PIZZA & BURGERS

Admit it—nothing tastes better after a long night of drinking beer, dancing, and laughing than a loaded-up pizza or burger *and* a nightcap! The recipes in this chapter, and their suggested beer pairings, will take everything you know about pizza and burgers to a whole new level of satisfaction.

The Beer & Pizza Bar is spinning with your choice of slices and sips, including Taco Night Pizza with a toasty Vienna Lager; Flying Buffalo at the Tap Pizza with a hopped-up, citrus-accented India Pale Lager; Alfredo's White Garlic Pub Pizza with a hoppier Barley Wine; Mushroom Lover's Pizza Party with a lightly hopped Belgian Abbey Dubbel; Pepper Lover's Pizza Palooza with a sweet Dunkel; or The Veggie Lover's Last Call Pizza with that Rauchbier you've been wanting to try.

And get ready to reimagine the traditional burger in many new tasty forms. The Beer & Burgers Bar will have you and your guests flipping out over the likes of Beer Garden Veggie Burgers with a moderately hoppy American or English Pale Ale; Sweet Onion Sliders with a dark, malty Dunkelweizen; Cheesy Eggplant Burgers with a low-hops German Hefeweizen; Grilled Cauliflower Burgers with a sweet and nutty Brown Ale; Fried Potato Sliders with a robust Doppelbock; Grilled Tomato-Basil Sliders with an easygoing Golden Ale; and Sauerkraut & Portobello Burgers with an Oktoberfest.

Also, to upgrade your burger into a platter fit for a king or queen of Beer Town, simply add a side from The Roadhouse Fries Bar (pages 87 to 90) or The Tavern Chips Bar (pages 68 to 72), and a few Crunchy Pickled Dills (page 96) or Deep-Fried Dills (page 92).

The Beer & Pizza Bar

⊷Taco Night Pizza⊶

By pairing with an ice-cold Pale Lager, Pilsner, or Vienna Lager, you can then easily turn this south-of-the-border-inspired taco pizza into a theme night. Start with the Guac 'n' Roll (page 134), a selection of salsa on pages 123 to 127, homemade tortilla chips (page 69), South of the Border Popcorn (page 75), and a few of the other bar snacks throughout the book that are fired up with jalapeños.

Pair with:
Pale Lager (page 36), Pilsner (page 37), Vienna Lager (page 37)

1 (16-ounce) can kidney beans, rinsed and drained, divided	1 yellow bell pepper, sliced into thin rings
3/4 cup salsa (use recipes on pages 123 to 127 or store-bought salsa)	1 small jalapeño or habanero, sliced into thin rings or chopped (optional)
1 (12-inch) prebaked thin pizza crust	1 red onion, sliced into thin rings
1 1/2 cups shredded Cheddar cheese (optional) (use recipe on page 15 or store-bought cheese)	2 tablespoons chopped fresh cilantro
	2 cups tortilla chips, broken into bite-size pieces (optional) (use recipe on page 69 or store-bought chips)
1 red bell pepper, sliced into thin rings	

Preheat the oven to 425°F. Partially mash 3/4 cup of the beans in a small bowl. Add the salsa, mixing well. Spread the bean mixture evenly over the pizza crust. Top with the Cheddar cheese, if using, remaining beans, bell peppers, jalapeño, if using, and onion. Place the pizza on a baking sheet, and bake for 12 minutes, or until the cheese is melted and the crust is golden brown. Scatter the cilantro and the tortilla chips, if using, over the top of the pizza before serving.

Yields 1 pizza or 8 to 10 slices

Flying Buffalo at the Tap Pizza

The sizzle of Frank's RedHot–infused toppings balanced by the cool arugula, carrots, cucumber, and tomatoes on top of this baked crust will get your pizza night soaring. The perfect counterpoint to this hot and cool blend of ingredients is an American or English Pale Ale with its malty overtones and slightly bitter edge, a hoppy IPA, or a sweeter, medium-hops Oktoberfest.

Pair with:
American or English Pale Ale (pages 33 and 34, respectively), India Pale Ale (page 34), Oktoberfest (page 36)

1/2 cup ketchup

1/4 cup Frank's RedHot Cayenne Pepper Sauce

1 teaspoon liquid smoke

2 teaspoons extra-virgin olive oil

1/2 cup chopped yellow onion

8 ounces seitan, cut into 1/2-inch cubes, or tofu, pressed, drained, and cut into 1/2-inch cubes (page 28)

2 cups quartered cremini mushrooms

1 (12-inch) prebaked pizza crust

1 1/2 cups arugula or spinach, julienned

2 carrots, shredded

1/2 cucumber, peeled and diced

2 tomatoes, cut into 1/4-inch-thick slices

Place an oven rack in the lower third of the oven, and preheat the oven to 450°F. Combine the ketchup, hot sauce, and liquid smoke in a small bowl, stirring well. Set aside.

Heat the olive oil in a large skillet over medium heat. Add the onion, and cook for 2 to 3 minutes. Add the seitan and mushrooms, and cook over medium-high heat for 3 to 4 minutes, or until the mushrooms are soft. Remove from the heat. Combine the seitan mixture and ketchup mixture in a medium-size bowl, mixing gently to coat well.

Spread the seitan mixture over the crust. Bake for 15 minutes, or until the crust is golden and crisp. Top with the arugula, carrots, cucumber, and tomatoes before serving.

Yields 1 pizza or 8 to 10 slices

Alfredo's White Garlic Pub Pizza

Mamma mia! With its Alfredo sauce, sun-dried tomato pesto, and herbs, this pizza will be a showpiece from the minute it's slipped out of the oven. Keep a good thing rolling by pairing the Alfredo-topped pizza with an amber-hued Belgian Ale, a toasty Barley Wine, or a hoppy Amber Lager.

Pair with:
Belgian Ale (page 34), Barley Wine (page 33),
Amber Lager (page 35)

---

2 tablespoons margarine, melted (use recipe on page 23 or store-bought margarine)

1 tablespoon extra-virgin olive oil

4 tablespoons garlic, crushed

3 tablespoons sun-dried tomato pesto (see note)

6 fresh basil leaves, stacked and sliced into a fine chiffonade (page 22)

1 1/2 teaspoons dried oregano

1 tablespoon grated Parmesan cheese (optional) (use recipe on page 17 or store-bought cheese)

1 cup Alfredo sauce (use the recipe that follows or store-bought sauce, see note)

1 (12-inch) prebaked thin pizza crust

1 medium tomato, sliced

Note: *Sun-dried tomato pesto can be found in many grocery stores, and several homemade recipes are available online. Likewise, while a homemade, nondairy Alfredo sauce recipe follows, Alfredo sauce is also widely available in stores. Just be sure to carefully read the label to make sure you are comfortable with all the ingredients.*

Preheat the oven to 375°F. Mix together the margarine, olive oil, garlic, pesto, basil, oregano, Parmesan cheese, if using, and Alfredo sauce in a small bowl. Spread the mixture evenly over the pizza crust. Top with the tomato slices. Bake for 10 to 15 minutes, or until the crust is lightly browned and the tomato slices are well softened.

Yields 1 pizza or 8 to 10 slices

Homemade Alfredo Sauce

1/2 cup margarine (use recipe on page 23 or store-bought margarine)

2 tablespoons cornstarch, divided

8 ounces cream cheese, at room temperature, cut into 1/2-inch cubes (use recipe on page 16 or store-bought cream cheese)

1 cup soy or almond milk

1 tablespoon white vermouth

3 cloves garlic, crushed

1 teaspoon onion powder

1 teaspoon kosher salt

Freshly ground black pepper, to taste

Melt the margarine in a medium-size saucepan over medium heat. Add 1 tablespoon of the cornstarch, and whisk well until thickened, adding more cornstarch to thicken if needed. When the margarine and cornstarch are thoroughly blended, add the cream cheese cubes, a few at a time. Stir continuously until the cream cheese has melted. Add the soy milk, vermouth, garlic, onion powder, salt, and pepper, and stir until well mixed. Reduce the heat to medium-low, and cook the mixture for 10 to 15 minutes.

Yields about 2 1/2 cups

❦ Mushroom Lover's Pizza Party ❦

Here, proper homage, bar style, is paid to a highly sought-after ingredient by giving the home chef his or her choice of mushrooms to create a super deluxe veggie pizza that is particularly irresistible when paired with a rich and nutty Brown Ale, a lightly hopped Belgian Abbey Dubbel, or a classic Amber Lager.

Pair with:
Brown Ale (page 34), Belgian Abbey Dubbel (page 33), Amber Lager (page 35)

Your choice of toppings, chopped and sliced as desired, with quantities to suit your taste:

- A mixture of mushrooms, such as: White mushrooms, Cremini mushrooms, Portobello mushrooms, Shiitake mushrooms, Enoki mushrooms
- Onions
- Garlic
- Red, yellow, and/or green bell peppers
- Banana peppers
- Tomatoes
- Broccoli
- Zucchini
- Sautéed spinach
- Jalapeño peppers

---

1 (12-inch) prebaked thin pizza crust
Extra-virgin olive oil, for brushing the crust
3 to 4 cups (or more) pizza sauce (use recipe on page 195 or store-bought pizza sauce)
Nutritional yeast, to taste

1 teaspoon finely chopped fresh rosemary leaves
1/2 teaspoon hot red pepper flakes
1 teaspoon dried oregano
1 tablespoon minced fresh basil leaves

Preheat the oven to 400°F. Brush the top of the pizza crust with the olive oil. Cover it with the sauce and your choice of toppings. Sprinkle the nutritional yeast, rosemary, red pepper flakes, and oregano on top of the pizza.

Bake the pizza until it's hot and all the mushrooms are softened, 10 to 15 minutes. Sprinkle the basil on top of the pizza after it's removed from the oven.

Yields 1 pizza or 8 to 10 slices

Pepper Lover's Pizza Palooza

From mild to downright singeing, peppers have captured hearts and imaginations, *and* appetites, the world over. For this pepper-tastic party pizza, go as wild as you want with your choice of peppers, from bell and banana to jalapeño and habanero. Just be sure the higher the heat factor, the more Amber Lager, Porter, and Dunkel you have on ice nearby!

 Pair with:
Amber Lager (page 35), Porter (page 37), Dunkel (page 36)

Your choice of toppings, chopped and sliced as desired, with quantities to suit your taste:

- A mixture of peppers, such as: Red, yellow, and/or green bell peppers, Banana peppers, Jalapeño peppers, Habanero peppers, Anaheim chile peppers
- Mushrooms
- Onions
- Garlic
- Tomatoes
- Broccoli
- Zucchini
- Sautéed spinach
- Fresh arugula leaves

Nutritional yeast

1 (12-inch) prebaked thin pizza crust

Extra-virgin olive oil, for brushing the crust

3 to 4 cups (or more) pizza sauce (use recipe on page 195 or store-bought pizza sauce)

1 teaspoon finely chopped fresh rosemary leaves

1/2 teaspoon hot red pepper flakes

1 teaspoon dried oregano

1 tablespoon minced fresh basil, especially if using fresh tomatoes

Preheat the oven to 400°F. Brush the top of the pizza crust with the olive oil. Cover the crust with the sauce, the toppings of your choice, and the herbs, except the basil. Roast the pizza until the sauce is bubbly and the crust is darkening, about 10 to 15 minutes. Sprinkle the basil on top of the pizza after it's removed from the oven.

Yields 1 pizza or 8 to 10 slices

The Veggie Lover's Last Call Pizza

Head to your backyard garden, local farmers market, roadside veggie stand, or nearest produce section, and start building your dream pizza with as many fresh veggies as you can pile on for a feast with friends or the perfect snack after the bars close. For an unexpected pairing choice, opt for a Rauchbier, or go old school with a favorite Pilsner or Pale Lager.

Pair with:
Rauchbier (page 39), Pilsner (page 37), Pale Lager (page 36)

Your choice of toppings, chopped and sliced as desired, with quantities to suit your taste:

- Mushrooms
- Onions
- Garlic
- Red, yellow, and/or green bell peppers
- Tomatoes
- Broccoli
- Asparagus
- Avocado (Add before or after pizza has been baked, as desired)
- Zucchini, yellow summer squash, or eggplant
- Sautéed spinach
- Fresh arugula leaves
- Banana peppers
- Jalapeños

I (12-inch) prebaked thin pizza crust

Extra-virgin olive oil

3 to 4 cups (or more) pizza sauce (use the recipe that follows or store-bought pizza sauce)

Nutritional yeast, to taste

I teaspoon finely chopped fresh rosemary leaves

1/2 teaspoon hot red pepper flakes

I teaspoon dried oregano

I tablespoon minced fresh basil

Preheat the oven to 400°F. Brush the top side of the pizza crust with the olive oil. Cover the crust with the sauce and toppings of your choice. Sprinkle the nutritional yeast and herbs over top, except the basil.

Bake the pizza until the toppings are softened and/or lightly browned, about 10 to 15 minutes. Sprinkle the basil on top of the pizza after it's removed from the oven.

Yields I pizza or 8 to I0 slices

DIY Pizza Sauce

2 tablespoons extra-virgin olive oil

2 cloves garlic, crushed

1 medium sweet onion, such as Vidalia, finely chopped

1 (6-ounce) can tomato paste

2 teaspoons dried basil or 1 bunch fresh basil leaves, minced

2 tablespoons beer of your choice, preferably the same beer you're pairing with the dish

3 (28-ounce) cans crushed tomatoes, or 2 (28-ounce) cans crushed tomatoes and 1 (28-ounce) can tomato sauce

1 cup water

2 teaspoons sugar, or to taste

1 teaspoon fresh minced oregano leaves, or to taste

Salt, to taste

Freshly ground black pepper, to taste

2 tablespoons grated Parmesan cheese (use recipe on page 17 or store-bought cheese)

Note: *This sauce also works as a spaghetti sauce and freezes well.*

Heat the olive oil in a large pot over medium-low heat. Gently sauté the garlic and onion in the oil until the mixture is golden brown. Add the tomato paste and basil, and sauté for 5 minutes. Add the beer, tomatoes, water, sugar, oregano, salt, pepper, and Parmesan cheese. Stir gently, and bring to a simmer. Simmer for at least 5 hours, stirring occasionally.

Yields 12 cups

The Beer & Burgers Bar

Beer Garden Veggie Burgers

This zesty black bean–bell pepper–onion veggie burger, served on a bun or solo with all the trimmings, is best accompanied by a chilled Pilsner, Amber Lager, or an American or English Pale Ale that leans to the mighty malt side.

Pair with:
Pilsner (page 37), Amber Lager (page 35),
American or English Pale Ale (pages 33 and 34, respectively)

1 (16-ounce) can black or kidney beans, drained	Egg replacer equal to 1 egg (page 19)
	1 tablespoon chili powder, or to taste
1/2 green bell pepper, or 1 whole Anaheim chile pepper, sliced into 2-inch pieces	1 tablespoon ground cumin
1/2 red onion, cut into 1/4-inch slices	1 teaspoon Tabasco sauce
	1/2 cup plain breadcrumbs
3 cloves garlic	4 potato bread rolls/buns, toasted

Preheat the oven to 400°F. Line a baking sheet with aluminum foil, and coat lightly with canola oil.

Place the beans in a medium-size bowl, and mash with a fork until they're no longer lumpy. Finely chop the pepper, onion, and garlic in a food processor. Stir the pepper mixture into the beans.

Whisk together the egg replacer, chili powder, cumin, and Tabasco sauce in a small bowl. Stir the egg mixture into the beans. Add the breadcrumbs, and stir with a fork until the mixture holds together. Divide the mixture into four patties.

Place the patties on the prepared baking sheet, and bake for about 8 minutes on each side, until lightly browned. Split the toasted potato buns, place a patty in each bun bottom, and garnish as desired with ketchup, mustard, and other condiments.

Yields 4 burgers

Sweet Onion Sliders

When you get your hands on large, luscious sweet onions, fire up the grill and transform them into backyard or tailgating sliders topped with mayonnaise, parsley, and capers. Not only will these sliders surprise and impress your guests, but the accompanying nutty Brown Ale, sweet Dunkel, or malty Dunkelweizen will bring these sliders right into home plate!

Pair with:
Brown Ale (page 34), Dunkel (page 36), Dunkelweizen (page 38)

---

16 slider buns, about 2 1/2 to 3 inches in diameter, split and toasted

16 tablespoons unsalted margarine, room temperature (use recipe on page 23 or store-bought margarine)

4 large sweet onions, such as Vidalia, sliced into 16 (1/3-inch thick) slider-size patties

Extra-virgin olive oil, for brushing the onion patties

Sea salt, to taste

2 tablespoons mayonnaise (use recipe on page 24 or store-bought mayo)

4 tablespoons finely minced fresh parsley leaves

2 tablespoons chopped capers (optional)

Spread each bun with 1 tablespoon of the margarine. Brush each onion patty with the olive oil. Heat a grill to medium-high heat, or place a grill pan over a burner set to medium-high. Cook the onion patties until just tender and grill marks form, about 10 minutes.

Place 1 onion patty on each bun bottom. Lightly season the onions with the salt. Spread some of the mayonnaise around the inside top of each bun, sprinkle with the parsley and the capers, if using, and close each bun. Serve immediately.

Yields 16 sliders

Grilled Portobello Burgers

Grilled portobello burgers are popping up on menus everywhere, but none of them can hold a candle to this marinated version boasting a culinary treasure trove of ingredients—balsamic vinegar, vermouth, Old Bay, soy sauce, and chiles, to name a few. The only thing that can possibly make this burger better is its sidekick of a Belgian Ale, American Wheat Ale, or American or English Pale Ale. And that's before you even hit up the potential variations that follow, including a Portobello Fire Burger, Buffalo-Style Portobello Burger, and Sauerkraut & Portobello Burger. Also, you can use the marinades and beer pairing suggestions from The DIY Kebab Bar on page 160 to create even more grilled portobello burgers.

Pair with:
Belgian Ale (page 34), American Wheat Ale (page 38),
American or English Pale Ale (pages 33 and 34, respectively)

1/4 cup canola or vegetable oil

1/4 cup balsamic vinegar

2 tablespoons dry white vermouth

2 teaspoons garlic powder

2 teaspoons onion powder

1 teaspoon Old Bay Seasoning

2 teaspoons low-sodium soy sauce

1/2 to 1 teaspoon Tabasco sauce

1 teaspoon freshly ground white pepper, divided

2 Anaheim chile peppers, seeded, each pepper carved into 2 wedges

2 jalapeños, finely chopped

8 portobello mushrooms (about 1 pound), black gills under the caps scraped away

4 potato bread rolls/buns or regular hamburger buns

2 to 3 teaspoons chopped fresh tarragon leaves

1/4 cup mayonnaise (use recipe on page 24 or store-bought mayo)

4 romaine lettuce leaves, halved and trimmed to fit inside the rolls

1 tomato, sliced

1 red onion, thinly sliced

Whisk the canola oil with the balsamic vinegar, vermouth, garlic powder, onion powder, Old Bay Seasoning, soy sauce, Tabasco sauce, and 1/2 teaspoon pepper in a large bowl. Add the Anaheim chile wedges, jalapeños, and mushrooms, and toss to coat thoroughly. Marinate the mixture at room temperature for 45 minutes.

Lightly oil the grates, if necessary, and heat the grill to medium. Grill the pepper wedges, skin side down, until blackened, about 10 minutes, turning after 5 minutes to create crisscross grill marks. Set aside until cool enough to handle, then rub off the skins with paper towels.

Meanwhile, grill the mushrooms, covered, until tender, about 8 minutes, turning once after about 6 minutes. Remove from the heat and set aside.

Split the buns and toast them. Stir the tarragon into the mayonnaise in a small bowl. Generously spread the mayonnaise mixture on both insides of the toasted buns. Place two grilled mushrooms on the bottom half of each hamburger roll, and top with a lettuce leaf, and tomato and red onion slices. Close the burgers, and serve promptly.

Yields 4 burgers

Variations:

Mushroom Lover's Burger

Pair with:
Amber Lager (page 35)

Heat extra-virgin olive oil or canola oil in a medium-size skillet. Sauté 2 to 3 cups chopped white mushrooms (or any other mushrooms, or a combination of mushrooms, on page 29) in the oil until tender, 6 to 8 minutes. Spoon the mushrooms onto inverted grilled portobello mushrooms before placing them on the toasted buns.

Portobello Fire Burger

Pair with:
Chili Beer (page 39)

Place 2 tablespoons of canola oil in a medium-size cast-iron skillet over medium-high heat. Slice a red onion into rings, and sauté the rings until firm-tender, about 7 minutes, stirring once. Transfer the rings to a plate, and let cool slightly. Mince 2 to 3 jalapeño peppers and 1 habanero pepper. Transfer the chopped peppers to the skillet.

Sauté for 5 to 6 minutes over medium heat, stirring often, until the peppers are very tender. Stir in a few squeezes of Sriracha Hot Chili Sauce, and then immediately remove the peppers from the pan. Spoon the peppers onto inverted grilled portobello mushrooms, and top with the onion rings. Place the portobello mushrooms onto the toasted buns.

Buffalo-Style Portobello Burger

 Pair with:
India Pale Ale (page 34)

Place 4 portobello mushroom caps in a medium-size bowl. Combine 1/2 cup Frank's RedHot Cayenne Pepper Sauce, 1 tablespoon white or cider vinegar, and 1 tablespoon low-sodium soy sauce in a small bowl, mixing well. Pour this mixture over the mushrooms, and cover. Let the mushrooms marinate for 30 minutes. Grill the mushrooms over medium-high heat for 8 minutes, until they're tender and browned, turning once and brushing on any leftover marinade sauce. Tuck two of the mushrooms inside two toasted burger buns, and serve with extra Frank's RedHot Cayenne Pepper Sauce on the side. Double the recipe for 4 burgers.

Sauerkraut & Portobello Burger

 Pair with:
Oktoberfest (page 36)

Rub 4 large portobello mushroom caps with canola oil. Grill the mushroom caps over medium-high heat, turning once, until tender and browned on both sides, about 8 minutes. Heat 2 or more cups sauerkraut (sprinkled with caraway seeds, if you wish) in a small saucepan or in the microwave oven until fairly hot. Spoon the sauerkraut onto the inside surface of the mushrooms. Tuck one mushroom into each of four toasted buns, and serve at once.

Cheesy Eggplant Burgers

The beauty of these fried or grilled eggplant cheeseburgers, with all the fixings, is that they stand alone with an accompanying Pilsner, Amber Lager, or German Hefeweizen, or you can easily transform them into Pizza Burgers by piling on pizza sauce (use the recipe on page 195 or store-bought pizza sauce), onions, bell peppers, mushrooms, and any other desired toppings.

 Pair with:
Pilsner (page 37), Amber Lager (page 35),
German Hefeweizen (page 38)

I eggplant, peeled and sliced into 6 (3/4-inch)
    rounds
I tablespoon margarine (use recipe on page
    23 or store-bought margarine)
6 slices Cheddar cheese (use recipe on page
    I5 or store-bought cheese)
6 hamburger buns, split and toasted
6 leaves lettuce or mixed greens

6 slices tomato
1/2 onion, sliced
12 to I8 (depending on size) thin dill pickle
    slices
Ketchup, to taste
Mayonnaise, to taste (use recipe on page 24
    or store-bought mayo)
Mustard, to taste

Place the eggplant slices on a microwave-safe plate, and cook them in the microwave for about 3 to 5 minutes (depending on your oven's wattage), or until the centers are just cooked through and tender when pierced with a toothpick.

Melt the margarine in a large skillet or grill pan over medium-high heat. Add the eggplant slices, and fry until they are lightly toasted on each side, about 6 to 8 minutes. Place 1 slice of cheese onto each eggplant slice, and cover the skillet. Cook until the cheese has melted, and remove the eggplant from the skillet. Place the eggplant slices on the toasted buns, and allow each guest to garnish the burgers with their choice of lettuce, tomato, onion, pickles, ketchup, mayonnaise, and mustard.

Yields 6 burgers

Grilled Cauliflower Burgers

The humble cauliflower becomes the center of attention when it hits the grill for its very own signature burger. Slather it with a homemade mayonnaise and herb mixture, and pile it high with slices of tomato, onion, and jalapeño. The only thing left to knock this burger out of the ballpark is a frosted mug brimming with Brown Ale, Barley Wine, or your favorite American Wheat Ale.

Pair with:
Brown Ale (page 34), Barley Wine (page 33), American Wheat Ale (page 38)

I medium-size head cauliflower, core, stem, and leaves removed, and sliced into 6 to 8 slices

1/4 cup extra-virgin olive oil

Seasoned salt, such as Lawry's, to taste

Smoked Spanish paprika, to taste

2 tablespoons chopped fresh tarragon leaves, or I tablespoon fresh thyme leaves, chopped

1/4 cup mayonnaise (use recipe on page 24 or store-bought mayo)

6 to 8 burger buns, split and toasted

I tomato, sliced

I red onion, thinly sliced

I to 2 jalapeños, thinly sliced

Pickapeppa Sauce, to taste (optional) (page 22, see "Ketchup")

Bring a medium-size saucepan full of water to a boil. Blanch the cauliflower slices in the gently boiling water for 8 to 10 minutes, or until firm-tender. Drain and let cool.

Heat a grill to medium or medium-high. Rub the olive oil all over the cauliflower slices, and sprinkle them with the seasoned salt and paprika.

Grill the cauliflower slices for about 3 minutes per side, or until they're as tender as you like.

Meanwhile, stir the tarragon or thyme leaves into the mayonnaise in a small bowl, and sprinkle with additional seasoned salt. Let the mayonnaise rest for at least 10 minutes, and then spread it on both sides of the split buns.

Place one cauliflower slice on each bun. Top each cauliflower patty with the tomato, onion, and jalapeño slices, and the Pickapeppa Sauce, if using.

Yields 6 to 8 burgers

Fried Potato Sliders with Saffron Sauce

Saffron is earthy, and it tends to the bitter side if too much is used, so stick to the large pinch of saffron called for here and let your appetite reap the benefits alongside a few rounds of your favorite Stout, Amber Lager, or Doppelbock.

 Pair with:
Stout (page 38), Amber Lager (page 35),
Doppelbock (page 36)

---

3 cups low-sodium vegetable broth

Large pinch of saffron

1/2 teaspoon turmeric

1 teaspoon finely grated orange zest, or to taste

1 1/2 tablespoons margarine (use recipe on page 23 or store-bought margarine)

1 large sweet onion, cut into 1/4-inch slices

Seasoned salt, such as Lawry's, to taste

Freshly ground black pepper, to taste

1 large potato, cut into 4 or 5 (1/2-inch-thick) slider-size slices

2 tablespoons minced fresh parsley leaves

4 to 5 slider buns, about 2 1/2 to 3 inches in diameter, split and toasted

Bottled pickled green tomato slices, to taste

Potato chips, seasoned or not, to taste

Pickled sliced jalapeños, to taste

Place the vegetable broth in a medium-size saucepan over medium-high heat and bring to a boil. Continue to boil until the vegetable broth is reduced to about 3/4 cup, 8 to 12 minutes. Stir in the saffron, turmeric, and orange zest. Set aside.

Melt the margarine in a medium-size frying pan over medium heat, allowing the margarine to coat the surface of the frying pan. Add the onions, seasoned salt, and pepper, and slowly sauté the onions for 3 to 4 minutes, until they are soft. Add the potato slices, seasoning them with more seasoned salt and pepper. Stir the potatoes, coating them thoroughly with the seasoned margarine.

Fry the potatoes until the juices are absorbed and the potatoes are browned, about 8 to 10 minutes. Remove the pan from the heat. Sprinkle the parsley flakes on top of the potatoes. Place one potato patty on each bun. Top with the green tomato slices, potato chips, and pickled jalapeños. Dribble judiciously with the saffron sauce.

Yields 4 to 5 servings

Grilled Tomato-Basil Sliders

Grilled tomatoes transform a luncheon classic from plate to bun, and turn it into a new backyard-tailgating-bar snack standard. Match the seasoned tomato, Cheddar, and basil slider note for flavorful note with a go-to Pale Lager, Golden Ale, or hoppier Vienna Lager.

Pair with:
Pale Lager (page 36), Golden Ale (page 34),
Vienna Lager (page 37)

---

4 ripe but fairly firm medium tomatoes, halved crosswise and cut into 1/3-inch-thick slices slightly larger than the slider buns

Extra-virgin olive oil, for rubbing on the tomatoes and drizzling

Kosher salt, to taste

Freshly ground black pepper, to taste

8 slider buns, about 2 1/2 to 3 inches in diameter, split and toasted

4 Cheddar cheese slices, or more to taste (use recipe on page 15 or store-bought cheese) (optional)

8 fresh basil leaves, cut into chiffonade (page 22) or several large spinach leaves, if you prefer instead of basil

---

Heat the grill to high heat. Rub the cut sides of the tomatoes with the olive oil, and season well with the kosher salt and pepper. Using a fine grill grate (if possible) or grilling screen, place the tomatoes, cut sides down, over the heat. Cover the grill, and let the tomatoes cook for about 3 minutes, checking for doneness after 1 minute. (The rate of cooking will depend on the ripeness of the tomatoes and their temperature.) Gently lift the tomatoes off the grill with a thin metal spatula.

Arrange the tomato slices on the slider buns, and cover each tomato with a slice of the Cheddar cheese, if desired. Drizzle with the olive oil, and sprinkle on a bit more salt and pepper. Finish with a showering of basil chiffonade or a layer of spinach leaves. Close the buns, and serve promptly.

Yields 8 servings

⫸Dance to the Beet Sliders⫷

Whether served picnic-style or at your own home bar, these beet burgers, simmered in a lively seasoning mix, will have you doing a victory dance all through mealtime. And when served up beside rounds of icy Maibock, Cream Ale, or a good ole Pilsner, you will hear nothing but cheers from all your guests!

 Pair with:
Maibock (page 36), Cream Ale (page 34), Pilsner (page 37)

---

2 teaspoons dried dill

2 teaspoons chopped fresh tarragon leaves

6 canned chipotles in adobo, well chopped, with 2 teaspoons of the adobo sauce

3 tablespoons coriander seeds, toasted and ground

1 large carrot, roughly chopped

2 stalks of celery, roughly chopped

1 medium yellow onion, roughly chopped

3 vegetable bouillon cubes

8 medium whole beets

Extra-virgin olive oil, for sautéing

Salt, to taste

16 to 18 slider buns, about 2 1/2 to 3 inches in diameter, split and toasted

Mayonnaise, to taste (use recipe on page 24 or store-bought mayo)

1 large red onion, thinly sliced, for serving

Bring a large (4-quart) pot of generously salted water to a boil. Add the dill, tarragon, chipotles and adobo sauce, coriander, carrots, celery, onion, bouillon cubes, and beets. Bring the mixture to a boil, and let simmer for 1 hour.

Remove the beets from the pot, and let them cool. Discard the cooking liquid. When the beets have cooled, put on a pair of latex gloves, put down several layers of newspaper or waxed paper, and remove the beets' skins with a vegetable peeler. Be careful—the beets will stain any surface once they're peeled. Cut the beets into 1/4-inch slices.

Place a large sauté pan over medium heat, and pour in about 1/8 inch of olive oil. When the oil is hot, carefully place 1 layer of the beets into the skillet, and salt them lightly. Raise the heat to high, and sauté the beets until cooked through, about 3 minutes on each side. Transfer the beets to a warm plate, and repeat with the remaining beet slices until all are cooked through.

Spread the insides of the toasted slider buns with the mayonnaise. Place a beet slice on the bottom of each bun, and top with slices of red onion. Close the buns, and serve promptly.

Yields 16 to 18 sliders

Part 2

The Ultimate

BEER LOVER'S PARTY DRINKS

Chapter 6

BEER COCKTAILS

B eer cocktails are all the rage now as professional and at-home bartenders find ever new and inventive ways to use the expansive traditional, seasonal, craft, and home-brews available today. Each style of beer, as well as the nuanced flavorings within each style and their brands, offers endless excitement and gratification when mixed and matched, shaken, and stirred with all the other superstars of the bar circuit—vodka, gin, rum, whiskey, tequila, Kahlúa, liqueurs, wine, and so on.

Each cocktail recipe that follows offers you the choice of three different styles of beer to use as an ingredient. Feel free to experiment with these suggestions, especially if any of them are new to you, or invoke your inner bartender and try another beer that's not on the list. The combinations and potential for a new cocktail with every new beer that's used are limited only by the imagination.

What follows in this chapter and onward through chapter 10 is one of the largest collections of beer cocktails and other beer-infused drinks ever compiled in one place. It's your very own party drinks handbook! There is something within these pages to suit everyone's tastes for a boozy thirst quencher…

Buzzy Navel, Hoola Juice, Peach Fizz, Sweet Caroline, Pacific Coast Highway, Eeking Monkey, The Original Beer Margarita, The Lush's Iced Tea, Dive Bar Mimosa, Beertini, Under the Table Daiquiris, Red-Headed Mary, Dreamsicle, Sour Momma, Wild Thing, Hootinanny Sunrise, Truth or Dare?, Daredevil's Brew, Nineteenth Hole, Route 66, The Celebrewtante, and Sweet Home Amaretto.

Seven & Lime

7UP and fresh lime juice add extra fizzle and pizzazz to the beer in this refreshing cocktail, which works just as well served poolside or tailgating on a sunny afternoon as it does while laughing the night away with friends under the stars. You can use a go-to Pale Lager or Pilsner, or mix it up for an added burst of flavor by choosing a Fruit Beer.

10 ounces Pale Lager (page 36), Pilsner (page 37), or Fruit Beer (page 39)

2 ounces 7UP or ginger ale

1/2 teaspoon fresh squeezed lime juice

Crushed ice

1 lime slice or wedge, for garnishing

Combine all the ingredients, except the lime slice or wedge, in a Collins glass, stirring well. Garnish with the lime slice or wedge.

Yields 1 cocktail

Buzzy Navel

The *buzzzz* of fun is always in the air when vodka, peach schnapps, and orange juice mix and match with a classic wheat beer—American Wheat Ale or Belgian Witbier—or a Pale Lager on the rocks.

1/3 ounce vodka

1/3 ounce peach schnapps

1/3 ounce American Wheat Ale (page 38), Belgian Witbier (page 38), or Pale Lager (page 36)

Orange juice

1 orange slice or wedge, for garnishing (optional)

1 peach wedge, for garnishing (optional)

Combine the vodka, peach schnapps, and beer in a highball glass on the rocks, stirring well. Fill the remainder of the glass with the orange juice. Garnish with the orange slice or wedge and peach wedge, if using, either by fixing them on the rim of the glass or using a skewer.

Yields 1 cocktail

Jukebox

I double-dog dare you! Just try to resist this tempting rabble-rouser of beer, apple cider, and raspberry liqueur. My advice: hit PLAY on this cocktail by using a lively Fruit Beer, Herb/Spiced Beer, or Amber Lager, and let the sweet and spicy notes carry you into the night.

> 2 ounces Fruit Beer (page 39), Herb/Spiced Beer (page 39), or Amber Lager (page 35)
> 2 ounces apple cider
>
> Dash of raspberry liqueur
> Ice

Combine all the ingredients in a shaker. Shake well, and then strain into a lowball glass.

Yields I cocktail

Lemon Jack

Lemon gets the ultimate triple power punch of flavor here when it meets whiskey, vodka, and the complex flavor mix of a Belgian Abbey Tripel or German Hefeweizen, or the slight hoppiness of a Vienna Lager, for a cocktail that will take any occasion from good to great in one sip.

> I ounce vodka
> I ounce whiskey
> I ounce freshly squeezed lemon juice
>
> I ounce Belgian Abbey Tripel (page 33), German Hefeweizen (page 38), or Vienna Lager (page 37)
> I lemon wedge, for garnishing (optional)

Combine all the ingredients, except the garnish, in a lowball glass on the rocks, stirring well. Garnish with the lemon wedge, if using.

Yields I cocktail

Jungle Juice

When gin and vodka get the tropical treatment from white rum, triple sec, and the fruitiness of a Kölsch, Dunkelweizen, or Fruit Beer, you better have your best Tarzan call ready to roll.

1 1/2 ounces white rum	1 teaspoon grenadine
1 1/2 ounces gin	1 teaspoon Kölsch (page 35), Dunkelweizen
1 1/2 ounces vodka	(page 38), or Fruit Beer (page 39)
1 ounce triple sec	Maraschino cherries, for garnishing
1 1/2 ounces sour mix	(optional)

Layer the ingredients in a hurricane or pilsner glass, following the order in the ingredients list and serving over the rocks. Garnish with the maraschino cherries on a long skewer, if using.

Yields 1 cocktail

Wild Thing

Vodka, a few sparks of Tabasco, and a favorite Pilsner or Pale Lager, or the smooth maltiness of a Maibock, are all you need to ignite this wild and fiery party starter.

2 ounces vodka	Dash of Tabasco sauce
12 ounces Pilsner (page 37), Pale Lager	
(page 36), or Maibock (page 36)	

Combine all the ingredients on the rocks in a beer mug or pilsner glass, stirring well.

Yields 1 cocktail

The Sweet Nut

Meet your new party pals: amaretto, vodka, rum, Dr. Pepper, and the original golden rock star: beer. Here, the rum and popular sweet soda blend well with a nutty, sweet, and spicy Belgian Abbey Dubbel, a malty Dunkelweizen, or a light-bodied Cream Ale.

1 ounce amaretto

1 ounce vodka

1 ounce rum

1 ounce Dr. Pepper

1 ounce Belgian Abbey Dubbel (page 33), Dunkelweizen (page 38), or Cream Ale (page 34)

Combine the amaretto, vodka, and rum on the rocks in a Collins glass. Stir in the Dr. Pepper and beer.

Yields 1 cocktail

Hoola Juice

Make island time anytime and anywhere you are with this tropical mix of icy pineapple juice and a spicy and fruity Saison, Fruit Beer, or classic Amber Lager, all topped with pineapple chunks and cherries.

Pineapple juice (frozen into ice cubes)

12 ounces Saison (page 35), Fruit Beer (page 39), or Amber Lager (page 35)

4 tablespoons crushed pineapple

Pineapple chunks, for garnishing

Maraschino cherries, for garnishing

Place the pineapple juice ice cubes in a blender, and crush them. Pour the crushed pineapple ice into a hurricane or pilsner glass. Add the beer, stirring well. Top with the crushed pineapple. Alternate the pineapple chunks and cherries on a short skewer, and garnish by laying the skewer across the top of the glass.

Yields 1 cocktail

The Lush's Iced Tea

This *ain't* your momma's iced tea! A Pilsner, Oatmeal Stout, or Dunkel, along with lemon and mint garnishes, transforms this iced tea into the perfect companion for watching all those glorious lazy, hazy days of summer drift right on by.

4 ounces unsweetened iced tea
Sugar, to taste
12 ounces Pilsner (page 37), Oatmeal Stout (page 37), or Dunkel (page 36)

Lemon slices, for garnishing
Sprigs of mint, for garnishing

Combine the iced tea and sugar in a small pitcher. Add the beer, stirring to mix and dissolve the sugar. Pour into pilsner glasses or Collins glasses over ice. Garnish with the lemon slices and sprigs of mint.

Yields 2 cocktails

Malibu Rumble

Taste the good life in this tall, cool rum cocktail with blue curaçao, Mountain Dew, and every season's best accessory—beer—here in the form of a Kölsch, Cream Ale, or Fruit Beer.

5 ounces rum
2 ounces blue curaçao, or another orange liqueur
2 ounces coconut rum

Splash of Kölsch (page 35), Cream Ale (page 34), or Fruit Beer (page 39)
Crushed ice
Mountain Dew

Combine all the ingredients, except the Mountain Dew, in a hurricane glass, stirring well. Fill the remainder of the glass with the Mountain Dew.

Yields 1 cocktail

Hootinanny Sunrise

The. Best. Wake-up. Call. Ever. If sunshine came in a glass, this beer, amaretto, and orange juice cocktail would be it! The nutty and citric notes of the amaretto and orange juice correspond especially well to a citrus-accented IPL, a malty Dunkelweizen, or a rich and sweet Brown Ale.

12 ounces India Pale Lager (page 36), Dunkelweizen (page 38), or Brown Ale (page 34)

1 ounce amaretto
1 ounce freshly squeezed orange juice
1 orange slice, for garnishing

Combine all the ingredients in a pilsner or Collins glass, serving on the rocks. Stir well. Garnish with the orange slice.

Yields 1 cocktail

Truth or Dare?

Truth or dare, *indeed*! Regardless of which you choose, tequila, Kahlúa, whiskey, and a commanding Porter, Stout, or Oatmeal Stout will help you coast through any revelation or challenge.

2 ounces tequila
1 ounce Kahlúa
1 ounce whiskey

1 ounce Porter (page 37), Stout (page 38), or Oatmeal Stout (page 37)
1 ounce Mountain Dew

Combine all the ingredients in a lowball glass, stirring well. Add ice, if desired.

Yields 1 cocktail

⇒Root Beer⇐

When this drink's sweet anise flavor meets Kahlúa, cola, club soda, and a favorite Pale Lager, Oatmeal Stout, or Amber Lager, you'll rediscover just how amazing it is to throw all caution to the wind.

I ounce anise-flavored liqueur
I ounce Kahlúa
I ounce cola
Crushed ice

2 1/2 ounces club soda
I teaspoon Pale Lager (page 36), Oatmeal Stout
    (page 37), or Amber Lager (page 35)

Combine the anise-flavored liqueur, Kahlúa, cola, and crushed ice in a shaker, shaking well. Strain into a highball glass, and add the club soda and beer. Serve on the rocks.

Yields I cocktail

⇒BBQ Buddy⇐

It's not a BBQ without everyone's favorite sidekick, beer! Here, a Pale Lager, an Amber Lager, or an extra adventurous Chili Beer tops off a fitting grill-side cocktail of whiskey, V8 juice, barbecue sauce, and lemon juice.

I ounce whiskey
2 ounces V8 juice, preferably the Spicy Hot
    V8 juice
I teaspoon barbecue sauce (preferably a
    smoky-flavored barbecue sauce)

I teaspoon freshly squeezed lemon juice
Dash of liquid smoke (optional)
Pale Lager (page 36), Amber Lager (page 35),
    or Chili Beer (page 39)
I celery stalk, for garnishing

Combine all the ingredients, except the beer and celery, in a highball or hurricane glass. Fill the remainder of the glass with the beer. Garnish with the celery. Add ice, if desired.

Yields I cocktail

Red-Headed Mary

She's eccentric yet familiar, original yet classic, and always, *always* ready to party. Be prepared to make pitchers full of these Red-Headed Marys for weekend brunches or anytime you want to light up the room! For an extra-spicy Mary, grab a Chili Beer, or go with a lighter Pilsner or smooth Amber Lager.

8 ounces tomato juice or V8 juice, preferably the Spicy Hot V8 juice

Splash of Tabasco sauce

Splash of Worcestershire sauce (use recipe on page 30 or store-bought Worcestershire sauce)

4 ounces Chili Beer (page 39), Pilsner (page 37), or Amber Lager (page 35)

Seasoned salt, to taste

Freshly ground black pepper, to taste

I celery stalk, for garnishing

Layer the ingredients over the rocks in a highball or pilsner glass, following the order in the ingredients list. Garnish with the celery.

Yields I cocktail

Neon

A few pitchers of this glowing gin and Pale Lager–, Fruit Beer–, or Vienna Lager–infused lemonade will give a whole new meaning to getting lit.

6 ounces gin

I (12-ounce) can lemonade concentrate

12 ounces Pale Lager (page 36), Fruit Beer (page 39), or Vienna Lager (page 37)

Water (optional and to taste)

4 lemon slices, for garnishing

Combine all the ingredients, except the lemon slices, on the rocks in a pitcher, stirring well. Serve in pilsner glasses, and garnish with the lemon slices.

Yields 4 cocktails

Peach Fizz

This beer cocktail with schnapps, whiskey, and your choice of a Fruit Beer, a fruity and hop-heavy Saison, or a refreshing Kölsch is peachy keen on making sure you and your pals have a great time.

7 ounces peach schnapps
3 ounces Fruit Beer (page 39), Saison (page 35), or Kölsch (page 35)
1 ounce whiskey
3 ounces ginger ale
2 ounces lemonade
Ice

Combine all the ingredients in a shaker. Shake well, and strain into highball or lowball glasses, depending on your preferred serving size.

Yields 2 to 3 cocktails

Red Carpet

All the biggest and booziest superstars—vodka, rum, gin, tequila, brandy, and beer—are lined up in this cocktail for the ultimate march down the red carpet to a good time for all. This high-octane amalgamation pairs well with a stronger Porter or Stout, or a lighter Fruit Beer.

1/2 ounce vodka
1/2 ounce rum
1/2 ounce gin
1/2 ounce tequila
1/2 ounce triple sec
1/2 ounce brandy
1/2 ounce coconut rum
2 ounces Porter (page 37), Stout (page 38), or Fruit Beer (page 39)
1/2 ounce freshly squeezed lime juice
Splash of grenadine
Maraschino cherries, for garnishing

Combine all the ingredients, except the cherries, in a lowball glass on the rocks. Stir well. Garnish with the cherries on a short skewer.

Yields 1 cocktail

Sweet Caroline

Summertime (or anytime) just got a whole lot sweeter with this sudsy berry beer blast. The various sweet notes of the berries play nicely with a Golden Ale, Fruit Beer, or American Wheat Ale.

1 1/2 cups strawberries (fresh or frozen, thawed), plus more for garnishing
1 1/2 cups raspberries (fresh or frozen, thawed), plus more for garnishing
1 1/2 cups blueberries (fresh or frozen, thawed), plus more for garnishing
1 1/2 cups blackberries (fresh or frozen, thawed), plus more for garnishing
Freshly squeezed juice of 3 lemons, divided
1/2 cup confectioners' sugar
Crushed ice
3 (12-ounce) bottles Golden Ale (page 34), Fruit Beer (page 39), or American Wheat Ale (page 38)

Combine all the berries in a blender. Blend to reduce the mixture to juice. Add two-thirds of the lemon juice, mixing well. Place the remaining lemon juice in a small bowl, and place the confectioners' sugar in a separate small bowl. Dip the rim of 4 to 6 frosted pilsner or hurricane glasses in the bowl of lemon juice, and then in the confectioners' sugar. Fill each glass halfway with the crushed ice. Pour the berry–lemon juice mixture into the glasses, covering the ice. Fill the remainder of each glass with the beer. Garnish each glass by alternating berries on a skewer.

Yields 4 to 6 servings

⚒️Beer Over Cherry Rocks⚒️

The real cherry on top of any party is this simple pairing of an American Wheat Ale, Fruit Beer, or Kölsch and cherry-flavored 7UP over special cherry ice cubes.

> Cherry 7UP
> Maraschino cherries
>
> 12 ounces American Wheat Ale (page 38),
> Fruit Beer (page 39), or Kölsch (page 35)
> 2 ounces Cherry 7UP

To make the cherry rocks, pour the cherry-flavored 7UP into an ice cube tray. Place one cherry in each ice tray cube, and freeze. Fill a hurricane glass or large frosted beer mug with the frozen cherry rocks. Pour the beer and Cherry 7UP into the glass, stirring well.

Yields 1 large cocktail or 2 smaller cocktails

⚒️Ginger Ale⚒️

There's ginger ale, then there is *this* ginger ale. Equal parts Pilsner, Saison, or Amber Lager and ginger ale in a frosted glass take a classic thirst quencher from every day to extraordinary, sip after delicious sip!

> 6 ounces Pilsner (page 37), Saison (page
> 35), or Amber Lager (page 35)
> 6 ounces ginger ale
>
> 1 lemon slice, for garnishing
> 1 maraschino cherry, for garnishing

Combine the beer and ginger ale in a frosted pilsner or highball glass, stirring well. Garnish with the lemon slice and cherry.

Yields 1 cocktail

V Beer

This vanilla-infused vodka and Stout, Russian Imperial Stout, or Amber Lager combo over ice is classic enough for cocktail hour, yet simple enough for a few rounds around the pool or campfire.

2 ounces vanilla vodka	12 ounces Stout (page 38), Russian Imperial Stout (page 37), or Amber Lager (page 35)

Combine both ingredients on the rocks in a pilsner or highball glass, stirring well.

Yields I cocktail

A Beer Sour

Fresh lime juice paired with a Fruit Beer, Pale Lager, or Pilsner will really give you something to pucker about in the best way possible!

1/2 ounce freshly squeezed lime juice I lime slice, for garnishing	8 ounces Fruit Beer (page 39), Pale Lager (page 36), or Pilsner (page 37)

Stir the lime juice and beer together in a frosted beer mug. Garnish with the lime slice.

Yields I cocktail

Rum in the Dark

Brown Ale, Porter, or Russian Imperial Stout joins dark rum to make all those things that go bump in the night all the more exciting.

10 ounces Brown Ale (page 34), Porter (page 37), or Russian Imperial Stout (page 37)

1 ounce dark rum

Combine both ingredients on the rocks in a Collins or hurricane glass, stirring well.

Yields 1 cocktail

Dew Drop

This nice and easy mixture of Pale Lager, Pilsner, or Amber Lager, tequila, dark rum, and anise-flavored liqueur topped off with the jolt of Mountain Dew is custom-made for sipping the day away without a care in the world.

3 ounces Pale Lager (page 36), Pilsner (page 37), or Amber Lager (page 35)
2 ounces tequila

1 ounce dark rum
1 ounce anise-flavored liqueur
Mountain Dew

Combine all the ingredients, except the Mountain Dew, in a highball glass. Top with the Mountain Dew. Add ice, if desired.

Yields 1 cocktail

⫷⫸ The Big O ⫷⫸

The orange-flavored curaçao and orange juice add a twist of citrus and summer to the Belgian Abbey Tripel, IPL, or American Wheat Ale that's welcome year-round.

I ounce curaçao or another orange liqueur
Splash of freshly squeezed orange juice
Ice

12 ounces Belgian Abbey Tripel (page 33), India Pale Lager (page 36), or American Wheat Ale (page 38)
I orange slice or wedge, for garnishing

Combine the curaçao, orange juice, and ice in a shaker, shaking well. Add the shaker mixture to the beer in a chilled pilsner glass or beer mug, stirring well. Garnish with the orange slice or wedge.

Yields I cocktail

⫷⫸ Lemon Tickler ⫷⫸

Are you ticklish? You're about to find out after a few rounds of this tongue tingler. A liqueur made from several botanical ingredients (including artichokes) and boasting a bitter edge, cynar—as aperitif *and* digestif—makes this an especially nice beer cocktail to bookend a meal with. For the beer, keep it simple with a lighter Pilsner or Pale Lager, or you can go a little heavier with a Maibock.

I ounce cynar (see note)
1/3 ounce lemon syrup (page 243)

12 ounces Pilsner (page 37), Pale Lager (page 36), or Maibock (page 36)

Note: *If you can't find a nearby source to buy cynar, it's available online.*

Combine the cynar and lemon syrup in a frosted beer mug. Add the beer, filling the mug and stirring well. Add ice, if desired.

Yields I cocktail

223

⪢Daredevil's Brew⪡

This gin drink is good for what *ales* you, with the addition of a favorite American or English Pale Ale, India Pale Ale, or Vienna Lager—especially if you're the daring type!

3 ounces American or English Pale Ale (pages 33 and 34, respectively), India Pale Ale (page 34), or Vienna Lager (page 37)

4 ounces gin
Ice

Combine all the ingredients in a shaker, shaking well. Strain the liquid into a lowball glass.

Yields I cocktail

⪢Hound Dog⪡

A round or two of this vodka and Southern Comfort cocktail infused with Dry Stout, Porter, or Russian Imperial Stout will have you and your friends saying bow-wow-WOW all night long.

3 ounces vodka
4 ounces Southern Comfort

12 ounces Dry Stout (page 37), Porter (page 37), or Russian Imperial Stout (page 37)

Combine all the ingredients on the rocks in 2 to 4 pilsner or Collins glasses, stirring well.

Yields 2 to 4 cocktails

Tongue Tingler

Whether you serve this drink for cocktail hour, after dinner, or simply as an after-hours treat to yourself, your palette will thank you again and again when you sip this sophisticated libation of Everclear, vodka, gin, rum, peppermint schnapps, and your choice of Stout, Russian Imperial Stout, or Amber Lager.

2 ounces Everclear	I ounce peppermint schnapps
2 ounces vodka	2 ounces Stout (page 38), Russian Imperial
2 ounces gin	Stout (page 37), or Amber Lager (page 35)
I ounce dark rum	Cola

Combine all the ingredients, except the cola, in a highball glass on the rocks. Fill the remainder of the glass with the cola, stirring well.

Yields I cocktail

Grizzly

Pale Lager along with a Stout or Porter help bring out your wild side when the following lineup of bar favorites is brought together for a growling good time.

I/4 ounce triple sec	I/4 ounce bourbon
I/4 ounce rum	I/4 ounce scotch
I/4 ounce vodka	Pale Lager (page 36)
I/4 ounce gin	Stout (page 38) or Porter (page 37)
I/4 ounce tequila	

Combine all the ingredients, except the Pale Lager and Stout or Porter, in a beer mug, stirring well. Fill the remainder of the mug with equal parts of the Pale Lager and Stout or Porter, stirring to combine.

Yields I cocktail

Skip & Go Naked

American Wheat Ale, Dunkelweizen, or Fruit Beer, gin, and sour mix keep this classic cocktail skipping happily along for any occasion, great or small.

1 ounce gin 2 ounces sour mix	American Wheat Ale (page 38), Dunkelweizen (page 38), or Fruit Beer (page 39)

Fill a Collins glass with ice. Stir the gin and sour mix into the glass. Fill the remainder of the glass with the beer, stirring lightly.

Yields 1 cocktail

Dive Bar Mimosa

Add a shiny golden buzz to morning meals and anytime get-togethers with this sudsy twist on a traditional brunch mimosa, starring Golden Ale, Belgian Abbey Tripel, or Fruit Beer.

4 ounces Golden Ale (page 34), Belgian Abbey Tripel (page 33), or Fruit Beer (page 39) 4 ounces orange juice	Splash of champagne Fresh strawberries or raspberries (optional)

Pour the beer into a champagne flute. Add the orange juice, stirring well. Top with the champagne. Drop in a few strawberries or raspberries, if desired.

Yields 1 cocktail

Blue Moon

There's nothing sad or lonely about this blue moon when vodka, blue curaçao, and a Belgian Witbier, Fruit Beer, or Pilsner join forces to light up the night.

I ounce vodka

2 teaspoons blue curaçao or another orange liqueur

Belgian Witbier (page 38), Fruit Beer (page 39), or Pilsner (page 37)

Pour the vodka and blue curaçao into a pilsner glass. Fill the remainder of the glass with the beer. Stir gently.

Yields I cocktail

Fire & Ice

Sweet cinnamon liqueur and cool peppermint schnapps get kicked up a few notches more when paired with vodka, cola, and malty Brown Ale, Amber Lager, or Vienna Lager.

5 ounces vodka

I ounce cinnamon liqueur

I ounce peppermint schnapps or creme de menthe

1/4 cup Brown Ale (page 34), Amber Lager (page 35), or Vienna Lager (page 37)

1/2 cup cola

Combine all the ingredients in a lowball glass on the rocks, stirring well.

Yields I cocktail

Pacific Coast Highway

The coconut rum, peach schnapps, and fruit juices in this cocktail set the stage for your choice of a light and fun Fruit Beer, spicy and citric Belgian Abbey Tripel, or hearty Russian Imperial Stout that will take you and your pals cruising on waves of flavor.

I ounce coconut rum

I ounce peach schnapps

Orange juice

Pineapple juice

Pineapple chunks, for garnishing

I teaspoon Fruit Beer (page 39), Belgian Abbey Tripel (page 33), or Russian Imperial Stout (page 37)

Maraschino cherries, for garnishing

I orange slice, for garnishing

Combine the rum and peach schnapps in a shaker, shaking well. Strain the mixture into a frosted hurricane glass filled with crushed ice. Pour in equal amounts of each juice. Top with the beer. Garnish by alternating the pineapple chunks and cherries on a skewer and placing it along with the orange slice on the side of the glass.

Yields I cocktail

Jumping Jack

Southern Comfort, whiskey, and the complementary flavor notes of Belgian Abbey Dubbel, Amber Lager, or Dunkelweizen will get any party started and have you and your guests jumping for joy in no time flat.

I cup Southern Comfort

I cup whiskey

16 ounces Belgian Abbey Dubbel (page 33), Amber Lager (page 35), or Dunkelweizen (page 38)

Combine all the ingredients in 2 to 4 lowball glasses on the rocks, stirring well.

Yields 2 to 4 cocktails

Beer Cinner

This one is so good, it should be a sin! But luckily, it only sounds like one, so feel free to indulge. Enjoy as many of these guilt-free cinnamon schnapps and American Wheat Ale, Amber Lager, or Belgian Witbier cocktails as you desire.

2 parts cinnamon schnapps (chilled)
I part American Wheat Ale (page 38), Amber
    Lager (page 35), or Belgian Witbier (page 38)

Splash of grenadine
Cinnamon sticks, for garnishing

Pour the cinnamon schnapps and then the beer into a lowball glass, on the rocks. Top with the grenadine, and add the cinnamon stick as a stirrer and garnish.

Yields will vary

Beertini

Whether served straight up or on the rocks, this sophisticated vermouth–gin–whiskey–beer–blue curaçao–vodka concoction will dazzle even the biggest martini snobs you know. Either keep it simple by using a lighter Pilsner or Pale Lager, or add a heartier twist with a new Oktoberfest that you've been wanting to try.

3 parts dry vermouth
3 parts sweet vermouth
3 parts gin
3 parts whiskey

8 parts Pilsner (page 37), Pale Lager (page
    36), or Oktoberfest (page 36)
Splash of blue curaçao or another orange
    liqueur
Splash of vodka

Combine the vermouths, gin, and whiskey in a shaker, shaking well. Add the beer, followed by the blue curaçao and vodka, shaking well. Strain into a martini or lowball glass on the rocks.

Yields will vary

⤳ Eeking Monkey ⤳

This tropical refresher of rums, fruit juices, and your choice of Fruit Beer, American Wheat Ale, or Amber Lager will have you swinging from the rafters, the chandeliers, and anything else you can get your hands on.

3 shots rum

4 shots spiced rum

1 ounce freshly squeezed lime juice

1 ounce freshly squeezed lemon juice

1 ounce freshly squeezed papaya juice

2 ounces freshly squeezed orange juice

3 ounces coconut milk

Crushed ice

4 ounces Fruit Beer (page 39), American Wheat Ale (page 38), or Amber Lager (page 35)

Shredded coconut (for toasted shredded coconut, see page 19)

Papaya chunks, for garnishing

2 lime slices, for garnishing

2 lemon slices, for garnishing

Combine the rum and spiced rum in a shaker, shaking well. Pour in the juices, coconut milk, and ice, shaking well. Combine the rum mixture with the beer in 2 hurricane glasses, stirring well. Top with the shredded coconut. Garnish with the papaya chunks on a skewer, and place the lime and lemon slices on the side of the glasses.

Yields 2 cocktails

Nineteenth Hole

A round of this sweet and citrusy cocktail—rum and lime combined with a lighter Pilsner, Pale Lager, or Fruit Beer—will guarantee you a boozy hole-in-one winner at your next get-together or party.

I shot rum

2 tablespoons freshly squeezed lime juice

12 ounces Pilsner (page 37), Pale Lager (page 36), or Fruit Beer (page 39)

Add the rum to the beer in a frosted beer mug or pilsner glass. Add the lime juice, stirring well.

Yields I cocktail

Hangover

This light and yummy seasoned vodka, tomato juice, and beer cocktail will be a welcomed sight at the breakfast or brunch table, regardless of how you arrived there. Spice it up even more by choosing a Chili Beer, or go a little lighter with a Pale Lager or Vienna Lager.

2 ounces vodka

3 ounces Chili Beer (page 39), Pale Lager (page 36), or Vienna Lager (page 37)

Salt, to taste

Seasoned salt, to taste

4 ounces tomato juice or V8 juice, preferably the Spicy Hot V8 juice

I celery stalk, for garnishing

Combine all the ingredients, except the celery, in a Collins glass, stirring well. Garnish with the celery.

Yields I cocktail

⚞ Love Potion #7 ⚟

The combination of grenadine, 7UP, and a few swigs of Golden Ale, Belgian Ale, or Fruit Beer proves that true love is really a state of mind.

Splash of grenadine
1/3 glass 7UP or ginger ale

2/3 glass Golden Ale (page 34), Belgian Ale (page 34), or Fruit Beer (page 39)

Pour each ingredient into a pilsner glass over the rocks, proceeding in the order listed in the ingredients list. Stir well.

Yields 1 cocktail

⚞ Sour Momma ⚟

This sour momma is going to put a huge smile on your face with the help of gin, vodka, grenadine, and sour mix, which all blend nicely with the flavor profiles of a Pale Lager, Pilsner, or Amber Lager.

1 ounce gin
1 ounce vodka
1 ounce grenadine

1 ounce sour mix
Pale Lager (page 36), Pilsner (page 37), or Amber Lager (page 35)

Combine the gin, vodka, grenadine, and sour mix in a shaker, shaking well. Pour the mixture into a highball glass filled with ice, filling about 1/2 to 3/4 of the glass. Fill the remainder of the glass with the beer.

Yields 1 cocktail

Beer Bender

This unlikely combination of ingredients—vodka, gin, Gatorade, Crown Royal, and a Pilsner, Belgian Abbey Tripel, or Amber Lager—is packed with swagger and flavor while serving as a playful bar top conversation piece.

I shot vodka

1/2 shot gin

2 ounces Lemon-Lime Gatorade

4 ounces Crown Royal

I teaspoon salt

Splash of freshly squeezed lemon juice

6 ounces Pilsner (page 37), Belgian Abbey Tripel (page 33), or Amber Lager (page 35)

Combine all the ingredients on the rocks in a highball glass, stirring well.

Yields I cocktail

Beer Crush

Slushy lemonade with a lively whiskey-beer bite—you'll have a crush on this cocktail right from the beginning. For the beer, go with a favorite Pale Lager, bold IPL, or an earthy and spicy Saison.

12 ounces whiskey

12 ounces Pale Lager (page 36), India Pale Lager (page 36), or Saison (page 35)

12 ounces frozen lemonade concentrate

I cup crushed ice

4 lemon slices, for garnishing

Combine all the ingredients, except the lemon slices, in a blender, blending well. Serve in 4 highball or pilsner glasses, and garnish with the lemon slices.

Yields 4 cocktails

⊰∰⊱ Sour Puss ⊰∰⊱

The sour mix adds a little pucker and jive to the almond-flavored amaretto and American Wheat Ale, Stout, or Belgian Abbey Dubbel, delivering a cozy little cocktail that you'll return to again and again.

I 1/2 ounces amaretto
I teaspoon American Wheat Ale (page 38), Stout (page 38), or Belgian Abbey Dubbel (page 33)

3 ounces sour mix
Splash of lemon-lime soda, such as Sprite, or ginger ale

Combine the amaretto, beer, and sour mix in a lowball glass filled with ice. Top with the lemon-lime soda or ginger ale, stirring well.

Yields I cocktail

⊰∰⊱ Twist & Shout ⊰∰⊱

You'll be ready to bust a move for sure when vodka and lemon soda do a little twist and shout with cola and an American Wheat Ale, Kölsch, or Pilsner.

I ounce vodka
American Wheat Ale (page 38), Kölsch (page 35), or Pilsner (page 37), to taste

2 ounces lemon soda
Cola, to taste

Combine the vodka and lemon soda in a frosted pilsner or Collins glass. Add the beer and cola as desired.

Yields I cocktail

Back Alley Dame

Vodka, gin, rum, Grand Marnier, coffee-flavored liqueur, and Kahlúa topped with a crown of your favorite beer foam will grab everyone's attention in proper fashion.

1/2 ounce vodka

1/2 ounce gin

1/2 ounce rum

1/2 ounce Grand Marnier

1/4 ounce coffee-flavored liqueur

1/4 ounce Kahlúa

1 ounce sour mix

Splash of cranberry juice

Crushed ice

Draft foam from the beer of your choice
(pages 32 to 39)

Combine all the alcohol, except the beer draft foam, in a lowball glass. Add the sour mix. Add the cranberry juice and crushed ice, stirring well. Top with the draft foam from the beer.

Yields 1 cocktail

Cranberry Beer

A holiday must, cranberry juice gets all holly jolly with your choice of a Golden Ale, Pale Lager, or Vienna Lager to make any season all the brighter.

12 ounces Golden Ale (page 34), Pale Lager
(page 36), or Vienna Lager (page 37)

1 ounce cranberry juice

Combine both ingredients on the rocks in a pilsner or highball glass, stirring well.

Yields 1 cocktail

After-Dinner Mint

Time to drink your dessert! This cool, minty after-dinner cocktail with cognac, crème de menthe, and Pale Lager, Pilsner, or a nutty and spicier Belgian Abbey Dubbel is the perfect nightcap to any evening.

1/3 part cognac
1/3 part crème de menthe
Ice

1/3 part Pale Lager (page 36), Pilsner (page 37), or Belgian Abbey Dubbel (page 33)

Combine all the ingredients in a shaker, shaking well. Strain into a lowball glass. Add ice to the cocktail, if desired.

Yields will vary

The Original Beer Margarita

One of the most iconic cocktails in the world gets a sudsy visit from the golden rock star here with your choice of Pale Lager, Fruit Beer, or Amber Lager, making those glorious days of summer even tastier and more refreshing.

1 pitcher ice
12 ounces frozen limeade concentrate
12 ounces Pale Lager (page 36), Fruit Beer (page 39), or Amber Lager (page 35)

12 ounces tequila
3 splashes margarita mix
1/4 cup salt
4 to 6 lime slices, for garnishing

Pour the ice into a blender until it is 3/4 full. Add the limeade concentrate, beer, and tequila, blending until smooth. Add the margarita mix, and blend again. Salt the rims of 4 to 6 margarita glasses. Pour the mixture into the glasses, and garnish with the lime slices.

Yields 4 to 6 cocktails

Red, White & Brewski

Whether declaring your independence or celebrating like there's no tomorrow, Pale Lager, Fruit Beer, or Golden Ale teams up with blueberry brandy, peach schnapps, vodka, and Everclear to give all of us boozy patriots something to really cheer about.

6 ounces Pale Lager (page 36), Fruit Beer (page 39), or Golden Ale (page 34)
1/2 ounce blueberry brandy
2 ounces peach schnapps
1 ounce vodka
1/2 ounce Everclear
Crushed ice

Combine all the ingredients in a pilsner or highball glass, stirring well.

Yields 1 cocktail

Apple Tree Cider

Autumn in a cup, this simple beer cocktail with apple cider is a perfect treat after raking all those leaves, or when simply sitting under a favorite old tree and watching the leaves all swirl down around you. Carry that autumn feeling through by using an Herb/Spiced Beer, or opt for a favorite American Wheat Ale or Pilsner.

6 ounces Herb/Spiced Beer (page 39), American Wheat Ale (page 38), or Pilsner (page 37)
6 ounces apple cider

Combine both ingredients in a pilsner or highball glass, stirring well.

Yields 1 cocktail

Volcano

Get ready for an epic eruption of fun and pleasure when a go-to Pale Lager, Fruit Beer, or fruity and hoppy Saison, coconut rum, vodka, triple sec, and melon liqueur join forces.

> 2 parts Pale Lager (page 36), Fruit Beer (page 39), or Saison (page 35)
> 2 parts coconut rum
>
> I part vodka
> I part triple sec
> 2 parts melon liqueur

Combine all the ingredients on the rocks in a hurricane glass, stirring well.

Yields I cocktail

Beer Gypsy

Set your spirit free with this minty and creamy beer cocktail, and let the road to adventure lead where it may. The Jägermeister, Irish cream, and crème de menthe pair effortlessly with the warm flavor points of a Pilsner, Amber Lager, or Belgian Abbey Dubbel.

> 3 parts Jägermeister
> 2 parts gin
> I part Irish cream (use recipe on page 18 or store-bought Irish cream)
>
> Pilsner (page 37), Amber Lager (page 35), or Belgian Abbey Dubbel (page 33)
> Crème de menthe

Combine the Jägermeister, gin, and Irish cream on the rocks in a lowball glass. Top with equal amounts of the beer and crème de menthe.

Yields I cocktail

Brewdriver

This beer lover's take on a classic screwdriver, starring an ice-cold Pilsner, Pale Lager, or Fruit Beer, is a tipsy tool everyone can easily operate, round after round after round.

2 ounces vodka

8 ounces orange juice

12 ounces Pilsner (page 37), Pale Lager (page 36), or Fruit Beer (page 39)

Combine the vodka and orange juice in a small pitcher, stirring well. Pour into 2 to 4 pilsner or lowball glasses on the rocks. Stir in the beer.

Yields 2 to 4 cocktails

Goodnight, Sweetheart!

Perfect for cold winter afternoons or evenings by the fire, this warm and cozy Brown Ale, Porter, or Russian Imperial Stout and agave drink is the perfect nightcap, sending you off to dreamland with every sip.

1 gallon Brown Ale (page 34), Porter (page 37), or Russian Imperial Stout (page 37)

8 ounces agave nectar

Pepper, enough to fill an infuser

Combine the beer and agave in a large saucepan over medium-high heat, stirring and heating the mixture until the agave is dissolved. Remove from the heat. Place the pepper in an infuser, and steep it in the mixture overnight on the counter. Serve the drink hot in mugs.

Yields 6 to 8 cocktails

⇒Pleather & Lace⇐

Your choice of an American Wheat Ale, Fruit Beer, or Amber Lager and cream soda create a sloshed soft drink that is equal parts comfort and buzz-worthy.

> I part American Wheat Ale (page 38), Fruit Beer   I part cream soda
> (page 39), or Amber Lager (page 35)

Combine both ingredients on the rocks in a pilsner glass, stirring well.

Yields I cocktail

⇒Route 66⇐

This mixture of grape brandy, cola, lemon juice, and a dash of American Wheat Ale, Pilsner, or Fruit Beer will turn every sip into a carefree road trip to fun and mischief.

> I 1/2 ounces pisco   Dash of American Wheat Ale (page 38),
> 2 ice cubes   Pilsner (page 37), or Fruit Beer (page 39)
> Cola (to fill the glass)   Splash of freshly squeezed lemon juice

Layer the ingredients in a lowball glass in the order specified in the ingredients list.

Yields I cocktail

⚜ Under the Table Daiquiri ⚜

Nothing says, "Summer party!" quite like a round of strawberry daiquiris! Here, your choice of a Pilsner, Fruit Beer, or Pale Lager adds a sudsy touch of awesome to a classic hot day cocktail, letting your guests know you mean business.

1/2 cup ice

5 ounces Pilsner (page 37), Fruit Beer (page 39), or Pale Lager (page 36)

1/2 ounce tequila

1/2 ounce light rum

6 ounces strawberry daiquiri mix (use the recipe that follows or store-bought mix)

Fresh strawberries

Add the ingredients (including some of the fresh strawberries) to a blender in the order listed in the ingredients list, blending until frothy. Pour into 1 to 2 frosty hurricane glasses, depending on size, and garnish with the remaining fresh strawberries on a skewer.

Yields 1 to 2 cocktails

DIY Strawberry Daiquiri Mix

1/2 cup water

1/2 cup sugar

1/4 cup freshly squeezed lime juice

2 1/2 cups fresh strawberries, sliced

Create a simple syrup by combining the water and sugar in a small saucepan over medium heat, stirring until the sugar dissolves. Combine the lime juice, strawberries, and simple syrup in a blender, pureeing until smooth.

Yields about 2 to 2 1/2 cups of daiquiri mix

The Celebrewtante

The flavor range of a light-bodied Pale Lager to a darker, maltier Scotch Ale or smooth Maibock paired with tequila, rum, and vodka offers you a few choices for celebrating the dawn of a great time for all.

4 ounces tequila, divided 1 ounce rum 1 ounce vodka	8 ounces Pale Lager (page 36), Scotch Ale (page 35), or Maibock (page 36)

Pour 2 ounces of the tequila over ice in a shaker, and shake well. Add the rum and vodka, and shake well again. Add this mixture to the beer in 1 highball glass or 2 low-ball glasses. Add the rest of the tequila, pouring it over the back of a spoon.

Yields 1 to 2 cocktails

Tailgater

Together, the tequila, dash of bitters, and Pale Lager, Amber Lager, or Pilsner here let your taste buds crisscross the borders of flavor and fun.

2 ounces tequila Dash of bitters	Pale Lager (page 36), Amber Lager (page 35), or Pilsner (page 37)

Combine the tequila and bitters in a pilsner or highball glass, stirring well. Fill the remainder of the glass with the beer.

Yields 1 cocktail

⫸ Pussycat ⫷

Here, an orange-flavored liqueur, lemon syrup, and the fruity and spicy notes of a Saison or Belgian Abbey Tripel, or a mellow Golden Ale, add a citrusy *purr* to any cocktail hour or backyard get-together.

I ounce orange-flavored liqueur

1/3 ounce lemon syrup (use the recipe that follows or store-bought syrup)

Saison (page 35), Belgian Abbey Tripel (page 33), or Golden Ale (page 34)

Combine the orange-flavored liqueur and lemon syrup in a frosty beer mug. Fill the remainder of the mug with the beer, stirring well.

Yields I cocktail

DIY Lemon Syrup

1/2 cup sugar

1/2 cup water

3/4 cup freshly squeezed lemon juice

Create a simple syrup by combining the sugar and water in a small saucepan, bringing the mixture to a boil. Simmer, stirring, until the sugar dissolves. Pour the simple syrup into a small bowl, allowing it to cool to room temperature. Add the lemon juice, mixing well.

Yields I 1/2 cups

Spicy Tomato

For this spicy tomato cocktail, feel free to increase the flame factor by adding more Tabasco sauce, or even some minced jalapeños, and using a Chili Beer. Or temper it a bit with a Pilsner or Pale Lager.

Pinch of salt

Dash of freshly squeezed lemon juice

Pinch of freshly ground black pepper

1 ounce Tabasco sauce, or to taste

6 ounces tomato juice or V8 juice, preferably the Spicy Hot V8 juice

6 ounces Chili Beer (page 39), Pilsner (page 37), or Pale Lager (page 36)

Combine the salt, lemon juice, and pepper in a beer mug. Add the tomato juice. Slowly add the beer. Add the Tabasco sauce. Serve on the rocks.

Yields 1 cocktail

Butter Beer

Smooth and sweet, this butter beer is pure comfort by the mugful. The butterscotch schnapps is nicely balanced by a Belgian Abbey Dubbel, Scotch Ale, or Pale Lager.

10 ounces Belgian Abbey Dubbel (page 33), Scotch Ale (page 35), or Pale Lager (page 36)

1 ounce butterscotch schnapps

Combine both ingredients in a beer mug, stirring well.

Yields 1 cocktail

Dreamsicle

Warm afternoons were made for this icy smooth dreamboat of amaretto and orange juice paired with the nuttiness of a Belgian Abbey Dubbel or Scotch Ale, or a chilled Fruit Beer.

I ounce amaretto

4 ounces Belgian Abbey Dubbel (page 33), Scotch Ale (page 35), or Fruit Beer (page 39)

4 ounces freshly squeezed orange juice

1/2 teaspoon simple syrup (recipe follows)

Crushed ice

Combine all the ingredients in a hurricane glass, stirring well. Or combine all the ingredients in a blender, blending until smooth, and then pour into a hurricane glass.

Yields I cocktail

DIY Simple Syrup

I part water

I part sugar

Combine the water and sugar in a small saucepan over medium heat, stirring until the sugar dissolves. Let cool to room temperature.

Yields will vary

Sweet Home Amaretto

Add an extra down-home flare to this cocktail by using a Porter, Scotch Ale, or Belgian Abbey Dubbel brewed in the South.

2 ounces amaretto

3 ounces Southern Comfort

6 ounces Porter (page 37), Scotch Ale (page 35), or Belgian Abbey Dubbel (page 33)

Combine all the ingredients in a frosted Collins glass, stirring well.

Yields I cocktail

Head Trip

Everclear, butterscotch schnapps, root beer, and an assertive Russian Imperial Stout, Doppelbock, or American Dark Lager conspire to give you and your friends 190-proof fun in every gulp!

I ounce Everclear

2 tablespoons Russian Imperial Stout (page 37), Doppelbock (page 36), or American Dark Lager (page 35)

2 ounces butterscotch schnapps

Root beer

Combine the Everclear, beer, and butterscotch schnapps on the rocks in a pilsner or highball glass, filling the remainder of the glass with the root beer and stirring well.

Yields I cocktail

Hottie

Worcestershire and Frank's RedHot sauces bring on the spiciness to either balance a cool, refreshing Pale Lager or Amber Lager, or go spark for spark with a fiery Chili Beer in this new brunch-time standard.

7 ounces tomato juice or V8 juice, preferably the Spicy Hot V8 juice (room temperature)

12 ounces Pale Lager (page 36), Amber Lager (page 35), or Chili Beer (page 39)

Celery salt, to taste

Frank's RedHot Cayenne Pepper Sauce, to taste

Worcestershire sauce (use recipe on page 30 or store-bought Worcestershire sauce), to taste

2 celery stalks, for garnishing

Shake the tomato juice, and then pour it into 2 pilsner glasses. Pour the beer down the side of the glasses. Garnish with the seasonings and the celery.

Yields 2 cocktails

Chapter 7

BEER CHUGGERS

Beer chuggers are all about getting the party started, keeping the party going, and adding an exclamation point to a great night. Whether you're knocking one back as part of a turbocharged toast or in celebration of good friends and a great time, the various combinations of liquor shots and beer in the following recipes deliver ultimate flavor, instant impact, and unforgettable moments you may (or may not) remember the next morning.

Get ready to redefine what "bottoms up!" and "living for the moment" really mean with beer chuggers like the Boilermaker with Belgian Abbey Tripel, Depth Charge with Doppelbock, Tequila Rocket with Belgian Witbier, Jäger Beer Bomb with Altbier, The Rebel's Yell with Amber Lager, Strawberry Jolt with American Wheat Ale, Red Vodka Chugger with India Pale Lager, Barroom Blitz with Scotch Ale, Craig's Outhouse Slammer with Fruit Beer, Skinny-Dipper with Belgian Abbey Dubbel, Coconut Bonfire with Saison, and Sake Boom Boom with Pilsner.

Boilermaker

Feel the heat rise with every gulp of this potent whiskey and Pale Lager, Belgian Abbey Tripel, or Stout chug fest.

2 ounces whiskey

10 ounces Pale Lager (page 36), Belgian Abbey Tripel (page 33), or Stout (page 38)

Pour the whiskey into a shot glass and the beer into a mug. Drop the shot glass into the mug, and chug.

Yields I chugger

Powwow

When vodka and your choice of Pale Lager, Pilsner, or Fruit Beer conspire for this high-voltage chugger, you'll know what it feels like to have the earth move under your feet!

I ounce vodka

16 ounces Pale Lager (page 36), Pilsner (page 37), or Fruit Beer (page 39)

Pour the vodka into a shot glass and the beer into a mug. Drop the shot glass into the mug, and chug.

Yields I chugger

Kahlúa Chug

Boasting complementary flavor profiles, this Kahlúa and Stout, Porter, or Bock chugger may tempt you to sip and savor its hearty punch, maybe even as a brunch starter.

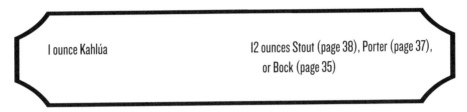

I ounce Kahlúa

12 ounces Stout (page 38), Porter (page 37), or Bock (page 35)

Pour the Kahlúa into a shot glass and the beer into a mug. Drop the shot glass into the mug, and chug.

Yields I chugger

Depth Charge

When Southern Comfort hits the robust Stout, Doppelbock, or IPL, get ready for an explosion of flavor that will rock your world.

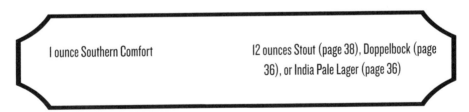

I ounce Southern Comfort

12 ounces Stout (page 38), Doppelbock (page 36), or India Pale Lager (page 36)

Pour the Southern Comfort into a shot glass and the beer into a mug. Drop the shot glass into the mug, and chug.

Yields I chugger

Licorice Beer

The anise-flavored liqueur and strong, earthy Stout, Russian Imperial Stout, or Dunkelweizen will twist and turn your palate into fits of utter glee.

I ounce anise-flavored liqueur	12 ounces Stout (page 38), Russian Imperial Stout (page 37), or Dunkelweizen (page 38)

Pour the anise-flavored liqueur into a shot glass and the beer into a mug. Drop the shot glass into the mug, and chug.

Yields I chugger

Woodpecker

Mountain Dew, vodka, and your choice of American Wheat Ale, Pilsner, or Fruit Beer will supercharge any occasion, ensuring that the fun and mischief keep coming at Mach speed.

10 ounces Mountain Dew 2 ounces vodka Dash of agave nectar	12 ounces American Wheat Ale (page 38), Pilsner (page 37), or Fruit Beer (page 39)

Combine all the ingredients in a pitcher, stirring well. Pour into pilsner glasses or beer mugs, and chug.

Yields 2 chuggers

Tequila Rocket

This chugger is perfect for Mexican-themed parties and get-togethers, or as a quick filler in between all those pitchers of The Original Beer Margarita (page 236). Get ready to soar when this tequila and Pale Lager, Belgian Witbier, or Fruit Beer trailblazer hits your mouth!

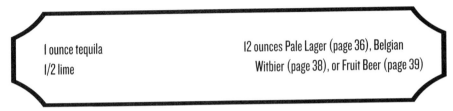

I ounce tequila
1/2 lime

12 ounces Pale Lager (page 36), Belgian Witbier (page 38), or Fruit Beer (page 39)

Pour the tequila into a shot glass and the beer into a mug. Drop the shot glass into the mug, squeeze the lime on top, and chug.

Yields I chugger

Beer Beer Chugger

Sweet, spicy, and sudsy are all wrapped in one neat little chugger when root beer schnapps takes the plunge into a tall, cool mug of Pale Lager, Pilsner, or Cream Ale.

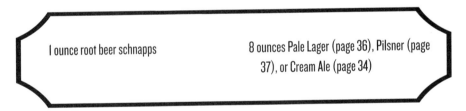

I ounce root beer schnapps

8 ounces Pale Lager (page 36), Pilsner (page 37), or Cream Ale (page 34)

Pour the root beer schnapps into a shot glass and the beer into a mug. Drop the shot glass into the mug, and chug.

Yields I chugger

The Electric Slider

When the infamous anise-flavored absinthe and cinnamon schnapps shot hits the Golden Ale, Pale Lager, or Vienna Lager, you'll really glide across the floor exclaiming, "It's electric!"

1/2 ounce absinthe or another anise-flavored liqueur

1/2 ounce cinnamon schnapps

12 ounces Golden Ale (page 34), Pale Lager (page 36), or Vienna Lager (page 37)

Pour the absinthe and cinnamon schnapps into a shot glass and the beer into a mug. Drink a quarter of the beer, drop the shot glass into the mug, and chug.

Yields I chugger

Dancin' Momma

Nothing will get you on the dance floor quicker than when rum and tequila go swimming in a sturdy Stout or Porter, or take a dip in your favorite Pale Lager.

1/2 ounce dark rum

1/2 ounce tequila

6 ounces Stout (page 38), Porter (page 37), or Pale Lager (page 36)

Pour the dark rum and tequila into a shot glass, stirring well. Pour the beer into a mug. Drop the shot glass into the mug, and chug.

Yields I chugger

Jäger Beer Bomb

Thanks to the addition of a Pale Lager, Altbier, or Amber Lager, a popular classic chugger gets the party started in a whole new way. Another option for this chugger is to eliminate the energy drink and use 6 to 8 ounces of beer with the shot of Jägermeister.

I tall shot Jägermeister

4 ounces Pale Lager (page 36), Altbier (page 33), or Amber Lager (page 35) (see headnote)

4 ounces energy drink of choice, preferably Red Bull energy drink (see headnote)

Pour the Jägermeister into a tall shot glass, stirring well. Pour the beer and energy drink into a mug. Drop the shot glass into the mug, and chug.

Yields I chugger

Lunch Box

This sweet, citrusy beer chugger offers a whole new way to get over that midday hump. The nutty amaretto goes down especially well with a Belgian Abbey Dubbel, Scotch Ale, or Amber Lager.

I/2 ounce amaretto

I/2 ounce freshly squeezed orange juice

4 ounces Belgian Abbey Dubbel (page 33), Scotch Ale (page 35), or Amber Lager (page 35)

Pour the amaretto into a shot glass. Pour the beer and orange juice into a mug, stirring well. Drop the shot glass into the mug, and chug.

Yields I chugger

The Rebel's Yell

This cinnamon and citrusy beer chugger is definitely one rebel *with* a cause: to make sure you have a blast! Balance the intense Rebel Yell 101 with an easygoing Pale Lager, Amber Lager, or Pilsner for maximum chug.

3/4 ounce Rebel Yell 101 or another cinnamon liqueur

Bacardi Limón

6 ounces Pale Lager (page 36), Amber Lager (page 35), or Pilsner (page 37)

Splash of cola

Pour the Rebel Yell 101 into a shot glass, and then fill the rest of the shot glass with the Bacardi Limón. Pour the beer into a mug, filling the mug halfway, and add the cola. Drop the shot glass into the mug, and chug.

Yields 1 chugger

Hot Sake Beer Plunge

Hot Sake and your choice of a Pilsner, Pale Lager, or Vienna Lager dive deep when it comes to infusing your night with an exotic flavor.

1 ounce hot Sake (page 38)

6 ounces Pilsner (page 37), Pale Lager (page 36), or Vienna Lager (page 37)

Pour the Sake into a shot glass and the beer into a mug. Drop the shot glass into the mug, and chug.

Yields 1 chugger

⫸Strawberry Jolt⫷

This chugger is sweet enough to serve as a liquid dessert or summertime cocktail, but for a real jolt of the fantastic, open wide and take the plunge with strawberry liqueur when it hits a chilled Pilsner, Golden Ale, or American Wheat Ale.

1 1/2 ounces strawberry liqueur	12 ounces Pilsner (page 37), Golden Ale (page 34), or American Wheat Ale (page 38)

Pour the strawberry liqueur into a shot glass and the beer into a mug. Drop the shot glass into the mug, and chug.

Yields 1 chugger

⫸Melon Burst⫷

The melon-flavored liqueur, combined with a Pilsner, Fruit Beer, or Amber Lager and 7UP, offers you and your guests the choice of a lazy afternoon sipper or a late-night mug and chugger.

1 ounce melon liqueur 1/2 glass 7UP	1/2 glass Pilsner (page 37), Fruit Beer (page 39), or Amber Lager (page 35)

Pour the melon liqueur into a shot glass. Pour the beer into a mug, then add the 7UP. Drop the shot glass into the mug, and chug.

Yields 1 chugger

Green Goblin

Get ready to see green when you chug this rich and spirited concoction of gin, sweet vermouth, lime juice, melon liqueur, and Pilsner, Saison, or Belgian Abbey Tripel.

I part gin

I part sweet vermouth

I part lime juice

I part melon liqueur

16 ounces Pilsner (page 37), Saison (page 35), or Belgian Abbey Tripel (page 33)

Pour all the ingredients, except the beer, into a shot glass. Pour the beer into a mug. Drop the shot glass into the mug, and chug.

Yields I chugger

Gobble Gobble

All your inhibitions will be set free to run wild like they're meant to with the help of this galvanizing assortment of rum, tequila, bourbon, vodka, Wild Turkey, and Pale Lager, Pilsner, or Amber Lager.

I shot 151 proof rum or regular dark rum

I shot tequila

I shot bourbon

I shot vodka

2 shots Wild Turkey

4 to 6 ounces Pale Lager (page 36), Pilsner (page 37), or Amber Lager (page 35)

Combine all the ingredients in a big, frosty beer mug, stirring well. Chug.

Yields I chugger

Red Vodka Chugger

A nice festive holiday chugger, nothing says "Ho ho ho!" better than grenadine-dressed vodka and American Wheat Ale, Saison, or IPL tossed down the hatch.

> 3 ounces American Wheat Ale (page 38), Saison (page 35), or India Pale Lager (page 36)
>
> 1 1/2 ounces vodka
> Dash of grenadine

Combine all the ingredients in a lowball glass, stirring well. Chug.

Yields 1 chugger

Irish Car Race

You'll get lucky every time with this Irish chugger, especially when using rich, delicious Irish cream with the whiskey and a scene-stealing Stout or Porter, or a lighter-bodied Cream Ale.

> 3/4 ounce Irish whiskey
> 3/4 ounce Irish cream (use recipe on page 18 or store-bought Irish cream)
>
> 6 ounces Stout (page 38), Porter (page 37), or Cream Ale (page 34)

Pour the whiskey and Irish cream into a shot glass and the beer into a mug. Drop the shot glass into the mug, and chug.

Yields 1 chugger

Barroom Blitz

Bring the barroom home with this amaretto, root beer schnapps, and corresponding Pale Lager, Scotch Ale, or Belgian Ale chugger, with its almond, sassafras, and wholesome earthy notes of flavor.

1/3 ounce amaretto	12 ounces Pale Lager (page 36), Scotch Ale
2/3 ounce root beer schnapps	(page 35), or Belgian Ale (page 34)

Pour the amaretto and root beer schnapps into a shot glass and the beer into a mug. Drop the shot glass into the mug, and chug.

Yields 1 chugger

Amaretto-Rum Chugger

Instead of chugging, it's okay if you give into the temptation to sip this scrumptious almond and rum-flavored shot and then chase it with a Pale Lager, Golden Ale, or Stout. Just be sure to savor every bit of it one way or another.

3/4 ounce amaretto	1/2 cup Pale Lager (page 36), Golden Ale
1/4 ounce rum	(page 34), or Stout (page 38)

Combine the amaretto and rum in a shot glass. Pour the beer into a tall mug. Drop the shot glass into the mug, and chug.

Yields 1 chugger

Flamemaker

Everclear is like liquid fire, and when it meets an icy Pale Lager, Amber Lager, or Fruit Beer, the combination is an eruption of pure bliss.

2 ounces Everclear

12 ounces Pale Lager (page 36), Amber Lager (page 35), or Fruit Beer (page 39)

Pour the Everclear into a shot glass. Pour the beer into a tall mug. Drop the shot glass into the mug, and chug.

Yields I chugger

Craig's Outhouse Slammer

Don't give this fire water–cola–beer chugger a second thought: pour one for each of your buddies using a favorite Stout, Fruit Beer, or Pale Lager, and slam the night away.

I ounce Everclear

3 ounces cola

2 ounces Stout (page 38), Fruit Beer (page 39), or Pale Lager (page 36)

Pour the Everclear into a shot glass. Combine the cola and beer in a tall mug, stirring well. Drop the shot glass into the mug, and chug.

Yields I chugger

Barn Burner

The Everclear and Doppelbock, American or English Pale Ale, or Russian Imperial Stout play well with the almond milk to deliver a creamy chugger that slides right down the hatch.

32 ounces Everclear

16 ounces almond milk

6 ounces Doppelbock (page 36), American or English Pale Ale (pages 33 and 34, respectively), or Russian Imperial Stout (page 37)

Combine all the ingredients in a pitcher, stirring well. Pour the mixture into 6 tall glasses. Pass around the glasses, and on the count of three, chug.

Yields 6 chuggers

Burning Bush

Whether celebrating the fall harvest, admiring the colorful falling leaves, or inviting all those ghosts and witches to come out and play, this chugger, especially when made using an Herb/Spiced Beer, has autumn written all over it. A standard Pale Lager or that German Hefeweizen you've been wanting to try also spin their own brand of yummy mischief with the cinnamon schnapps and apple cider.

1 ounce cinnamon schnapps

1/2 mug apple cider

1/2 mug Herb/Spiced Beer (page 39), Pale Lager (page 36), or German Hefeweizen (page 38)

Pour the cinnamon schnapps into a shot glass. Combine the beer and apple cider in a tall mug. Drop the shot glass into the mug, and chug.

Yields 1 chugger

Skinny-Dipper

The best thing to do with this chugger is just hold on tight and enjoy the ride! The trio of amaretto, whiskey, and Everclear is best paired with a frosty mug of Pale Lager, Pilsner, or Belgian Abbey Dubbel.

I/2 ounce amaretto
I/2 ounce whiskey
Dash of Everclear

8 ounces Pale Lager (page 36), Pilsner (page 37), or Belgian Abbey Dubbel (page 33)

Combine the amaretto and whiskey in a shot glass. Top the shot glass mixture with the Everclear. Pour the beer into a tall mug. Drop the shot glass into the mug, and chug.

Yields I chugger

Raspberry Comet

This is a great stand-alone chugger or a sweet side-by-side sip-and-sip combo. To really savor the raspberry liqueur and rum pairing, keep the shot and chilled mug of Golden Ale, Fruit Beer, or Pilsner separate, taking one sip of the shot followed by one sip of the beer to make this shooting star last as long as possible.

3/4 ounce raspberry liqueur
I/4 ounce rum

8 ounces Golden Ale (page 34), Fruit Beer (page 39), or Pilsner (page 37)

Layer the liqueur and rum in a shot glass. Pour the beer into a tall mug. Drop the shot glass into the mug, and chug.

Yields I chugger

Coconut Bonfire

Sometimes you just have to break the rules. Good thing there aren't any in this book! In addition to serving as a chugger, you can also opt to turn this amaretto–coconut rum–beer lineup into a slow motion chugger enjoyed over time, or keep the shot and mug of Stout, Porter, or Saison separate for a side-by-side sip-and-sip.

1/2 ounce amaretto	8 ounces Stout (page 38), Porter (page 37),
1/2 ounce coconut rum	or Saison (page 35)

Layer the amaretto and rum in a shot glass. Pour the beer into a tall mug. Drop the shot glass into the mug, and chug.

Yields I chugger

Sake Boom Boom

Sake and Everclear transform the melon liqueur and Pilsner, Pale Lager, or Amber Lager combo into the ultimate playground to be downed in as few gulps as possible for optimal impact.

3/4 ounce Sake (page 38)	16 ounces Pilsner (page 37), Pale Lager (page
1/4 ounce Everclear	36), or Amber Lager (page 35)
1/2 ounce melon liqueur	

Pour the Sake into a shot glass, and top it with the Everclear. Combine the melon liqueur and beer in a tall mug. Drop the shot glass into the mug, and chug.

Yields I chugger

Dice Run

If this tequila-rum-lager chugger doesn't sizzle all the way going down, then you've already had too many! Pair the tequila and rum with a go-to Pale Lager, Fruit Beer, or darker Vienna Lager.

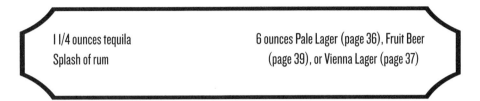

1 1/4 ounces tequila

Splash of rum

6 ounces Pale Lager (page 36), Fruit Beer (page 39), or Vienna Lager (page 37)

Pour the tequila into a shot glass, and top it with the rum. Pour the beer into a tall mug. Drop the shot glass into the mug, and chug.

Yields 1 chugger

Chapter 8

BEER SHOTS, SHOOTERS & CHASERS

If you're like me, you often tend to sip your shots, especially the sweet, delicious concoctions that you can't bear to have disappear in a single gulp, such as the Tropical Nectar made with a German Hefeweizen, Sweetie made with a Kölsch, and Agave Drop made with a Fruit Beer.

Otherwise, the shots, shooters, and chasers that follow—like the Atomic Diva with Rye Beer, Wild Turkey Trot with Amber Lager, Hoot & Holler with Brown Ale, Shooting Stars with Pale Lager, Drunken Leprechaun with Stout, Hot Ballers with Pilsner, Beer Babbler with Belgian Abbey Dubbel, and many more—are the liquid magic that celebratory toasts and memories are made of, and are meant to be savored in a flash!

⊱Tropical Nectar⊰

Flavors like melon, pineapple, lemon, and orange, along with the American Wheat Ale, Fruit Beer, or German Hefeweizen, manage to squeeze everything great about a tropical island into one shot glass.

1/3 ounce melon liqueur

1/6 ounce American Wheat Ale (page 38), Fruit Beer (page 39), or German Hefeweizen (page 38)

1/3 ounce pineapple juice

1/5 ounce lemonade

Freshly squeezed orange juice, to taste

Combine all the ingredients in a shot glass, stirring well.

Yields I shot

⊱Gin Blast⊰

Calling all gin lovers! Add a little Pilsner, Pale Lager, or Amber Lager to your favorite bar star and toss back your new signature shot.

I ounce gin

1/2 ounce Pilsner (page 37), Pale Lager (page 36), or Amber Lager (page 35)

Combine both ingredients in a shot glass, stirring well.

Yields I shot

Sweetie

The sweetness of the Southern Comfort kicks back with the vodka and Scotch Ale, Amber Lager, or Kölsch to give you a smooth shot with lots of punch.

---

4 parts Southern Comfort

2 parts vodka

2 parts Scotch Ale (page 35), Amber Lager (page 35), or Kölsch (page 35)

Combine all the ingredients in a shot glass, stirring well.

Yields I shot

Short & Stout

Creamy with a vodka-beer twist, this shot will have you setting your sights on a great night in no time. The vodka and Irish cream pair well with a rich, dark Stout or Porter, or a lighter Cream Ale.

1/4 shot vodka

1/2 shot Irish cream (use recipe on page 18 or store-bought Irish cream)

Splash of Stout (page 38), Porter (page 37), or Cream Ale (page 34)

Layer the vodka and Irish cream in a shot glass. Top with the beer.

Yields I shot

⋙~Atomic Diva~⋘

Warning: not to be sipped! This almighty shot of intense aquavit and your choice of Pilsner, Rye Beer, or Amber Lager is meant for rapid firing down the hatch—the quicker, the better.

17 ounces aquavit	7 ounces Pilsner (page 37), Rye Beer (page 35), or Amber Lager (page 35)

Combine the beer and aquavit in a pitcher, stirring well. Serve as shots.

Yields 8 to 12 shots

⋙~Agave Drop~⋘

Head south of the border in T-minus one gulp with this sweet agave-accented tequila and Fruit Beer, Belgian Abbey Tripel, or Pale Lager shot.

2 parts tequila 1 part Fruit Beer (page 39), Belgian Abbey Tripel (page 33), or Pale Lager (page 36)	Freshly squeezed juice of 1 lime 1/2 teaspoon agave nectar

Combine the tequila, beer, and lime juice in a shot glass, mixing well. Pour the agave in a teaspoon. Drop the agave into the shot glass, and drink quickly.

Yields 1 shot

Hell-O Beer Shots

The beauty of these beer-centric gelatin shots is that you can easily use a different fla-vored beer (such as strawberry, blueberry, or orange) every time for an endless array of choices. Not to mention, making the portion sizes larger offers the flexibility of serving these as light snacks or desserts.

I cup water

I cup coconut milk

I (3-ounce) packet Lieber's Unflavored Jel (page 13)

I cup beer of your choice (preferably a Fruit Beer [page 39], such as strawberry, blueberry, orange, or pineapple)

Combine the water and coconut milk in a medium-size pan, bringing the mixture to a boil. Mix 1/2 packet of Lieber's Jel into the coconut milk mixture, and stir to dissolve. Stir in the beer. Divide among 8 (2-ounce) cups. Refrigerate the cups until the gelatin has set, several hours to overnight. Serve cold.

Yields 8 shots

Honky Tonk

The chase is on big time when Pale Lager, Pilsner, or Amber Lager follows a shot of tequila, triple sec, and whiskey.

1/2 ounce tequila

1/2 ounce triple sec

1/2 ounce whiskey

8 ounces Pale Lager (page 36), Pilsner (page 37), or Amber Lager (page 35)

Combine the tequila, triple sec, and whiskey in a shot glass. Down the shot, and chase it with the beer.

Yields I shot and chaser

Pickled Vodka

Depending on the pickle juice, you may find that you will enjoy sipping this shot as much as throwing it back, so making extras is always a wise option to cover all your bases. In either case, be sure you have plenty of Pale Lager, Pilsner, or Chili Beer nearby.

I ounce vodka

1/2 ounce pickle juice of your choice, or more to taste

8 ounces Pale Lager (page 36), Pilsner (page 37), or Chili Beer (page 39)

Combine the vodka and pickle juice in a shot glass, stirring well. Down the shot, and chase it with the beer.

Yields I shot and chaser

Extra Dirty!

My advice: make two of these shots because you're going to be tempted to sip it. Indulge and sip the first one (maybe even add an olive), but then do yourself a big favor and toss back the second shot and chase it like there's no tomorrow with an icy Pale Lager, Pilsner, or Amber Lager!

I ounce vodka

I ounce green olive juice, or more to taste

8 ounces Pale Lager (page 36), Pilsner (page 37), or Amber Lager (page 35)

Combine the vodka and olive juice in a shot glass, stirring well. Down the shot, and chase it with the beer.

Yields I shot and chaser

☙ Wild Turkey Trot ❧

This rum and Wild Turkey shot, with its Pale Lager, Pilsner, or Amber Lager chaser, will get you and your guests moving full-speed ahead into a memorable night.

> I ounce rum
> I ounce Wild Turkey
>
> 8 ounces Pale Lager (page 36), Pilsner (page 37), or Amber Lager (page 35)

Combine the rum and Wild Turkey in a shot glass, stirring well. Down the shot, and chase it with the beer.

Yields I shot and chaser

☙ Hoot & Holler ❧

The proper way to consume a Hoot & Holler: down the triple sec–Kahlúa–tequila combo in one gulp, let loose a loud shout-out to the good life, and then chug the Brown Ale, Pale Lager, or Stout. *Ahhhhhh!* Now that's what I'm talking about!

> I/2 ounce triple sec
> I/2 ounce Kahlúa
> I/2 ounce tequila
>
> Ice
> 6 ounces Brown Ale (page 34), Pale Lager (page 36), or Stout (page 38)

Combine the triple sec, Kahlúa, tequila, and ice in a shaker, shaking well. Strain the mixture into a shot glass. Down the shot, and chase it with the beer.

Yields I shot and chaser

Shooting Stars

Get ready to make a lot of wishes fast when you toss back these shooting stars one right after another, followed by a Pale Lager, Pilsner, or Amber Lager.

I ounce Jägermeister
I ounce whiskey
I ounce Everclear

I ounce cinnamon liqueur
8 ounces Pale Lager (page 36), Pilsner (page 37), or Amber Lager (page 35)

Pour the Jägermeister, whiskey, Everclear, and cinnamon liqueur into separate shot glasses. Down each shot separately in the order listed in the ingredients list, and chase them with the beer.

Yields 4 shots and a chaser

Drunken Leprechaun

It's almost impossible to consume just one Drunken Leprechaun. I mean, come on: Irish cream and crème de menthe! Consider making a pitcher—some to sip with friends before and after dinner, and some to shoot and chase with a sturdy Stout, Bock, or Porter.

1/3 ounce Irish cream (use recipe on page 18 or store-bought Irish cream)
2/3 ounce crème de menthe

I ounce Stout (page 38), Bock (page 35), or Porter (page 37)

Combine the Irish cream and crème de menthe in a shot glass, stirring well. Down the shot, and chase it with the beer.

Yields I shot and chaser

Hot Ballers

Your palate is about to get a sizzling wake-up call that it's time to throw caution to the wind and laugh the night away, all capped with a refreshing flood of Pale Lager, Pilsner, or Amber Lager.

20 drops Tabasco sauce

I shot tequila

I shot peppermint schnapps

8 ounces Pale Lager (page 36), Pilsner (page 37), or Amber Lager (page 35)

Pour the Tabasco sauce, tequila, and peppermint schnapps into 3 different shot glasses. Down each shot separately in the order listed in the ingredients list, and chase them with the beer.

Yields 3 shots and a chaser

Motor Mouth

The tequila and peppermint schnapps shot paves the way for the equally refreshing Pale Lager, Pilsner, or Amber Lager to clear your mind and let all your problems go far, far away, at least for the moment.

I part tequila

I part peppermint schnapps

Ice

8 ounces Pale Lager (page 36), Pilsner (page 37), or Amber Lager (page 35)

Combine the tequila, peppermint schnapps, and ice in a shaker, shaking well. Strain the mixture into a shot glass. Down the shot, and chase it with the beer.

Yields I shot and chaser

273

Beer Babbler

After a few of these amaretto and Southern Comfort shots and the Pale Lager, Stout, or Belgian Abbey Dubbel chasers, any slurring and babbling will make perfect sense.

1/2 ounce amaretto	8 ounces Pale Lager (page 36), Stout (page
1/2 ounce Southern Comfort	38), or Belgian Abbey Dubbel (page 33)

Combine the amaretto and Southern Comfort in a shot glass. Down the shot, and chase it with the beer.

Yields 1 shot and chaser

Aunt Reggie

It doesn't get much more classic than this pioneer of the shot and chaser circuit, pairing whiskey with beer—Pale Lager, Pilsner, or Amber Lager. This was my Great-Great Aunt Reggie's signature combo, and she lived to be 104 years old. Draw your own conclusions!

1 shot whiskey	8 ounces Pale Lager (page 36), Pilsner (page
	37), or Amber Lager (page 35)

Down the shot, and chase it with the beer.

Yields 1 shot and chaser

~~Spinal Tap~~

This shot and chaser may contain more ingredients than any other recipe in this book, considering that Green Chartreuse is made using some 130 different herbs and plants! Lucky for us, all of those come in a convenient, delicious green liqueur that, when combined with 151 proof rum and chased by a Pale Lager, Pilsner, or Amber Lager, will light up your world!

1/2 ounce Green Chartreuse

1/2 ounce 151 proof rum

8 ounces Pale Lager (page 36), Pilsner (page 37), or Amber Lager (page 35)

Combine the Green Chartreuse and rum in a shot glass, stirring well. Down the shot, and chase it with the beer.

Yields I shot and chaser

Chapter 9
BEER PARTY PUNCHES

I n the recipes that follow, you'll discover just how well beer rocks out with fruit juices and other mixers. The beauty of many of these recipes is that they can also easily be converted into family-friendly, nonalcoholic (NA) punches by eliminating the alcohol and perhaps increasing the fruit juices and other ingredients to serve alongside the more potent, high-octane versions. And, whether boozy-*licious* or NA, they can all easily be doubled and tripled.

Fruit Beer can especially be explored in this chapter by matching the fruit- and berry-brewed flavors, such as orange, strawberry, blueberry, raspberry, cherry, pineapple, pumpkin, and apricots, of those beers to the other fruity ingredients and alcohols in the punches. For example, use one or a mixture of fruit-flavored beer for such punches as Citrus Sunsation, New Year's Punch, Good for What Ales You! Fruit Punch, The Berry Bucket, Beach Party Punch, Orange Fizz, Double Trouble, Orange Tattoo Punch, and Beer Bottle Punch.

Or showcase your love of a favorite beer or the latest seasonal or craft brew you're obsessed with by serving Gin Mill & Ginger Punch with Pilsner, The Wine Snob's Beer Punch with Pale Lager, Three Sheets to the Wind Punch with American Wheat Ale, Home Sweet Home with Herb/Spiced Beer, Party Like a Rock Star! with Amber Lager, Double Trouble with Kölsch, Dart Board Punch with Saison, and Trick-or-Treat Candy Punch with Porter.

⫸—Citrus Sunsation—⫷

Light and refreshing, this easy combination of lemons, orange juice, 7UP, and your choice of American Wheat Ale, Fruit Beer, or Belgian Abbey Tripel served from a pitcher is perfect for lunches with friends, afternoon gab sessions, or backyard barbecues.

2 cups sugar

2 cups water

6 lemon peels, sliced (use the peels from the lemons you juice)

Freshly squeezed juice of 6 lemons

I cup freshly squeezed orange juice

24 ounces American Wheat Ale (page 38), Fruit Beer (page 39), or Belgian Abbey Tripel (page 33)

7UP (frozen into ice cubes)

Orange slices, for garnishing

Combine the sugar and water in a medium-size saucepan over high heat. Bring to a boil. Add the lemon peels, remove from the heat, and cover for 5 minutes. Remove the peels. Add the lemon and orange juices. Stir well. Pour into a large pitcher, and refrigerate for several hours. Stir in the beer and 7UP ice cubes just before serving the punch. Garnish with the orange slices.

Yields 8 to 10 servings

 # Beer-Tang

With its high notes of orange, lime, ginger, and a Belgian Abbey Tripel, American Wheat Ale, or Amber Lager, this is a party punch that will make every guest feel welcome.

10 ounces Belgian Abbey Tripel (page 33), American Wheat Ale (page 38), or Amber Lager (page 35)

12 ounces orange juice

4 cups ginger ale

2 tablespoons freshly squeezed lime juice

3 ounces sugar

Lemonade (frozen into ice cubes)

Orange slices, for garnishing

Lime slices, for garnishing

Combine all the ingredients, except the garnishes, in a medium-size punch bowl, stirring well. Either float the orange and lime slices in the punch bowl, or garnish each serving with them.

Yields 10 to 12 servings

Pretty in Pink

Perfect for any occasion, this pink punch is a particular favorite for wedding and baby showers, girls' nights out, and '80s movie nights. For the beer, go with a lighter Pale Lager or Pilsner, or a hoppier Amber Lager.

I (12-ounce) can pink lemonade concentrate

12 ounces water

12 ounces vodka

Pink lemonade (frozen into ice cubes)

12 ounces Pale Lager (page 36), Pilsner (page 37), or Amber Lager (page 35)

Maraschino cherries (frozen into each ice cube as well, if desired)

Pour the lemonade concentrate into a medium-size punch bowl or large pitcher. Add the water and vodka. Stir well. Add the beer and pink lemonade–maraschino cherry ice cubes. Mix well.

Yields 6 to 8 servings

Gin Mill & Ginger Punch

With its double blast of ginger combined with gin and a Pale Lager, Pilsner, or Amber Lager, this pitcher punch is a sophisticated way to start and finish a meal or any other get-together.

1 1/2 ounces gin

12 ounces Pale Lager (page 36), Pilsner (page 37), or Amber Lager (page 35)

12 ounces ginger beer

Freshly squeezed juice of 1/2 lemon

Splash of soda water

Ginger ale (frozen into ice cubes)

Combine all the ingredients in a large pitcher, stirring well.

Yields 2 to 4 servings

Lemon & Lager Punch

This is basically the most amped up lemonade in a punch bowl you'll find anywhere, thanks to the rum and American Wheat Ale, Pale Lager, or Pilsner.

I (12-ounce) can lemonade concentrate

36 ounces water

Lemonade (frozen into ice cubes)

24 ounces American Wheat Ale (page 38), Pale Lager (page 36), or Pilsner (page 37)

1 1/2 cups rum

Lemon slices, for garnishing

Maraschino cherries, for garnishing

Sprigs of mint, for garnishing

Combine the lemonade concentrate and water in a medium-size punch bowl, stirring well. Add the lemonade ice cubes. Add the beer and rum, stirring well. Garnish with the lemon slices, cherries, and sprigs of mint.

Yields 8 to 10 servings

4th of July Parade Punch

A lot of vodka and your choice of Pale Lager, Pilsner, or Cream Ale ensure that this fruity array is fireworks in a bowl, and after a few glasses, you'll even see fireworks in broad daylight!

I gallon vodka

8 cups Pale Lager (page 36), Pilsner (page 37), or Cream Ale (page 34)

4 (12-ounce) cans lemonade concentrate

4 cups water

8 cups fruit punch

Blueberry Kool-Aid (frozen into a star-shaped ice mold)

Fresh blueberries (frozen inside the ice mold)

Fresh strawberries (frozen inside the ice mold)

Combine all the ingredients, except the ice mold, in a large punch bowl, stirring well. Add the star-shaped ice mold just before serving.

Yields 45 to 50 servings

Sour Patch Punch

The lemons and grapefruit in this punch will give you and your guests a fun little pucker to play around with, tempered nicely by the ginger ale and Pale Lager, Pilsner, or Amber Lager.

I cup sugar

I cup water

Zest of 3 lemons (use the zest from the lemons you juice)

Freshly squeezed juice of 3 lemons

1/2 cup chilled grapefruit juice

12 ounces Pale Lager (page 36), Pilsner (page 37), or Amber Lager (page 35)

Ginger ale (frozen into ice cubes)

Lemon slices, for garnishing

Maraschino cherries, for garnishing

Combine the sugar and water in a saucepan over high heat, and bring to a boil. Stir until the sugar is dissolved. Add the lemon zest, and remove the mixture from the heat. Cover and let cool for 10 minutes. Remove the lemon zest, and allow the mixture to cool to room temperature. Add the lemon and grapefruit juices to the sugar mixture. Chill for 2 to 3 hours. Stir in the beer and ginger ale ice cubes before serving. Garnish the servings with the lemon slices and cherries.

Yields 2 to 4 servings

New Year's Punch

Before the stroke of midnight, when champagne claims the spotlight, this vodka and beer punch extravaganza will be one heck of an opening act for the New Year! Go with a fun Fruit Beer, a more citrusy American Wheat Ale, or your favorite Pale Lager.

I gallon vodka

I gallon plus 16 ounces Fruit Beer (page 39), American Wheat Ale (page 38), or Pale Lager (page 36)

2 liters Sprite

I (19-ounce) can powdered lemonade mix

Sprite (frozen into ice cubes)

Maraschino cherries (frozen inside the ice cubes, see note)

Orange rinds or zest (frozen inside the ice cubes, see note)

Green grapes (frozen inside the ice cubes, see note)

Note: *For the ice cubes, use one cherry, orange rind/zest, or grape per ice cube, and create an equal amount of each.*

Combine all the ingredients in a large punch bowl, stirring well.

Yields 30 to 40 servings

The Wine Snob's Beer Punch

Calling all wine and beer *and* vodka snobs! You deserve the best of all worlds, right? Snob's choice of red wine, vodka, and Pale Lager, Pilsner, or Amber Lager brings home this stylish punch that will please everyone's taste for the good life.

4 cups vodka

1/2 gallon red wine, preferably a sweeter red wine

4 cups ginger ale, or more to taste

Ginger ale (frozen into ice cubes)

12 ounces Pale Lager (page 36), Pilsner (page 37), or Amber Lager (page 35)

Red and/or green grapes (frozen inside the ice cubes)

Combine all the ingredients, except the beer and ginger ale ice cubes, in a large punch bowl, stirring well. Add the beer. Add the ginger ale ice cubes. Stir well.

Yields 35 to 40 servings

Three Sheets to the Wind Punch

Want to know what freedom really tastes like? Vodka, beer—Pale Lager, Pilsner, or American Wheat Ale—and lemonade provide the loud and clear answer.

1 fifth vodka

8 cups plus 8 ounces Pale Lager (page 36), Pilsner (page 37), or American Wheat Ale (page 38)

1 cup powdered lemonade, or more to taste

Water, to taste

Sugar, to taste

Ice

Raspberries (frozen inside the ice cubes)

Lemon slices, for garnishing

Combine all the ingredients, except the lemon slices, in a large punch bowl, stirring well. Garnish with the lemon slices.

Yields 35 to 40 servings

⚛ Cloud 9 ⚛

Is it so far-fetched to believe that the sensation of floating on cloud nine really tastes like a mixture of vodka, brandy, gin, rum, red wine, and Pale Lager, Pilsner, or Amber Lager? Sit back, sip, and find out for yourself.

4 cups vodka

4 cups brandy

4 cups gin

4 cups light rum

4 cups semisweet, dry red wine

3 gallons fruit punch

Ice

8 cups plus 8 ounces Pale Lager (page 36),
    Pilsner (page 37), or Amber Lager (page 35)

Combine all the ingredients in a large punch bowl, adding the beer last, and stir well.

Yields 50 to 60 servings

⚛ Home Sweet Home ⚛

A perfect autumn through winter punch, this cozy blend of nutmeg, ginger, apples, and a well-chosen Herb/Spiced Beer, a rich and subtly sweet Brown Ale, or the roasted maltiness and hoppiness of a Porter is sure to warm your heart even on the coolest days and nights.

1/4 cup margarine (use recipe on page 23 or
    store-bought margarine)

1 cup sugar

1/2 teaspoon freshly ground nutmeg

1/2 teaspoon ground ginger

8 red apples, sliced

8 cups Herb/Spiced Beer (page 39), Brown
    Ale (page 34), or Porter (page 37)

Melt the margarine in a large saucepan over medium heat. Add the sugar, stirring well. Add the nutmeg and ginger, continuing to stir. Place the apple slices in the mixture. Top with the beer. Slowly heat, and serve warm in mugs.

Yields 12 to 14 servings

The Berry Bucket

One could declare this the official punch of summer, as the vodka and Pilsner, Fruit Beer, or American Wheat Ale play host to bunches of the season's freshest berries. Feel free to carry through the berry-*licious* theme by adding a few shots of berry-flavored liqueurs to the mixture, or arrange extra berries, fruit slices, and liqueurs next to the punch bowl to let guests add their own finishing touches and garnishes.

I fifth vodka

3 (12-ounce) bottles Pilsner (page 37), Fruit Beer (page 39), or American Wheat Ale (page 38)

2 (12-ounce) cans fruit punch

Ice (create using an ice mold)

Strawberries (frozen inside the ice mold), plus extra for garnishing

Blueberries (frozen inside the ice mold), plus extra for garnishing

Blackberries (frozen inside the ice mold), plus extra for garnishing

Raspberries (frozen inside the ice mold), plus extra for garnishing

3 lemons, sliced, for garnishing

3 limes, sliced, for garnishing

Combine the vodka, beer, fruit punch, and ice mold in a large punch bowl or large bucket. Garnish with the berries and fruit slices.

Yields 35 to 40 servings

Good for What Ales You! Fruit Punch

Vacation in a punch bowl! Feel free to take this punch in even more decadent directions (as if banana liqueur et al. isn't enough) by adding coconut shavings (for toasted ones, see page 19), strawberries, blueberries, kiwis, and anything else you'd like. For the beer, choose a favorite American Wheat Ale, Fruit Beer, or malty Dunkelweizen.

1 2/3 cups rum

12 ounces American Wheat Ale (page 38),
    Fruit Beer (page 39), or Dunkelweizen
    (page 38)

4 cups orange juice

3 cups pineapple juice

2 cups cranberry juice

Splash of banana liqueur

Ice

Pineapple chunks, for garnishing

Banana slices, for garnishing

Maraschino cherries, for garnishing

Papaya chunks, for garnishing

Orange slices, for garnishing

Combine all the ingredients, except the fruit, in a medium-size punch bowl or large pitcher, stirring well. Add all of the fruit, allowing it to float in the punch bowl, or use it to garnish each serving.

Yields 6 to 8 servings

Midnight Moon & Fiddle Punch

We all have those magical nights we'd like to live in forever. This special punch, with its rum, blackberry brandy, and Pale Lager, Pilsner, or Amber Lager infusion, captures those moments for our taste buds to savor again and again, anytime we wish.

16 ounces rum

16 ounces blackberry brandy

12 ounces Pale Lager (page 36), Pilsner (page 37), or Amber Lager (page 35)

1 (12-ounce) can cola

1 (12-ounce) can orange soda

1 (12-ounce) can 7UP or ginger ale

32 ounces pineapple juice

Ice (created using an ice mold)

Blackberries (frozen inside the ice mold), plus extra for garnishing (optional)

Combine all the ingredients in a medium-size to large punch bowl, stirring well.

Yields 12 to 14 servings

Party Like a Rock Star!

There will be no second thoughts or regrets once you hit center stage at any party with this perfect union of vodka, gin, rum, pink lemonade, and lots of the golden rock star—Pale Lager, American Wheat Ale, or Amber Lager.

7 cups vodka

7 cups gin

7 cups rum

10 quarts pink lemonade

Pink lemonade (frozen into ice cubes)

13 1/2 quarts Pale Lager (page 36), American Wheat Ale (page 38), or Amber Lager (page 35)

Combine all the ingredients in one or more large punch bowls, stirring well.

Yields 100 to 125 servings

Orange Fizz

Thick and slushy, this whimsical punch is cool enough for the hottest days or ready to add bursts of fun and flavor to any occasion year-round. Complement the orange soda and gin with a Fruit Beer, or go old school with a favorite Pale Lager or Pilsner.

8 ounces gin	16 ounces orange soda
11 ounces Fruit Beer (page 39), Pale Lager (page 36), or Pilsner (page 37)	Ice
	4 to 6 orange slices, for garnishing

Combine all the ingredients, except the orange slices, in a blender, blending for 3 minutes. Serve in 4 to 6 lowball or pilsner glasses, and garnish each serving with an orange slice.

Yields 4 to 6 servings

Plastered Peach Punch

Increase the peachy keen quotient of this vodka–peach schnapps–beer punch by seeking out some of the great peach-flavored juices that are widely available and also adding them to taste. For the beer, keep it simple with Pale Lager, American Wheat Ale, or Amber Lager.

2 cups vodka	4 cups water
12 ounces peach schnapps	1/2 cup Orange Tang powder
36 ounces Pale Lager (page 36), American Wheat Ale (page 38), or Amber Lager (page 35)	Ice
	14 to 16 peach wedges, for garnishing

Combine all the ingredients, except the peach wedges, in a medium-size to large punch bowl, stirring well. Garnish each serving with a peach slice.

Yields 14 to 16 servings

Beach Party Punch

Whether by beach, lake, creek, pool, or even rain puddle, for that matter, kick back and enjoy this punch, which takes the best that life has to offer and translates it into each lingering sip. Balance the rum, vodka, amaretto, and gin quartet with your go-to choice of Pale Lager, or a Fruit Beer or Kölsch you haven't gotten to try yet.

4 ounces rum

4 ounces vodka

4 ounces amaretto

4 ounces gin

24 ounces Pale Lager (page 36), Fruit Beer (page 39), or Kölsch (page 35)

1 (12-ounce) can Sprite or ginger ale

8 ounces orange juice

8 ounces pineapple juice

Ice

Garnish with your choice of orange slices, pineapple chunks, and maraschino cherries (optional)

Combine all the ingredients, except the optional garnishes, in a medium-size to large punch bowl, stirring well. Garnish as desired, including freezing some orange slices, pineapple chunks, and maraschino cherries inside an ice mold.

Yields 10 to 12 servings

Double Trouble

With its double dose of coconut rum, this punch made with Kölsch, Fruit Beer, or Amber Lager and all the trimmings is like drinking sunshine.

12 ounces Kölsch (page 35), Fruit Beer (page 39), or Amber Lager (page 35)

3 1/2 ounces coconut rum, divided

1 1/2 cups freshly squeezed orange juice

7 ounces 7UP

2 splashes freshly squeezed lemon juice

9 ounces Pale Lager (page 36)

6 ounces Mountain Dew

Orange juice (frozen into an ice mold)

6 to 8 lemon slices, for garnishing

Combine the Kölsch, Fruit Beer, or Amber Lager, 2 1/2 ounces of rum, orange juice, 7UP, and lemon juice in a medium-size pitcher or medium-size bowl, stirring well. Combine the Pale Lager, Mountain Dew, and remaining rum in a small pitcher or small bowl, stirring well. Combine both mixtures in a medium-size punch bowl, stirring well. Add the orange juice ice mold. Garnish each serving with a lemon slice.

Yields 6 to 8 servings

❧ Polka Punch ❧

Roll out the barrel of Pale Lager, Pilsner, or Amber Lager, *and* the vodka, Southern Comfort, sloe gin, and gin for this polka punch that promises the night will never end as long as you keep dancing and laughing.

Crushed ice

12 ounces Pale Lager (page 36), Pilsner (page 37), or Amber Lager (page 35)

2 ounces vodka

2 ounces Southern Comfort

2 ounces sloe gin

2 ounces gin

2 ounces grenadine

7UP

Orange juice

Place a layer of crushed ice at the bottom of a medium-size to large pitcher. Add the beer, followed by the vodka, Southern Comfort, sloe gin, gin, and grenadine. Top off the remainder of the pitcher with equal amounts of 7UP and orange juice. Stir well.

Yields 4 to 6 servings

❧ Dart Board Punch ❧

After a few glasses of this punch, boasting your choice of Pale Lager, Saison, or Amber Lager, everyone will be your best friend!

40 ounces Pale Lager (page 36), Saison (page 35), or Amber Lager (page 35)

12 ounces ginger ale

1/4 shot vodka

1/4 shot light rum

1/2 shot amaretto

Ice

Combine all the ingredients in a medium-size punch bowl, stirring well.

Yields 8 to 10 servings

Orange Tattoo Punch

After a long day of lazily lounging in the sun, indulge yourself and your guests further with this effortless lager–vodka–orange juice punch that will ensure it's always sunny wherever you are. While a Pale Lager or Amber Lager is always good to go here, also try experimenting with some Fruit Beers.

4 cups plus 8 ounces Pale Lager (page 36), Amber Lager (page 35), or Fruit Beer (page 39)

34 ounces vodka

2 gallons orange juice

Orange juice (frozen into an ice mold and crushed)

Combine all the ingredients in a large punch bowl, stirring well.

Yields 50 to 55 servings

Barstool Sipping Punch

For all those bar-side powwows and other gatherings when you aim to please and impress, this vodka, whiskey, and Pale Lager, Pilsner, or Amber Lager lemonade punch will get the job done.

12 (12-ounce) bottles Pale Lager (page 36), Pilsner (page 37), or Amber Lager (page 35)

2 (12-ounce) cans pink lemonade concentrate

13 ounces vodka

13 ounces whiskey

Pink lemonade (frozen into ice cubes)

Combine all the ingredients in a large punch bowl, stirring well.

Yields 20 to 25 servings

Trick-or-Treat Candy Punch

Ok, so the kiddies have *their* way of trick-or-treating, and we adults have *ours*. This bewitching punch is all the more spook-tacular when served in a witch's cauldron or a large plastic or ceramic pumpkin with your choice of Pale Lager. Or, for a dark punch, use Brown Ale or Porter. Bobbing for the candy garnishes, or the classic apple, in this punch is highly encouraged.

1 gallon cinnamon liqueur

11 ounces Pale Lager (page 36), Brown Ale (page 34), or Porter (page 37)

12 ounces orange-flavored whiskey

10 ounces sparkling wine

3 ounces 7UP

1/2 ounce apple juice

1 (12-ounce) can Dr. Pepper

4 ounces grenadine

Dr. Pepper (frozen into ice cubes)

Gummy worms and other candy, for garnishing (see note)

Note: *For the gummy worms and any other candy used to garnish this punch, read the labels to make sure you're comfortable with all the ingredients. An online source for vegan, gluten-free, allergen-free, and other candies is NaturalCandyStore.com.*

Combine all the ingredients, except the candy, in a large punch bowl, witch's cauldron, or hollow plastic or ceramic pumpkin. Garnish with the gummy worms and any other candy of your choice.

Yields 16 to 20 servings

Strawberry-Orange Sloshed Slush

Often a winter holiday favorite, this vodka- and Pale Lager–, Fruit Beer–, or American Wheat Ale–sloshed strawberry and orange slush is really best served during the summer, when you can use freshly picked strawberries instead of the frozen ones.

> 1 (.16 ounce) packet strawberry Kool-Aid
>
> 3 cups sugar
>
> 6 ounces orange juice
>
> 4 1/2 cups warm water
>
> 1 cup vodka
>
> Ginger ale, to taste
>
> 1 (10-ounce) package frozen strawberries, thawed, or 10 ounces freshly picked strawberries, plus more for garnishing
>
> 1/2 cup Pale Lager (page 36), Fruit Beer (page 39), or American Wheat Ale (page 38)

Place the Kool-Aid, sugar, orange juice, and warm water in a large saucepan over medium heat. Dissolve the Kool-Aid and sugar in the liquid, stirring occasionally. Remove from heat. Add all the remaining ingredients, except the ginger ale, stirring well. Pour into a medium to large container or two smaller containers, cover, and freeze for several hours to overnight. To serve, scoop the slushy mixture into glasses, and add the ginger ale to taste. Garnish with strawberry slices.

Yields 8 to 10 servings

Mojo Punch

The quickest way to ignite your party mojo is with this double rum–cherry brandy punch, with its hefty dose of Pale Lager, Pilsner, or Saison.

4 cups light rum

4 cups dark rum

16 ounces cherry brandy

4 cups plus 8 ounces Pale Lager (page 36), Pilsner (page 37), or Saison (page 35)

5 (12-ounce) cans 7UP or ginger ale

4 quarts pineapple juice

Ice

Maraschino cherries, for garnishing

Pineapple chunks, for garnishing (optional)

Combine all the ingredients, except the maraschino cherries and pineapple chunks, in a large punch bowl, stirring well. Garnish with the cherries and pineapple chunks, if using, floating in the punch bowl, or arrange the cherries and pineapple chunks on skewers to garnish each serving.

Yields 45 to 50 servings

Beer Bottle Punch

This punch is perfect for backyard BBQs or when playing beach bum. Just be sure that the Pale Lager, Fruit Beer, or Kölsch you pour out of each bottle goes into even more beer-infused thirst-quenchers from chapters 6 to 10.

40 (or so) ounces Pale Lager (page 36), Fruit Beer (page 39), or Kölsch (page 35), in bottles

4 cups SunnyD orange juice

Pour half of the beer out of each bottle (using it for other purposes, such as more cocktails), and fill the remainder of each bottle with the orange juice. Shake and drink.

Yields 4 to 6 servings

Chapter 10
BEER FLOATS & SHAKES

I scream, you scream, we all scream for…well, take your pick: a Root Beer Float, Strawberry & Ale Float, Minty Stout Float, Chocolate Beershake, Vanilla Cream Ale Float, Coconut Ale Float, or Irish Cream & Stout Float—all made with beer!

The secret to making the following beer floats and shakes into bona fide treats that everyone will enjoy is using the homemade vanilla ice cream recipe, with its chocolate and strawberry variations, on page 22. From there, your go-to, everyday brews, as well as the endless seasonal and craft beers available—like Doppelbock, American Wheat Ale, Kölsch, Russian Imperial Stout, Oatmeal Stout, Cream Ale, Herb/Spiced Beer, Scotch Ale, and others—will add new layers of flavor to these all-time favorite cool and creamy indulgences.

Root Beer Float

Talk about melt-in-your-mouth delish! A rich and hearty Stout, robust Doppelbock, or favorite Amber Lager will meld seamlessly with the vanilla and root beer flavors for one reason and one reason only: your pleasure.

12 ounces Stout (page 38), Doppelbock (page 36), or Amber Lager (page 35)
4 ounces root beer schnapps or root beer

6 tablespoons vanilla ice cream (use recipe on page 22 or store-bought ice cream)

Combine all the ingredients in a blender, blending until smooth. Serve in parfait or pilsner glasses.

Yields 2 floats

Strawberry & Ale Float

When you look up "summer treat" in the dictionary, you'll likely find this strawberry and American Wheat Ale, Fruit Beer, or Kölsch float, and with whipped cream to boot.

12 ounces American Wheat Ale (page 38), Fruit Beer (page 39), or Kölsch (page 35)
3 scoops strawberry ice cream (use recipe on page 22 or store-bought ice cream)

Whipped cream (use recipe on page 18 or store-bought whipped cream), for garnishing
Maraschino cherries or strawberries, for garnishing

Combine the beer and ice cream in a parfait glass. Garnish with the whipped cream and cherries or strawberries.

Yields 1 float

Minty Stout Float

A cool way to cap off a terrific meal, this triple-mint Stout float—using a rich Stout, Russian Imperial Stout, or Oatmeal Stout—is triple the pleasure and then some.

12 ounces Stout (page 38), Russian Imperial Stout (page 37), or Oatmeal Stout (page 37)

3 scoops chocolate ice cream (use recipe on page 22 or store-bought ice cream)

1 teaspoon crème de menthe

Chocolate chips or shaved chocolate (page 17)

1 sprig of mint, for garnishing

Combine the beer, ice cream, and crème de menthe in a blender, blending until smooth. Pour into a parfait or pilsner glass. Top with the chocolate chips or shavings, and garnish with the sprig of mint.

Yields 1 float

Chocolate Beershake

If you really, really, *really* want to dazzle your guests with the best chocolate shake ever, then enlist your choice of Stout, Doppelbock, or Amber Lager, along with whiskey and Kahlúa, as your secret weapons to becoming the dessert host or hostess with the mostess.

3 ounces Stout (page 38), Doppelbock (page 36), or Amber Lager (page 35)

Splash of whiskey

2 cups Kahlúa

2 cups almond milk

1 cup tonic water

4 cups chocolate ice cream (use recipe on page 22 or store-bought ice cream)

Chocolate shavings, for garnishing (page 17)

Maraschino cherries, for garnishing

Combine all the ingredients, except the chocolate shavings and cherries, in a blender, blending until smooth. Serve in parfait or pilsner glasses. Garnish with the chocolate shavings and cherries.

Yields 4 shakes

⇌Vanilla Cream Ale Float⇌

It doesn't get much more classic and delightful than this vanilla and Cream Ale float with whipped cream, marshmallows, and a cherry on top! To switch it up on occasion, use an Herb/Spiced Beer or Fruit Beer.

1/2 glass vanilla ice cream (use recipe on page 22 or store-bought ice cream)

1/2 glass Cream Ale (page 34), Herb/Spiced Beer (page 39), or Fruit Beer (page 39)

Whipped cream (use recipe on page 18 or store-bought whipped cream)

Small marshmallows (see note), for garnishing

1 maraschino cherry, for garnishing, or more to taste

Note: *Plant-based marshmallows, which don't contain gelatin, are available at SweetAndSara.com and NaturalCandyStore.com. While small marshmallows are only used for this one recipe, they are something you will always want to have on hand in both small and larger sizes, just like plant-based graham crackers, which are also available from Sweet & Sara. Think campfire s'mores paired with a favorite Stout (page 38), Porter (page 37), or Amber Lager (page 35), or simply marshmallows toasted over a campfire and served solo, especially since these marshmallows react to flame in the same way as traditional marshmallows.*

Place the ice cream in a parfait or pilsner glass. Pour the beer over the ice cream. Freeze the mixture for about 3 hours, or until slushy. To serve, top with the whipped cream, marshmallows, and a cherry (or two or three, if you wish).

Yields 1 float

Coconut Ale Float

CAUTION! It's very easy to go *coconuts* over this rummy vanilla float, with its generous dose of American Wheat Ale, Pale Lager, or a malty, even nutty Scotch Ale.

1/2 glass vanilla ice cream (use recipe on page 22 or store-bought ice cream)
2 tablespoons coconut rum
1/2 glass American Wheat Ale (page 38), Pale Lager (page 36), or Scotch Ale (page 35)
Shredded coconut (for toasted, see page 19), for garnishing

Whipped cream (use recipe on page 18 or store-bought whipped cream), for garnishing
1 maraschino cherry, for garnishing, or more to taste

Place the ice cream in a parfait or pilsner glass. Pour the rum and then the beer over the ice cream. Freeze the mixture for about 3 hours, or until slushy. To serve, top with the coconut, whipped cream, and a cherry (or two or three, if you wish).

Yields 1 float

Irish Cream & Stout Float

The only thing that can make your guests feel even luckier when enjoying this float, with its rich and heavy accent of Stout, Oatmeal Stout, or Russian Imperial Stout, is garnishing it with a four-leaf clover.

2 ounces Irish cream (use recipe on page 18 or store-bought Irish cream)
3/4 ounce vodka
Root beer, to taste

Stout (page 38), Oatmeal Stout (page 37), or Russian Imperial Stout (page 37), to taste
Vanilla ice cream, to taste (use recipe on page 22 or store-bought ice cream)

Combine the Irish cream and vodka in a parfait or pilsner glass. Add the root beer and beer, but do not mix. Add the ice cream.

Yields 1 float

Appendix 1
ALCOHOL GLOSSARY

For quick reference, these are descriptions of the main alcohol ingredients used throughout the book.

Absinthe: anise-flavored liqueur

Amaretto: almond-flavored liqueur

Aquavit: spirit distilled from grain or potatoes and flavored with caraway and other seeds

Bacardi Limón : lemon-lime-grapefruit-flavored Bacardi rum

Beer: see the "Beer Style Guide" on page 32

Bitters: mixture of bitter and aromatic plant products

Bourbon: American whiskey made from at least 51 percent corn and a blend of barley and rye or wheat (see also **Wild Turkey**)

Brandy: spirit distilled from wine or fermented fruit juice (see also **cognac** and **pisco**)

Champagne: sparkling wine made by using grapes from the Champagne region of France (see also **wine**)

Cognac: fine brandy named after the town of Cognac in France (see also **brandy**)

Crème de menthe: mint-flavored liqueur

Crown Royal: Canadian blend of rye whisky and a lighter corn whisky

Curaçao (also Blue Curaçao): orange-flavored liqueur

Cynar: herbal liqueur made using artichokes and other herbs and plants

Everclear: 190 proof/95 percent pure grain alcohol

Gin: liquor distilled from juniper berries and other botanicals (see also **sloe gin**)

Ginger beer: high to low alcohol content, even nonalcoholic, beverage made by the fermentation of root ginger, sugar, water, and yeast

Grand Marnier: orange-flavored, cognac-based liqueur

Irish cream: liqueur made from cream, whiskey, and sweetener (use the recipe on page 18 or store-bought Irish cream)

Jägermeister: German liqueur made with over 50 herbs and spices

Kahlúa: coffee-flavored liqueur

Liqueur: sweet spirit distilled from herbs, fruits, seeds, and peels

Pisco: brandy made from the muscatel grape (see also **brandy**)

Rebel Yell 101: double-cinnamon-spiced liqueur

Rum: liquor made from molasses or sugarcane

Sake: See page 38 of the "Beer Style Guide"

Schnapps: strong, flavored spirit

Scotch: malt or grain whisky made in Scotland

Sloe gin: red liqueur traditionally made from gin and sloe (blackthorn) drupes (see also **gin**)

Southern Comfort: peach-flavored bourbon liqueur

Tequila: liquor distilled from the sap of the mescal plant

Triple Sec: very sweet orange-flavored liqueur made by redistilling curaçao until it is clear

Vermouth: dry or sweet white wine flavored with herbs (see also **wine**)

Vodka: clear liquor made from grain and mash

Whiskey or Whisky: liquor distilled from the fermented mash of grain; some types, such as Canadian and Scottish, drop the "e" in the spelling, while other types, such as American and Irish, keep the "e" in the spelling. (see also **bourbon**, **scotch**, and **Wild Turkey**)

Wild Turkey: brand of bourbon whiskey (see also **bourbon** and **whiskey**)

Wine: beverage made from fermented grape or plant juices (see also **champagne** and **vermouth**)

STORE-BOUGHT PLANT-BASED CHEESE RESOURCE GUIDE

For those of you who are interested in nondairy cheese, I've included a few resources for finding them. In addition to using the DIY plant-based cheese recipes on pages 15 to 17, which are originally from my cookbook *The Cheesy Vegan,* you can use plant-based cheeses produced by the following companies for optimum results in cooking or creating any recipes from this book. These cheeses are becoming more widely available in grocery stores and online.

Bute Island Foods
www.buteisland.com

Chicago Vegan Foods
www.chicagoveganfoods.com

Daiya Foods
www.daiyafoods.com

Dixie Diners' Club
www.dixiediner.com

Dr-Cow
www.dr-cow.com

Edward & Sons (Road's End Organics)
www.edwardandsons.com

Fat Goblin (Nacho Mom's)
www.fatgoblin.com

Follow Your Heart
www.followyourheart.com

Galaxy Nutritional Foods (GO Veggie!)
www.goveggiefoods.com

Heidi Ho Veganics
www.heidihoveganics.com

Lisanatti Foods
www.lisanatti.com

Punk Rawk Labs
www.punkrawklabs.net

Sister River Foods
www.eatparma.com

Ste Martaen
www.stemartaen.com

Tofutti
www.tofutti.com

ACKNOWLEDGMENTS

I'd like to raise a big frosty mug in toast to the following people who helped me create the ultimate bar crawl on these pages:

Steve Troha, literary agent extraordinaire and longtime drinking buddy.

Stephanie Bowen, my editor at Sourcebooks, who well knows what it means to create the ultimate party-in-a-book.

Tom Steele, a culinary master with unparalleled expertise and flair.

Vince Assetta, a brilliant head brewer who knows beer like no one else.

The extraordinary team at Sourcebooks, including Jenna Skwarek in editorial, Rachel Gilmer and Melanie Jackson in production, and Liz Kelsch, Becca Smith, and Heather Moore in publicity.

Peter Straub, my great-great-grandfather, who at age nineteen left his home and family in Germany and set sail in search of the American dream, with little more than a few gold pieces sewn into his jacket and a recipe for beer. Because of his vision and courage, more than 140 years later, I'm savoring my own American dream one bite and sip at a time.

And, finally, to all my fellow beer lovers out there: The world is a brighter and happier place with all of you in it. May you always eat and chug to your heart's content!

ABOUT THE AUTHOR

John Schlimm is the international award-winning author of several books, including *The Ultimate Beer Lover's Cookbook* (awarded "Best Beer Book in the U.S." and "Best Beer Book in the World" by Gourmand International), *The Beer Lover's Cookbook, The Cheesy Vegan, Grilling Vegan Style, The Tipsy Vegan, The Seven Stars Cookbook*, and other titles. A member of one of the oldest and most historic brewing families in the United States (Straub Brewery), he has appeared on national media outlets including the *Ellen DeGeneres Show*, NPR's *The Splendid Table*, Martha Stewart's *Everyday Food*, QVC, and *Fox & Friends*. He holds a master's degree from Harvard University. Visit his website at www.JohnSchlimm.com.